In Resistance

In Resistance

*Studies in African, Caribbean, and
Afro-American History*

EDITED BY
GARY Y. OKIHIRO

The University of Massachusetts Press

Amherst, 1986

Copyright © 1986 by The University of Massachusetts Press
All rights reserved
Printed in the United States of America
Set in Linotron Aldus at G & S Typesetters, Inc.
Printed by Cushing-Malloy, Inc. and bound by John Dekker & Sons

Library of Congress Cataloging-in-Publication Data

Main entry under title:

In resistance.

   Chiefly papers presented at a conference held at
Stanford University in the spring of 1983.
   Bibliography: p.
   Includes index.
   1. Slavery—Insurrections, etc.—History—Congresses. 2. Slavery—
Insurrections, etc.—Historiography—Congresses. 3. Aptheker, Herbert,
1915–   American Negro slave revolts—Congresses. I. Okihiro, Gary Y.,
1945–
HT855.I5   1986   326'.09   85-28874
ISBN 0-87023-519-2 (alk. paper)
ISBN 0-87023-520-6 (pbk.: alk. paper)

To
Herbert and Fay

CONTENTS

Acknowledgments   ix

1   Introduction
     GARY Y. OKIHIRO   1

2   Resistance and Afro-American History: Some Notes on
     Contemporary Historiography and Suggestions for Further Research
     HERBERT APTHEKER   10

3   Herbert Aptheker's Achievement and Our Responsibility
     EUGENE D. GENOVESE   21

4   Resistance in Africa: From Nationalist Revolt to Agrarian Protest
     TERENCE RANGER   32

5   Kikuyu Women in the "Mau Mau" Rebellion
     CORA ANN PRESLEY   53

6   Fugitive Slaves: Resistance to Slavery in the Sokoto Caliphate
     PAUL E. LOVEJOY   71

7   From Caribs to Black Caribs: The Amerindian Roots of Servile
     Resistance in the Caribbean
     MICHAEL CRATON   96

8   "The Family Tree Is Not Cut": Women and Cultural Resistance in
     Slave Family Life in the British Caribbean
     BARBARA BUSH   117

9   Historiography and Slave Revolt and Rebelliousness in the United
     States: A Class Approach
     HERBERT SHAPIRO   133

10   Strategies and Forms of Resistance: Focus on Slave Women in the
     United States
     ELIZABETH FOX-GENOVESE   143

Contents

11 "The Dream Deferred": Black Freedom Struggles on the Eve of White
Independence
  PETER H. WOOD   166

12 Black Women in Resistance: A Cross-Cultural Perspective
  ROSALYN TERBORG-PENN   188

13 Bibliographical Comment
  BETTINA APTHEKER   210

  Notes on Contributors   221

  Index   225

ACKNOWLEDGMENTS

This book grew out of a conference that was made possible through the financial support of the following programs and agencies: the Ethnic Studies Program, University of Santa Clara; the California Council for the Humanities and the National Endowment for the Humanities; the University of California, Berkeley, and Stanford University Joint Center for African Studies; and the Comparative and International Studies Program, University of California, Santa Cruz. Grants from these institutions helped fund the conference on which the major portion of this book is based, and I thank them for their support.

I would also like to thank Joel Samoff and Judy Muchowski of the Center for African Studies at Stanford University for hosting the conference and undertaking all of the work associated with that responsibility. Finally, the editorial work on this book was aided in large part by a Faculty Grant from the Berkeley-Stanford Joint Center for African Studies. I am grateful for the assistance from all of these individuals and programs.

Peter Wood's chapter appears in this book with the permission of the journal *Southern Exposure*, which published an abridged version in its November-December 1984 issue.

G.Y.O.

In Resistance

1

Introduction

GARY Y. OKIHIRO

The data herein presented make necessary the revision of the generally accepted
notion that his [black people's] response [to bondage] was one of passivity and
docility. The evidence, on the contrary, points to the conclusion that discontent
and rebelliousness were not only exceedingly common, but, indeed,
characteristic of American Negro slaves.

HERBERT APTHEKER
American Negro Slave Revolts, New York, 1943; repr. 1983, 374.

In the spring of 1983, historians of Africa, the Caribbean, Latin America, and the
United States met on the campus of Stanford University to explore the subject of
resistance. The occasion that brought them together was the fortieth anniversary of the publication of Herbert Aptheker's pioneering *American Negro Slave
Revolts*. Most of the chapters that follow are based on papers presented at that
conference. The others were solicited specifically for this collection.

The conference and book represent the coming together of several streams.
First, the two are based on a recognition that struggle is the core of history and
that the principal dialectic in that struggle is between oppression and exploitation, on the one hand, and resistance on the other. Resistance thus constitutes a
fundamental theme of history. Second, the case studies presented in the following chapters were drawn from distinctive cultures and historical periods in
order to ensure the perspectives of several vantage points and provide a more
thorough view of resistance. And finally, the conference and book are tributes
to Herbert Aptheker through their building and expanding on his thesis that
resistance in the face of oppression is a self-evident truth. As he put it, the cause
of slave revolt was slavery. That essential humanism, which perceives individuals in terms of possibilities, resilience, persistence, and self-determination, com-

prises the starting point and corresponding path that link the diverse studies contained herein. From that common ground, the authors reveal resistance in its myriad forms.

The book begins with a review essay by Herbert Aptheker on recent writings on black resistance in the United States and a prescription for areas of future research. Aptheker reminds us of the uses of historical scholarship. On the one hand, historical writing "excused a barbarous past as it rationalized a putrid present," and, on the other, scholars "have been producing and will continue to produce a body of historical literature that will approach the grandeur of its subject." It is that latter body of writing which Aptheker addresses in his literature review. Despite the advances made in recent years, the subject of resistance requires much additional study, including a systematic search of plantation and government records, research on the various means of resistance, both individual and collective, and an appreciation of the struggles against racism by white people. The result of such scholarship, concludes Aptheker, will be both liberating and transforming.

In a companion piece, Eugene Genovese offers an assessment of Aptheker's *American Negro Slave Revolts* and reflects on his career and influence. Genovese points to the "astonishing fact" that despite criticism of the book, "for forty long years, marked by the Cold War, by the criminal exclusion of Aptheker and other Communists from the universities, and by especially fierce redbaiting attempts to denigrate the work of Communist historians, no one has even tried to replace Aptheker's book with a fresh synthesis and reinterpretation." Further, although banished from the Academy, Aptheker has continued to influence new generations of scholars through his thesis "that blacks never accepted slavery, never ceased to struggle against it, and periodically carried their struggle to the point of insurrection." Any assessment of Aptheker's achievements, writes Genovese, cannot be divorced "from his effort to interpret history from a Marxist-Leninist viewpoint." That Marxism which directed his scholarship viewed the black liberation movement as central in the struggle against imperialism, and it was influential in his insistence on "a politically responsible reading of history." Some have criticized Aptheker for that political commitment. Yet that commitment, "when properly disciplined, sharpens historical writing and strengthens the search for truth." In fact, Aptheker's dedication to historical truth and to social change points to our responsibility "to connect, without ideological superimpositions and wish fulfillments, our historical work to our politics." Such scholarship, in the final analysis, "will constitute the most appropriate tribute we can pay him and the only way we can render permanent what he has done for us."

The main body of this book is devoted to area studies on resistance. These are divided into sections on African, Caribbean, and Afro-American history. The chapters span regions and cultures and historical periods. Still, the central focus is on resistance to oppression and exploitation, whether in the form of slavery or colonialism, and the essays build on each other, adding different dimensions to the face of resistance. At the same time, the collection reveals the complexities and ambiguities of resistance largely because of the variable nature of oppression and the dynamics of the dialectic. That ambiguity, of course, has been one of the major points of controversy arising from the resistance paradigm. Despite those contextual differences and questions of interpretation, resistance is revealed as a single historical process, not through mechanistic or simple-minded parallels, but through an understanding of history in terms of struggle and the dialectic of oppression and resistance.

Terence Ranger, the principal architect of African "nationalist" histories emphasizing African agency and the continuities of resistance, calls for a new synthesis of an indigenous and a world view of African history. Nationalist historians arose in reaction to African histories that were mere extensions of European imperial history; in turn, "radical" historians have been critical of the nationalists and have enlarged the field of analysis primarily through dependence and world-system theory. Taking that criticism into account, Ranger argues that the articulation of precapitalist modes of production with international capitalism should be seen in terms of process, struggle, and the contradiction of oppression and resistance. Accordingly, Ranger foreshadows a new generation of resistance histories by pointing to the deficiencies of both the nationalist and dependence models.

Whereas Ranger points to the ambiguities of the anticolonial struggle caused by the co-optation of the postcolonial bourgeois regimes, Presley contends that black nationalism within the context of European colonialism is necessarily a liberation movement. She describes women's involvement in the anticolonial movement in twentieth-century Kenya, first in associational politics and then, with the increasing radicalization of resistance, in the militant armed phase of the struggle. Women's protest was directed against the system of forced labor as applied to women and children, the physical abuse of women committed under colonial labor laws, and the deculturation being promoted by European missionaries. Excluded from male-dominated political parties, women formed their own Mumbi Central Association, which, like the counterpart for men, sought an end to colonial rule. In the "Mau Mau" rebellion, the women formed a network to provide information and supplies to the guerrillas, served as soldiers in the fighting forces, and endured imprisonment and torture. Presley concludes that the roles of women in the rebellion not only contributed to the eventual demise of the colonial order but also led to significant changes in women's position within Kikuyu society.

Paul Lovejoy expands upon and provides a conceptual framework for the important phenomenon of flight as a form of resistance. His study of the Sokoto Caliphate in nineteenth-century West Africa reveals that "flight was perhaps the most effective form of resistance against slavery" because it involved massive numbers of people, and because it struck at the property aspect of slavery and represented a loss of human capital to the slaveholding class. For Lovejoy, that meaning of flight and slavery is most clearly delineated in Afro-American studies of slave resistance. With the insight derived from that literature, Lovejoy forces a consideration of African slavery from the perspective of a class struggle between masters and slaves, and compels a reconsideration of the generally accepted notion of a relatively benign variety of slavery in Africa. Further, Lovejoy offers an alternative to the concern of African historians with the conditions affecting flight, such as geography and the impact of political collapse, while ignoring the resistance function of flight itself. Finally, like Peter Wood's chapter in this book, Lovejoy notes that the ideology of equality and freedom encouraged flight; ironically, in the African case that potentially revolutionary idea failed to develop a class consciousness, thereby facilitating the imposition of British colonial rule.

Resistance, for Michael Craton in his study of Amerindian responses to European hegemony in the Caribbean, includes not only rebellion but also "apparent collaboration where such behavior was designed to frustrate the absolute domination of the master class." Recalling Orlando Patterson's most recent exposition on slavery in his *Slavery and Social Death* (Cambridge, 1982), Craton's focus on a question of wills takes on renewed significance. Further, Craton conceptualizes the continuities of resistance through both direct linkages and "structural similarities" in the patterns of Amerindian and Afro-Caribbean responses to European colonialism. These continuities provide bases for cross-cultural comparisons and underscore the significance of localized acts of resistance to European rule through their cumulative effect. Finally, Craton follows Aptheker in demonstrating the dialectical relationship of oppression and resistance, in which each framed and affected the other; even though the ruling class might have provided the social context, popular resistance altered that environment, thereby determining the opportunities and forms of class rule. By the 1700s, the Carib Indians perceived imported African slaves as allies rather than as invaders, and actively encouraged runaway slaves to settle among them. Miscegenation and acculturation resulted in new groupings, from distinctly Amerindian bands to the Black Caribs with a dominant African element.

Craton concludes, "The passionate resistance of the Black Caribs more than symbolically represents not just the Amerindian roots of Caribbean slave resistance but the continuities of resistance to European and capitalistic exploitation of the Caribbean and its peoples that have run from the coming of Columbus to the present day."

The role of Afro-Caribbean women in cultural resistance is the subject of the next chapter, by Barbara Bush. Previous authors have assumed the destruction of African patterns of kinship under slavery and have created myths of black women's sexuality; both assumption and stereotype have contributed to the maintenance of class rule and the sexual and economic exploitation of black women in particular. In contrast, the historical reality shows that "slaves struggled to recreate their traditional kinship bonds, for it was within the family and community that they found the strength to survive servitude." For Bush, then, resistance to European efforts at deculturation and dehumanization meant retaining the African cultural heritage and adapting it under slavery. Women, the principal exponents of African culture, were at the forefront of that struggle. Besides maintaining African and Afro-Caribbean culture, slave women resisted, among other impositions, the planters' emphasis on childbearing, for the reproduction of labor, through birth control and abortion. In that resistance, slave women asserted their basic humanity in the face of racist stereotyping and class and gender exploitation. Further, their central role in preserving the slave family and extended community through blood, affinal, and "fictive" kinship posed a formidable resistance to overall European hegemony.

In chapter 9, Herbert Shapiro expands on Aptheker's position on the class nature of the struggle of black slaves in the United States and international capitalism. Such an approach places slavery within the context of the class relationship that produced and sustained slavery—slavery and the rise of merchant capital, masters and slaves, and slavery and the emergence of industrial capitalism. When placed in class perspective, the nature of slavery and resistance becomes clear; the condition of slavery promoted rebellion and the source of resistance lay in the natural human will to be free. A class approach would view cultural resistance as a means of defying class rule and as "the struggles of slaves as a class to resist the will of the masters and to establish a measure of control over their own lives." Shapiro closes his discussion of a class view of slave resistance by urging consideration of its influence on the political arena and, conversely, of the functions of antiresistance scholarship in maintaining the American political economy and class rule.

The strategies and forms of slave women's resistance, as articulated by Elizabeth Fox-Genovese, varied over time and were affected by the changing social relations both within Afro-American culture and within the wider world defined by the master class. The disruptive uprooting and transplanting of African women from diverse African cultures probably delayed the formation of a collective identity, and the fluid and experimental relations of a frontier slave society similarly retarded the establishment of distinctive social patterns. Beginning with the initial third of the eighteenth century and accompanying the rise of industrial capitalism, however, increasingly rigid structures of white domination were imposed, reflecting harsher and more complex means for the maintenance of white supremacy. For Afro-Americans, the eighteenth century saw the emergence of violent resistance, notably arson and poison. Moreover, the period witnessed the subjugation of female slaves "to the same structural constraints that relegated white women to households and male supervision," resulting in, perhaps, a "sharpened . . . distinction between male and female forms of resistance and revolt." Thus by the nineteenth century, there was an apparent absence of North American slave women in the direct planning and implementation of the major slave revolts. "Revolt seems to have become even more a specialized political and insurrectionary male responsibility." Women's resistance was more individual than collective, and the forms of their resistance were frequently specific to their gender, for example, in controlling their reproductive capacities, and to their mode of work, for example, in the domestic area. At the same time, Fox-Genovese cautions that there might be a danger in insisting on "the specific experience of women as women: We can miss the recalcitrant and determined struggle of the individual soul or consciousness against reduction to the status of thing." In addition, Fox-Genovese might agree that as conceptualized by Aptheker and others, a correct rendering of Afro-American resistance would view the movement in its totality, women and men in struggle and contributing, individually and collectively, to their overall liberation. It is the connections that remain problematic.

Nonetheless, the evidence of continuities between the great slave revolts in the Americas during the nineteenth century and the bourgeois American and French revolutions is compelling. Peter Wood examines that tradition of resistance in his essay on slave resistance on the eve of white independence. "Between 1765 and 1776, a wave of hope and discontent welled among American blacks," not only among urban slaves and free blacks in the North but more importantly among blacks in the South. Further, that "wave of struggle" was purposeful, sustained, widespread, and influenced the parallel political unrest among whites. Black resistance was not simply between slave and master; it was a more complex three-way conflict among "the merchant-planter revolutionaries, the English officer-bureaucrats, and the black worker." In the revolutionary struggle between the patriot colonists and the British, the slave population was seen as a potential ally for one against the other. For blacks, the conflict offered an opportunity to seek their own freedom by applying the logic and sometimes the tactics of the white independence movement. Their struggle belies the lofty principles of the colonial leaders, who declared their independence from an oppressive and meddlesome monarchy while denying freedom to black people and failing to recognize the kinship of their revolution with the black struggle for liberation.

Rosalyn Terborg-Penn's chapter on African women's resistance from a diaspora perspective provides an appropriate conclusion to the studies in African, Caribbean, and Afro-American resistance history. The essay was written from an Afrocentric view, which holds that diaspora history is an extension of African history and that there is a "tradition of identity" with Africa among blacks in the diaspora. That identity contains common values originating in the African cultural context and retained in the diaspora. One such value was self-reliance, which in turn formed the essential basis for the people's resistance to slavery, peonage, and colonization in Africa and the Americas. Terborg-Penn engages in a cross-cultural examination of African women's resistance, including Ann Nzinga of Angola during the seventeenth century, "Grandy" Nanny of Jamaica during the eighteenth century, and Harriet Tubman of the United States. Although the illustrations are varied in time and place, they share unifying themes such as the leadership of older women, several of whom were revered "because of supernatural or spiritual powers." Such examples of African women's resistance show that these women adopted "strategies and . . . values rooted in African cosmology. Hence their activities not only reflected a tradition of identity with Africa but also provided an extension of African history—diaspora history." We have thus come full circle—the tracings of which are etched on the shores of Africa and the Americas.

The final chapter of this book is a bibliographical essay by Bettina Aptheker on the writings of Herbert Aptheker in Afro-American history. The commentary provides a fitting capstone to this collection of essays assembled on the fortieth anniversary of the publication of *American Negro Slave Revolts*. In addition, as pointed out by Genovese, Aptheker's writings have been informed by his Marxist reading of history and his paradigm of black resistance. Thus, a review of his scholarship in Afro-American history is both germane and felicitous. But beyond that, the essay celebrates the significance of the resistance paradigm to the historian's profession as a whole. In that sense, the chapter underscores the importance of the concept of resistance in historical explanation. Finally, the chapter is an affecting testimony by a historian on the labor and lifework of a colleague and father. Of continuities and the tradition of resistance, Bettina Aptheker concludes, "His lifework, too, will be passed on in meaningful ways." The struggle continues.

"Deny the existence of resistance," writes Herbert Aptheker in this volume, "and one negates the dynamic, the soul, the reality of that history." The studies included in this book testify to and reinforce the veracity of that warning; to paraphrase Aptheker, resistance, not acquiescence, constitutes the core of history. But the essays move beyond mere reaffirmation. Several members of the audience at the Stanford conference excoriated, in a constructive way, the participants for dwelling on the obvious—black people's resistance. They are correct insofar as the field, with few individual exceptions, has been won over. But their comments strike at a more fundamental issue: the advancement of knowledge and the efficacy of scholarship in promoting social change.

This present collection points to the varieties and complexities of resistance across cultures and historical periods. For Ranger, a reformulation of African history must include the dimension of rural protest and its interconnection with world history, and for Presley, African nationalism should be reexamined from the rural as opposed to the urban perspective, with a complete view of the involvement of women and men in the anticolonial struggle. Lovejoy and Wood connect the ideology of equality and freedom with slave flight, and Lovejoy reframes African slavery and flight in terms of the American emphasis on the property aspect of slavery. The dialectical relationship between oppression and resistance is demonstrated by Craton, whereas Genovese, Shapiro, and Wood point to the corresponding link between the black and white liberation struggles. Women's resistance, for Bush and Terborg-Penn, illustrates the continuities and adaptations of the African cultural heritage, and Presley notes that women's roles within the Kikuyu cultural context were altered by women's participation in the liberation movement. Further, Fox-Genovese describes a shifting of the terrain of the struggle largely resulting from changing structural conditions, and Ranger points out the ambiguities of resistance and the limitations of the continuist argument.

Resistance was thus rooted in "tradition" and modernity, continuous and interrupted, gender-specific and all-inclusive, individual and collective. The studies in this anthology exemplify these complexities and reflect new stages in historical scholarship, prefiguring entirely new historiographies. Finally, the criticisms raised at the conference pointed to the underlying question of scholarship and politics, which Genovese and Aptheker make explicit in their work. In his concluding statement to the conference, Aptheker addressed the subject of black-white unity against racism, specifically, white people's participation in antiracism and its intersection with the black liberation movement. "The struggle is a mutual one, not a paternal one," reminded Aptheker. Further,

The Afro-American struggle for freedom is *not* one to simply join U.S.

society as equal participants. Given the history and function of racism in our society, the crux of black history is the effort to *transform*, to revolutionize U.S. society, for by joining as equals black people simultaneously are transforming the society from a racist one to an egalitarian one. It is this fundamental nature of the challenge represented by the black freedom movement that explains the duration, ingenuity, and intensity of the opposition by the classes that have ruled and do rule this country.

This conclusion returns us to the individual streams that coalesce in this book. A historiography reflective of a people's resistance is not only enlightening; it is revolutionary and liberating.

2

Resistance and Afro-American History: Some Notes on Contemporary Historiography and Suggestions for Further Research

HERBERT APTHEKER

Professor Orlando Patterson, of the Sociology Department at Harvard University, published a lengthy study entitled "Slavery" in the *Annual Review of Sociology*, 3 (1977), 407–449. About 150 words were devoted to *American Negro Slave Revolts*. Here Professor Patterson referred to me as "the main survivor of . . . an early school of Marxist scholarship." I concentrated, we were told, "on the revolutionary aspects of American slave life," and found "revolution and rebellion where they can hardly be said to exist." Further, "out of a romantic conception of proletarian culture," I "draw conclusions about the revolutionary potential of the American slave that in no way relate to the facts of the case."

The remainder of Professor Patterson's remarks, however, are not entirely negative; they approach generosity and so I quote them in full:

> Even so, we think that the total rejection of Aptheker has gone too far. The man and his work have literally been purged from the company of polite scholars. For all its faults, *American Negro Slave Revolts* cannot be dismissed as some monstrous emanation of the Communist Party line. Like the work of [Stanley] Elkins (1959), it did break new ground; and like that work it was largely wrong in its conclusions and biased in its interpretations. We therefore find it difficult to understand why it is that Elkins

remains respectable and continues to be credited with the initiation of new studies in American slave studies, yet Aptheker is totally rejected, even ridiculed. Something is amiss here.

I am reminded of a story the late Carter G. Woodson told me; the source again is Harvard. Woodson's teacher, Edward Channing—not prone to excesses of speech or action—once startled Woodson by announcing that he could not think of Old John Brown without wanting to kick him in the backside!

Something was amiss there, too!

The authority on what it meant to be a slave in the United States, until about 1950, was the late U. B. Phillips. The people enslaved, wrote this scholar, suffered from "inherited inaptitude" and were stupid, negligent, docile, dilatory, and "by racial quality submissive." Such views were *not* held to be disqualifying!

This outlook was not an academic matter; it was fundamental to the racism, in idea and in practice, that characterizes the United States from its colonial past to its Reaganomic present. It characterized as it bulwarked the status quo; it excused a barbarous past as it rationalized a putrid present.

Therefore, a work that, while slandering the inhabitants of concentration camps, employed the rationalizations for that slander to suggest reality in the slaveowners' Sambo fantasy and appeared at the tail end of McCarthyism and in the midst of the Cold War would be thrice welcomed. Nothing is amiss here.

Writing in the Phillips-Elkins tradition, the distinguished novelist William Styron, reviewing *American Negro Slave Revolts* on the twentieth anniversary of its appearance, in the *New York Review of Books*, September 26, 1963, dismissed it as beneath serious contemplation, for slavery had in fact reduced its victims "to the status of children . . . tranquillized, totally defenseless, ciphers and ants."

That is one end of the tension characterizing our subject. Deny the existence of resistance and one negates the dynamic, the soul, the reality of that history. Racists, whose arrogance is exceeded only by their ignorance, can persist in shunning this reality, and in this society often gain wealth and win prizes for doing so. Others have been producing and will continue to produce a body of historical literature that will approach the grandeur of its subject. Let us examine some of the most consequential examples of this positive development during the past dozen years.

Robert E. May, a young professor at Purdue University, published in the *Journal of Southern History*, 46:4 (November 1980), 551–570, a fascinating account: "John A. Quitman and His Slaves: Reconciling Slave Resistance with the Proslavery Defense." Quite apart from how this Mississippi congressman, governor, and fire-eater accomplished the reconciliation, what Professor May

shows is that Quitman himself faced "persistent resistance by both house servants and field hands" and that his friends and neighbors experienced similar travail from the peculiar institution. Especially catching my eye was this
paragraph:

> One of the most significant discoveries in recent works about slavery is
> that black resistance to bondage was virtually universal throughout the
> Old South and that this resistance interfered with the functioning of
> southern plantations and households.

Each generation must make its own discoveries. Certainly much of the literature of the 1970s, no doubt reflecting the upheavals of the 1960s, helped explain Mr. May's "discovery" of 1980.

In June 1977 the New York Academy of Sciences sponsored a conference entitled "Comparative Perspectives on Slavery in New World Plantation Societies."[1] A considerable section of this conference was devoted to "slave revolts,
resistance, marronage, and implications for post-emancipation society"; papers
dealt with St. Kitts, Haiti, Jamaica, Venezuela, Mexico, Surinam, Guadeloupe,
and the United States. Alas, that on the United States was disappointing, but
the section as a whole demonstrated that wherever African and African-derived
peoples endured slavery, they forged a rich history of resistance.

Early in the decade was published Gerald W. Mullin's *Flight and Rebellion:
Slave Resistance in Eighteenth-Century Virginia*, New York, 1972, a volume
made more disappointing by its promising title. Better, fresher and fuller was
Peter H. Wood's detailed study of slave resistance culminating in the Stono Uprising in South Carolina, 1739–1740, *Black Majority: Negroes in Colonial
South Carolina from 1670 through the Stono Rebellion*, New York, 1974.[2] This
young scholar's work continues to be helpful; he has published studies of a similar kind on the revolutionary period and this past April (1983) offered a paper
entitled "Black Freedom Struggles on the Eve of White Independence" at the
Annual Meeting of the Organization of American Historians, reflecting continuing probing in this period. (See chapter 11 in this volume.) Similarly detailed and informative was Daniel E. Meaders's fine study of flight by South
Carolina slaves as revealed through an examination of newspapers from 1732
through 1801: "South Carolina Fugitives as Viewed through Local Colonial
Newspapers with Emphasis on Runaway Notices, 1732–1801," *Journal of Negro
History*, 60:2 (April 1975), 288–319.

Popularizations now at times do not omit accounts of slave resistance. An
example is the chapter entitled "Black Rebellions" in Sally Smith Booth's *Seeds
of Anger: Revolts in America, 1607–1771*, New York, 1977. A study of another
kind—detailed and heavily dependent on computers—also concluded that un-

rest and protest were characteristic; I have in mind Jeffrey J. Crow's study *The Black Experience in Revolutionary North Carolina*, Raleigh, 1977, issued by North Carolina's Department of Cultural Resources.

Representative of a growing literature on the special suffering that enslavement meant for black women—from class, racist, and gender aspects—is the essay by Dorothy Burnham entitled "The Life of the Afro-American Woman in Slavery," in the *International Journal of Women's Studies*, 1:4 (July-August 1978), 363–377.

Increasingly, now, state studies of slavery and antislavery pay attention to the activities of black people, free and enslaved. An example is Lowell Harrison's *The Antislavery Movement in Kentucky*, Lexington, 1978, with the useful chapter "Blacks against Slavery."

New works are focusing not only on slaves in particular areas but upon certain industries employing slaves. An important instance is Ronald Lewis's *Coal, Iron, and Slaves: Industrial Slavery in Maryland and Virginia, 1715–1865*, Westport, 1979, which reveals discontent and protest to have been chronic. Lewis's work is in the tradition of Robert S. Starobin's *Industrial Slavery in the Old South*, New York, 1970, and Charles B. Dew's "Disciplining Slave Ironworkers in the Antebellum South: Coercion, Conciliation, and Accommodation," *American Historical Review*, 79:2 (April 1974), 393–418, but offers more evidence than the earlier works on the extent of slave disaffection.

Paul D. Escott, in his *Slavery Remembered: A Record of Twentieth-Century Slave Narratives*, Chapel Hill, 1979, confirms and expands the work of John W. Blassingame's *Slave Testimony: Two Centuries of Letters, Speeches, Interviews, and Autobiographies*, Baton Rouge, 1977. Escott has computerized the enormous body of material collected by the Federal Writers Project Slave Narratives and the two collections of narratives produced by Fisk University, much of this edited by George Rawick. Escott finds that the slaves "did not passively accept treatment dictated by their masters," that they waged "a continual battle," that "in a thousand ways . . . they fought their owners," that women were at least as militant as men, that, to sum up, "slave resistance was both continual and shrewdly practical."

Later in 1979 came Eugene Genovese's work devoted to an analysis of the meaning of slave resistance in the Western Hemisphere. Here, happily, Genovese is past essentially sterile questions about whether or not these slaves sought freedom. Of course they did, is the stance of this volume. The meaning of this fact is the book's theme and its title is suggestive: *From Rebellion to Revolution: Afro-American Slave Revolts in the Making of the Modern World*, Baton Rouge, 1979. I have offered my views of this volume in an essay that is to be published in a book of various contributors examining much of Genovese's writing.[3] Here I wish only to point out that his 1979 book fits into the developing consensus on resistance as characteristic of the Afro-American people's response to enslavement.

Michael P. Johnson, of the University of California, Irvine, has produced important studies on our theme. Outstanding was his examination entitled "Runaway Slave and Slave Communities in South Carolina, 1799–1830," *William and Mary Quarterly*, 38:3 (July 1981), 418–441. One is reminded of Meaders's study of an earlier period in the same state; like that one, Johnson's study emphasizes the active, struggling, protesting reality that dominates Afro-American history.

The 1980s show no letup in the production of books illuminating this dramatic story of resistance. On the contrary, already we have had Vincent Harding's *There Is a River: The Black Struggle for Freedom in America*, New York, 1981; Mary Francis Berry and John W. Blassingame, *Long Memory: The Black Experience in America*, New York, 1982; and two books inspired by both the Afro-American and the women's efforts for full liberation—Angela Y. Davis, *Women, Race, and Class*, New York, 1981, and Bettina Aptheker, *Woman's Legacy: Essays on Race, Sex, and Class in American History*, Amherst, 1982.

Harding's *There Is a River*, the first in a two-volume effort, is an inspired prose-poem, in the tradition of Du Bois, and constitutes a celebration and an inquiry: "How in the midst of such death and suffering could we find so much strength to love, so much determination to live, fight on, and be free?" Harding sees in this struggle, quite rightly, an effort "for the re-creation of America." The Berry-Blassingame volume develops many themes; running through all of them is a sense of activity, creativity, dignity—and resistance. Specifically, on slavery, these authors conclude that the slaves "resisted bondage by every means available to them."

Angela Davis and Bettina Aptheker are on the sunny side of forty; they have not wasted these early years and surely they will not be idle in the coming decades. The slave women, writes Davis, were "never subdued"; and in battling they bestowed upon all who follow "a legacy of tenacity, resistance and insistence on sexual equality—a legacy spelling out standards for a new womanhood." Bettina Aptheker, in concluding her second chapter, writes that "woman's emancipation and Afro-American liberation are intimately and inexorably connected and that neither can ever be envisioned or achieved without the other."

Here is the heart of our theme, offered as confirmation to all the young Robert Mays who in 1980 came upon "the most significant discovery," namely, "black resistance." Its expression comes from Du Bois, and was uttered seventy years before May's discovery. He was speaking to black youth:

Grant us today, O God, that fearlessness that rests on confidence in the ultimate rightness of things. Let us be afraid neither of physical hurt, nor of the unfashionableness of our color, nor of the unpopularity of our cause; let us turn to the battle of life undismayed and above all when we have fought the good fight grant us to face the shadow of death with the same courage that has let us live. *AMEN.*

Slave Resistance

Despite the advance in the historical literature, slave resistance as such requires much additional investigation. There is need for examination of the archival material relevant to insurrection and conspiracy in the United States, especially legislative, judicial, executive, and auditor papers, as well as systematic combing of plantation records. What I was able to do, over forty years ago, was a beginning and was conceived as such. Except for the work of Henry Irving Tragle on the Nat Turner cataclysm—and even that was not exhaustive—there has been no systematic search of the sources such as I have suggested. Professor Louis Harlan remarked to me, in April 1983, that he was planning such a documentary search on the Gabriel Conspiracy in Virginia in 1800; I hope he is able to do so and that more such efforts—not ignoring relevant foreign archives—will be undertaken.

There is need for the same kind of full-scale investigation of maroons in the United States. The word *maroon* is still defined in Webster's *New Collegiate Dictionary* (1977) as "a fugitive Negro slave of the West Indies and Guiana in the 17th and 18th centuries"—a definition that is wrong in both geographical and chronological terms. Again, my study of this subject, first published in 1939, was meant to be a beginning of an investigation of this significant phenomenon, but except for brief references—for example, in the work of Eugene Genovese, Michael Johnson, and Peter Wood—there has been no essay, not to speak of the volume the subject deserves, for almost forty-five years.

Individual modes of resistance are noted in my *Negro Slave Revolts* and given important emphasis in the article on the subject by Raymond A. Bauer and Alice H. Bauer entitled "Day to Day Resistance to Slavery," published in the *Journal of Negro History*, 27 (October 1942), 388–419, but since the early 1940s only scattered references to these kinds of protest—among the most consequential—have appeared, with the exception, as noted in Lovejoy's paper published in this volume, of important studies of flight. That subject, of course, also appeared much earlier in books such as those by William Still, W. H. Siebert, and Henrietta Buckmaster. Some attention, too, has been given to the purchase of freedom, although this dramatic practice still awaits the full treatment its consequence merits. Very little attention, except cursory notice, has been given to slave sabotage, strikes, and slowdowns. Although the literature is sparse, the subject is rich.

Two forms of slave resistance that were especially common were arson and the use of poison. Both were sometimes so widespread and collective as to verge on insurrection. Slaves were responsible for heating the homes and cooking the meals; their "carelessness" often resulted in their lighting something other than ovens or fireplaces. And what slaves might put into soup was anybody's guess, as Richard Wright suggested to me when he spoke of his work in a New York City hotel. The fear and reality of poisoning were ubiquitous. In my research I noted, and reported, that newspaper accounts of the demise of this or that person often ascribed the passing to "the Negro disease," which was slaveholders' Aesopian language for death by poisoning.

Arson was especially common; it seems to have hastened the use of brick in home construction in the South, to have helped cause high premiums for fire insurance in the South, and to have prompted the introduction of an architectural novelty now called a fire escape. Even haphazard reading in sources turns up slave arson. Here is an example. In the third volume of *The Papers of John Marshall*, edited by W. C. Stinchcombe et al., Chapel Hill, 1979, there is a letter from the jurist's brother-in-law, Rawleigh Colston, dated August 5, 1796, from his plantation near Winchester, Virginia. One learns that Mr. Colston's home was damaged by fire the previous July by the hand of a thirteen-year-old slave, "a house servant" who had received "a slight chastisement." The editors' notes lead to the conclusion that this youngster was hanged. In the same letter, Mr. Colston expresses astonishment that some had thought such punishment to be excessive—he was surprised, he added, because "of the many *horrid* acts of the same kind" that had lately occurred. From this eighteenth-century incident involving the family of John Marshall to the slave-caused fire that nearly consumed the official residence of Jefferson Davis himself in 1864, sources of all kinds are filled with references to slave-created fires. This deserves a full study.

Antiracism

Slavery in the United States was a particular form of class exploitation and oppression; its special severity induced and required racism. Antiracism existed; its expression comes first and most persistently, of course, from its immediate victims. But antiracism was also present among white people—especially, I think the evidence indicated, nonpropertied white people. This is an important element in the history of resistance and it is one almost totally neglected in the literature. This subject has engaged a substantial share of my attention for the past dozen years. Here I shall cite three instances of a mishandling of history because of a blindness to the reality of opposition to racism.

In 1663 the Maryland legislature found it necessary to enact the following law:

> And forasmuch as divers free born English women, forgetful of their free condition and to the disgrace of our nation, do intermarry with Negro slaves, by which, also divers suits may arise, touching the issue of such women, and a great damage befall the master of such Negroes, for preservation whereof, [and] for deterring such free born women from such shameful matches, be it enacted, etc. that whatsoever free born woman shall intermarry with any slave, from and after the last day of the present assembly, shall serve the master of such slave during the life of her husband; and that all the issue of such free born women, so married, shall be slaves as their fathers were.

Laws of this nature were repeated by Maryland in 1681, 1684, 1715, and 1717. Their passage and repetition confirm the racism and racist practices of the rulers of Maryland; simultaneously, both the existence and the repetition show that at least for some white people, not of an exalted level, there was an absence of—even a resistance against—racism.

Virginia enacted a similar law in 1662 and later in that year increased the punishment for any white person "fornicating with a Negro man or woman" by doubling the fine. Warren M. Billings, commenting on this type of legislation in "The Cases of Fernando and Elizabeth Key: A Note on the Status of Blacks in Seventeenth-Century Virginia," *William and Mary Quarterly*, 30:3 (July 1973), 467–474, declared: "Once white Virginians perceived free blacks and miscegenation as serious threats to the public weal and to their own private interests, they moved to circumscribe the African bondsmen's approach to liberty." But this view is manifestly in error. It was not "white Virginians" who so behaved. Rather, it was those few whites who made the laws in Virginia who so acted. Further, they were not only circumscribing the African but also, and in particular, the white persons who chose black mates; indeed, the white rulers of Virginia in this act were intensifying existing penalties against *white people* for behavior reflecting an absence of racism.

The historical literature offers other instances of such misapprehensions. Thus, Roger A. Fischer published an essay entitled "Racial Segregation in Ante-Bellum New Orleans," in the *American Historical Review*, 74:3 (February 1969), 926–937. Professor Fischer observed that laws in that city forbade black people from "participating in white activities and using white facilities," but those who enacted such laws found themselves "powerless to prevent whites who so desired from mixing freely with Negroes in colored taverns, bawdy houses and dance halls." Here, "the color line broke down completely." As a result, in the 1850s, regulations were passed in New Orleans simply outlawing *all* interracial activity. Those guilty faced fines—if slaves, lashes—and the laws provided increasingly heavy penalties, as enacted in December 1856 and January and March 1857. The author concluded that this showed that "white New Orleanians grew increasingly suspicious of all activities that brought whites and Negroes together." Clearly, this misinterprets his own evidence, which shows that whites in New Orleans *who enacted laws*—or most of *them*—were "increasingly suspicious"; clearly, it also shows that *other* white people (objects of the laws) chose to socialize with black people, that this choice was mutual, and that such behavior had to be restrained by increasingly severe penalties against *both* black and white people.

Finally, as an example of dubious interpretation of historical data, I shall consider the literature dealing with the racism of white voters in the North and the West during the generation just before, during, and after the Civil War. This racism is the theme, for example, of V. Jacques Voegeli's *Free But Not Equal*, Chicago, 1967; Eugene H. Berwanger's *The Frontier against Slavery*, Urbana, 1967; James A. Rawley's *Race and Politics*, Philadelphia, 1969; and very recently, Phyllis F. Field's *The Politics of Race in New York*, Ithaca, 1982. These books—representative of dominant opinion in the profession—regard racism as ubiquitous, decisive, and basically self-generating. As Field writes, "It was the stereotype of the black man rather than slavery itself that served most effectively to condemn him" (p. 22). This is in accordance with the Phillipsian view of racism as "the central theme in the history of the South." The priority of this mysteriously self-generating racism was affirmed also by historians as varied and distinguished as the late Allan Nevins and, more recently, C. Vann Woodward and James M. McPherson.

This is not the place to argue at length against this position (I did so about thirty-five years ago) but it is one that, I am persuaded, throws United States history askew; among other pernicious results, it tends to feed notions of the inevitability of racism, of its ineradicability, or even—as Justice Brown held in *Plessy vs. Ferguson* (1896)—its "instinctual" character.

Certain relevant considerations may be brought forward on the basis of the very data offered by the authors cited. Thus, on the question of whether or not black men should have the suffrage—the main content of the books—one finds that in Minnesota in 1865 and 1867, the "yes" vote came to 45.2 percent and 48.8 percent, respectively; in Wisconsin in 1865 the "yes" vote came to 46 percent; in Connecticut in the same year, to 44.6 percent; in Ohio in 1867 to

45.9 percent; and in Missouri, in 1868, 42.7 percent. In New York State the affirmative vote in 1846 came to 28 percent; in 1860 to 36 percent; and in 1869 to 47 percent. In Iowa and in Minnesota, in 1869, suffrage for black men was *approved* by over 56 percent in each state. These percentages are of white men who voted to give the suffrage to black men. Certainly, they do not show the absence of racism; on the contrary, they show its great prevalence. But they also demonstrate, on the not-unimportant question of voting, that a substantial percentage of white men of that generation *favored* an antiracist position.

The ultimate expression of antiracism—putting one's life on the line in that effort, as did John Brown and his comrades—has marked the behavior of some white people more frequently than the almost total absence of literature on the subject would suggest. The schoolteacher Joseph Wood was hanged in New Orleans in 1812 for complicity in a slave rebellion; George Boxley was sentenced to death in Virginia in 1816 for the same offense (he escaped from prison, with the help of his wife, and they were never captured); four workers—Andrew Rhodes, William Allen, Jacob Danders, and John Igneshias—went to prison in Charleston in 1822 for expressing views sympathetic to the rebels in the Vesey plot; Jabez Brown was driven out of Georgia in 1804 for expressing hatred of slavery; Delia Webster, Calvin Fairbanks, and Patrick Doyle were jailed in Kentucky for participating in efforts of slaves to flee or to rebel; and a printer in Georgia and a sailor in South Carolina were driven out by lynch mobs for daring to agree with David Walker's revolutionary appeal of 1829.

This black-white unity certainly did not end with the Thirteenth Amendment. On the contrary, to one degree or another, it characterized every progressive movement in United States history, from that of labor to that of women to that against colonialism and against the madness of preparing for nuclear war. Nor did black militant resistance to racism stop with slavery's termination. The contrary is true and that, too, is a vast story awaiting chroniclers.

A special word is needed concerning the role of white women in the effort to cleanse the republic of racism. I have in mind the work of such people as Isabel Eaton, Florence Kelley, Inez Milholland, Mary Dunlop McLean, Mary White Ovington, Martha Gruening, Helen Boardman, Elizabeth Lawson, Henrietta Buckmaster, Bella Gross, Elizabeth Donnan, Helen T. Catterall, Gene Weltfish, and Anne Braden, to name a few.

This whole matter of black-white unity in struggle against racism brings dimensions to the history of resistance that are fundamental and require, not a short section in a brief paper, but rather a lengthy book or series of books. Here, two considerations are simply broached. Afro-American history is basic to United States history and the latter is central to Afro-American history. In addition, there is a specifically black history, just as there is a black church, a black press, a black aesthetics. Here one has a distinctive, but interpenetrating subject.

The relationship is, indeed, dialectical. The Afro-American struggle for freedom is *not* one to simply join United States society as equal participants. Given the history and function of racism in our society, the crux of black history is the effort to *transform*, to revolutionize United States society, for by joining as equals black people simultaneously are transforming the society from a racist one to an egalitarian one. It is this fundamental nature of the challenge represented by the black freedom movement that explains the duration, ingenuity, and intensity of the opposition by the classes that have ruled and do rule this country.

The struggle is a mutual one, not a paternal one. No one is doing anyone any favors. The opposite view was expressed by Chief Justice Warren, speaking for eight other white men, in the landmark *Brown vs. Topeka* (1954), repudiating *Plessy vs. Ferguson*. The repudiation was long overdue but all to the good. Still it was not complete, for the Court found that segregated education "deprives the children of the minority group." Quite apart from the constriction of legal procedure, the paternalism in that opinion assured the hesitancy that characterized its enforcement and rationalizes the overall failure to tear racism out of education in our country. If segregation hurts only the "minority children," there is no real urgency, so far as the parents of other children are concerned, in terminating it. But, of course, racist education is a negation of education; it is, as Carter G. Woodson wrote over sixty years ago, miseducation, and that miseducation assaults all who are subject to it. Until the poison of racism is faced up to in those terms, its extirpation will not be seriously undertaken in the United States. There, I think, is the ultimate direction of a salutary historiography in our country.

Notes

1 The fortieth-anniversary edition of *American Negro Slave Revolts*, New York, 1983, contains a bibliography of relevant literature from 1944 through 1974.

2 See the following recent studies: Darold D. Wax, " 'The Great Risque We Run': The Aftermath of Slave Rebellion at Stono, South Carolina, 1739–1745," *Journal of Negro History*, 67:2 (Summer 1982), 136–147; and P. J. Schwartz, "Gabriel's Challenge: Slaves and Crime in Late Eighteenth-Century Virginia," *Virginia Magazine of History and Biography*, 90:3 (July 1982), 283–309.

3 The volume is to be edited by Clarence E. Walker and Herbert Shapiro.

3

Herbert Aptheker's Achievement and Our Responsibility

EUGENE D. GENOVESE

A review of the way in which historians have discussed the theme of slave resistance in the United States quickly reveals the seminal character of Herbert Aptheker's *American Negro Slave Revolts* and supplementary studies. The literature falls easily into categories of "before" and "after." To be sure, as Aptheker has always insisted, he built on the work of such outstanding black scholars as W. E. B. Du Bois and Carter Woodson. Still, his own book broke fresh ground, theoretically as well as empirically, and it forced itself upon the white Academy, which had been able to ignore those black scholars and would before long wish that it had ignored Aptheker too. By the time it arrived at the conclusion that he was dangerous, it was too late: Too many people had read his book.

The literature on slavery published since World War II has reflected Aptheker's influence and has, with surprisingly few exceptions, demonstrated the acceptance of the principal theses of his book, notwithstanding ritual disclaimers and signs of acute discomfiture by scholars at being associated with a real live Communist. During the decade before Aptheker published, rumblings of revolt against the hegemony of Ulrich Phillips's racist reading of the slave experience were being heard even in the Academy, but it was *American Negro Slave Revolts* that openly and effectively challenged that hegemony and prepared the ground for such subsequent works as Kenneth Stampp's *Peculiar Institution*.

Aptheker laid down a straightforward but, at the time, controversial and startling thesis—that blacks never accepted slavery, never ceased to struggle against it, and periodically carried their struggle to the point of insurrection. That thesis has swept the field. Notwithstanding the temporary detour occasioned by the debate over the Elkins thesis, we would be hard pressed to find a reputable historian who has not had to end with a positive assessment of Aptheker's thesis. Indeed, even those historians who defended Elkins against what they perceived as misunderstandings and unfair criticism generally dissociated themselves from his thesis of slave docility and argued, instead, that his psychological model could prove heuristically useful for much more limited purposes.

For the most part the criticism of Aptheker's book has proceeded on a secondary level and has largely filed charges of exaggeration of the number and extent of the revolts. Whatever the merits of such criticism, which turns out to be much more complex than meets the eye, I should like to draw attention to an astonishing fact. For forty long years, marked by the Cold War, by the criminal exclusion of Aptheker and other Communists from the universities, and by especially fierce redbaiting attempts to denigrate the work of Communist historians, no one has even tried to replace Aptheker's book with a fresh synthesis and reinterpretation. Aptheker's book has stood up as the indispensable introduction to its subject, and no broad challenge is in sight. All subsequent work on the subject, no matter how critical of Aptheker on particulars, has had to build on it. It is easy to predict that when a new synthesis does appear, it will represent a deepening and broadening of his book on the basis of new materials and the posing of additional questions; there is no hint that a new synthesis will challenge its fundamental viewpoint and principal conclusions. Few books have exercised such dominion over a subject of prime importance. That fact speaks for itself. It provides the context for, and defines the limits of, all criticism worthy of attention.

Aptheker's *American Negro Slave Revolts* and subsequent work on black history present a number of theses and suggestions that illuminate American history as a whole and have yet to receive the credit they deserve. Not all his ideas have panned out as he would have liked, but virtually all have proven fruitful, and many have in fact panned out. Let me settle for a few of those that seem to me of particular importance: the thesis of continuity, cumulative effect, and mutual reinforcement in the slave revolts; the thesis of interracial unity and of the relation of the struggle of the slaves for freedom to the struggle of the Southern yeomen and poor whites for material advancement and democratic rights; and the thesis of the centrality of the struggle of the slaves for political democracy in the United States as a whole.

First, Aptheker has been cautious about arguing that the slave revolts were connected and cumulative and has admitted a paucity of direct evidence and the existence of substantial methodological difficulties. Forty years later the jury is still out and may never be able to reach a firm verdict. Yet by raising the question of a connection, Aptheker was led to develop a supporting thesis that has steadily been gaining empirical support: his strong but little-noticed thesis that what he calls the revolutionary philosophy of the American and French revolutions exercised a decisive influence in the encouragement and shaping of slave revolt during the late eighteenth and nineteenth centuries. As the evidence in support of this thesis mounts, it renders less important the interesting but narrower question of direct links among the revolts. In other words, the explanation for the dynamics to which Aptheker was, along with C. L. R. James, among the very first to draw attention might well have been rooted in the international revolutionary process as a whole, so that links between specific revolts need not be established in order to sustain the deeper argument.

Second, Aptheker's insistence upon a considerable measure of black-white unity in the antislavery struggle within the South—a thesis he also has advanced cautiously—has yielded good fruit up to a point. The excellent new work on the social history of the colonial South, especially the Chesapeake, has demonstrated that blacks and poor whites, especially indentured servants, were by no means initially hostile to each other and in fact displayed considerable unity in struggle against a common oppressor. Edmund Morgan's *American Slavery, American Freedom* argues, in consequence, that the ruling class was badly frightened and that it deliberately promoted racist ideology and practice in order to divide and rule. Morgan's work and the monographic literature thereby confirm one of Aptheker's earliest theses, although he certainly has not been inundated with credit for having pioneered on this matter.

When Aptheker pushes his thesis into the nineteenth century, it fares less well, although the very pushing has had the positive effect of turning up scattered evidence that might well have been ignored in its absence. Unfortunately, the poison of racism, as Aptheker well calls it, did its work. By the Nat Turner revolt—probably a good deal earlier and certainly thereafter—there was precious little interracial class unity. We shall have to live with that disappointment.

Aptheker's larger argument about class struggle in the South has, however, steadily gained ground. He is being proven right by the new work on antebellum political history. That work supports his conclusion that "growing internal disaffection is a prime explanation for the desperation of the slaveholding class which drove it to the expedient of civil war." And a forthcoming book by Armstead Robinson, director of Afro-American Studies at the University of Virginia, will demonstrate that the Confederate war effort collapsed in no small part because of the parallel struggles of slaves and yeomen against the slavocracy. That those struggles remained parallel and objectively reinforcing without becoming ideologically interlocked represents a tragedy that foreshadowed the defeat of black Reconstruction.

Third, Aptheker scores heavily with his thesis of the centrality of the black struggle to the larger political history of the United States. And in so doing, he makes a beginning—or rather, as usual, he develops a beginning blazed by Du Bois, to whose greatness he has consistently paid high tribute: the beginning of a political history of the slaves, however odd the notion of slaves' having had a political history might sound. In *American Negro Slave Revolts* he mentions the Louisiana Purchase, the Ostend Manifesto, and other matters, and in subsequent writings he makes some additions.

Here I would like to call attention to the censorship of the mails, the gag rule, the collapse of interstate comity in the judicial system, the furor over the Fugitive Slave Law, and the Southern insistence on the right to carry slaves into places as far away as Oregon, where no slaveholder in his right mind would have ventured. These and similar actions by the slaveholders drove a deep wedge between them and their all-too-complacent, not to say almost supine, allies in the Northern Democracy. Those actions sealed the slaveholders' fate in the Union and backed them into a corner in which their enemies could isolate, confront, and smash them. Why then, since the slaveholders were hardly stupid, did they do it? The answer to that question confirms Aptheker's judgment on the extent of the slave revolts and throws into relief the limited value of the attendant "numbers game."

For certain problems, most notably those connected with the comparative history of slave revolts in the Americas, that numbers game retains some value. It remains striking that if the criterion for a slave revolt is raised from ten to twenty participants, the number of revolts drops precipitously. Hence, critics, myself among them, have criticized Aptheker for exaggeration or for overestimating the incidence of noteworthy insurrection, in contradistinction to violent local disturbances. And there is a distinction to be made among a massive rising of thousands in Demerara, a dangerous and nearly successful rising of hundreds in Bahia, and a rising, if it should be called that, of ten in Virginia or South Carolina. I continue to think that tempered criticism is in order, although I am afraid that there has been little tempered about most of the criticism so far.

And there are problems that concern the interpretation of black history in the United States. Let me settle for an example in which Aptheker may be saying too much—too much, that is, for his own larger argument. I am less impressed than he with the evidence of slave revolt between 1831 and 1861 and would recall Du Bois's observation that the slaves' insurrectionary impulse was largely exhausted by the defeat of Nat Turner. But let Aptheker grant, for the sake of argument, that he overstated his case for this period. He could still point to enough violent actions to sustain his argument that the slaves never wholly lifted the threat of revolt from their masters, and, more important, he could still defend his larger argument that slave resistance remained militant and took new forms, most notably the massive support for the Union during the war.

That wartime refocusing of militant black struggle compels reconsideration of the antebellum slave revolts themselves. Let us turn the question of extent and numbers around and direct it to Aptheker's critics: Just how do we assess the historical significance of those slave revolts and conspiracies, no matter how defined and measured? From this point of view, Aptheker's analysis stands up well in its essentials and indeed appears stronger as we learn more about the political dynamics of the period.

The inescapable truth is that the slaveholders plunged into that suicidal course for one reason above all others. Their pervasive fear of slave revolt, which was rationally based on periodic experience with actual revolts and plots, no matter how scattered and small, convinced them that their slaves must be disabused of any idea that they had prospects, that they had allies, that their masters were politically isolated, that slavery was increasingly becoming moral anathema throughout the North and the whole civilized world. Thus the slaveholders had to assert a defense of Southern honor, as they called it. They had to require that the North silence all moral criticism of slavery and join in a celebration of its virtue. As early as the mid-1830s, James Hammond of South Carolina, one of the brightest and ablest of the slaveholding congressmen, told his shocked Northern colleagues that they had a moral responsibility to hang abolitionists. (It was Northern abolitionists he was talking about, mind you.) Nothing less would serve. But the measures required to allay the fears of the South necessarily spelled the end of civil liberties and democratic freedom in the North. The only way the Southerners could meet the challenge posed by the militancy of their slaves was to suppress the freedom of white Northerners. The slaveholders' Northern Democratic party allies were being asked to do the one thing they could not do, for reasons of conscience or political expediency or both. The abolitionists had long warned that slavery was incompatible with Northern freedom and democracy, but few believed them. It took the intransigence of the slaveholders to make that case look good. Thus the slaves, by their periodic direct challenges to the regime, forced their masters down a political road that led to their destruction as a class.

When, therefore, we finish with the refinements and settle on appropriate numbers for the solution of specific problems, Aptheker's principal thesis is sustained. There was, by the admission of the slaveholders themselves, a record of revolt and conspiracy adequate to make a decisive impact on the political history that ended with the emancipation of the slaves.

In view of Aptheker's achievements, only some of which I have touched upon, we might profitably turn to the political implications of his career and of his exclusion from the university appointment he so richly deserved. The Academy effectively excluded Aptheker, not simply because he is a Marxist and a political radical—during the 1960s those barriers were pierced—but because he is a Communist. That exclusion constitutes a tribute both to him and to his party. But it has also had perverse effects beyond the obvious blow against academic freedom and beyond the dishonoring of the universities and the historical profession. By excluding him and depriving him of a graduate seminar—the training ground for the next generation—the Establishment sought to arrest the development of his point of view. On balance, it did not succeed. There are, after all, less-formal ways to influence younger scholars and even to train graduate students. But no doubt it took its toll. And perhaps more dangerously, by excluding Aptheker from a university post, the Academy minimized the opportunities for a full airing of his specific viewpoint. For a long time, and to some extent even now, he could be treated as a nonperson, with his work sometimes cited and more often mined, but not seriously discussed.

To make matters worse, he has had more than his share of the Establishment's customary Catch-22. When he is perceived to make a mistake or perform poorly, he does so because he is a Communist, a Marxist-Leninist. When he is perceived to write a seminal book, like *American Negro Slave Revolts* or to perform well, as he normally does, then he does so in spite of his being a Communist, a Marxist-Leninist. Either way, Marxism-Leninism loses, and so does Aptheker. To get out of this bind, all he would have to do is to announce that his Communist politics and Marxist-Leninist theory are irrelevant to his work as a historian. The Establishment will wait a long time to hear that announcement.

When the time comes to evaluate Aptheker's life's work, his accomplishments and limitations will have to be encompassed within a framework that pays equal attention to his individual talent and performance and to the particular kind of Marxism that has informed his thought and guided his action, and to which he has contributed significantly. That full and proper evaluation can wait until his productive years are behind him, and, happily, that will take awhile. But even now, we cannot avoid partial and tentative discussion without risking uncalled-for compromises with the subtle redbaiting to which he has always been subjected. What must be insisted upon is that his effort on black history and other subjects, now widely recognized as formulative, not be divorced from his effort to interpret history from a Marxist-Leninist viewpoint. Accordingly, permit me to suggest a few relevant themes.

Aptheker's emergence as our country's first great white historian of the black experience cannot readily be separated from his development as a Communist. We may dismiss with contempt the attribution of political opportunism to the Communists for their concern with black people. We should also reject the honest error of attributing left-wing romanticism, which may well have merit when applied to some radical historians but misses the point when applied to the Communists. Not that special apologies are necessary for left-wing romanticism when it is embedded in a demand for justice for black people and for an end to racism. There are, after all, worse crimes, most notably the original injustice to black people and the racism that has accompanied it. But the criticism nonetheless misses the point.

For inherent in Aptheker's stance and manifest throughout his intellectual labors has been critical political insight that has deep roots in the international Communist movement. I refer to the insight, articulated in the Comintern as early as 1924 by Ho Chi Minh, who made the Negro Question, as it was called, central to the struggle against imperialism and for a socialist America. In general political terms, the Communists saw, before anyone else except, of course, an occasional prophet like Du Bois, that no challenge to American imperialism could arise in the United States without a great upsurge of the black liberation movement. The Communist party did not always adhere to its own insight consistently and did make some serious mistakes. Those inconsistencies and mistakes have periodically evoked harsh criticism from liberals and social democrats who, never having had the insight in the first place, have had nothing to be inconsistent about and have had no mistakes to make. It is, in any case, in this context that we would do well to note the recent remarks of William Styron. Recalling the bitter exchanges occasioned by his novel *The Confessions of Nat Turner* in 1968, he has written, in his new book of essays, *This Quiet Dust and Other Writings:*

> I bear no ill will against Aptheker and keep trying to remember—as it might behoove us all to do—that in the horrible dark night of racism at its worst in America, the 1930s, the Communists were among the few friends black people had.

The point at issue, as Aptheker has tirelessly insisted, is that the struggle for peace, for democracy, and ultimately for socialism cannot advance except in relation to the black liberation movement; that such a relation can only be based upon an uncompromising war against racism; and that a war against racism requires a clear view of the historical experience of black Americans. Thus, those who accuse Aptheker, and all serious Marxists whether Communist or not, of bringing a political commitment to their work are right. But what that proves, contrary to what these critics assert, is that political commitment, when properly disciplined, sharpens historical writing and strengthens the search for truth. For the record shows that the politically committed history of Du Bois and Aptheker has not in fact transformed black history into ideology; to the contrary, it has made a decisive contribution toward overthrowing the flagrantly ideological history of the Phillips and Dunning schools.

In the masterwork we here honor but also in his path-breaking work on the maroons, on the black contribution to militant abolitionism, on the postslavery development of the struggle against racism and imperialism, and on other subjects, Aptheker demonstrated that the struggles of black people have had, throughout the entire course of American history, a double aspect—as discrete struggles for black liberation and as an integral part of the struggle of the American people against reaction. The historical profession has found it possible, and indeed increasingly necessary, to accept that first aspect, but it has, for the most part, wanted no truck with the second. Instead, it has tried to absorb the black liberation struggle into mainstream liberalism and thereby to anesthetize it and draw its political teeth. Thus, to do full justice to Aptheker's achievement today requires concentrating our efforts on explicating and deepening that second aspect, which has always pointed toward the unity of thought and action—toward the indissolubility of the search for historical truth and the responsibility to make clear the political meaning of our historical research.

The emergence of assorted radical schools of thought since the 1960s has not solved the problem. Some of those schools and such individual efforts as Vincent Harding's stunning *There Is a River* have in fact contributed toward a restoration of the political dimension to social history. But much of the current work in black history, like that in social history in general, is in full retreat from its own political implications. Let me give a single illustration. The fine, impressive, often outstanding work on the cultural struggle of the slaves—on their family life, religion, community solidarity, and much else—bears heavily on the historical tension between the integrationist and nationalist tendencies in the black experience. Among other things, it buries the thesis, made popular by Theodore Draper and widely subscribed to in the Academy, that black nationalism should be understood as a pathological response to oppression rather than as an authentic expression of the black experience. The political uses to which this history will be put are not foreordained and may safely be left to the black liberation movement. I am not even sure that Aptheker and I would agree on the specifics, but I am sure that black people will make their own political judgment in good time. The point for us is that Aptheker has always insisted upon a politically responsible reading of history—upon the responsibility of the historian to draw out, to analyze, and to risk judgment upon the political implications of his intellectual work. To reread his work today is to recognize that it contains a powerful antidote to the political neutering of black history and to the distressing tendency to make social history a substitute for political history instead of an indispensable part of it.

There is one important matter, which concerns this relation of history to politics, on which I part company with my Marxist comrade and with the Leninist development of Marxism: the thesis that the black experience has extruded a revolutionary tradition, in contradistinction to a tradition of determined opposition to enslavement and racism. And on this matter I must frankly concede that Aptheker's Leninism, like Lenin's own thought, is closer to Marx's viewpoint than is my own Marxism. Aptheker would insist, I am sure, that a straight line runs from Marx's philosophical writings, which he produced early but never repudiated, to Lenin's *State and Revolution* and other political and philosophical writings. I object neither to the pedigree nor to the orthodoxy, for, whatever others may think, I consider myself an orthodox Marxist in essential respects. Rather, I object to Marx's philosophy of humanity, which I think wrong, inconsistent with his philosophical materialism, and a superimposition upon his interpretation of history. Obviously, that is a big quarrel for another day. For the moment I merely wish to indicate the nature of the family quarrel that I have with Aptheker and with other Marxists, including the great historian Eric Hobsbawm, the Communist character of whose work the American Academy also pretends not to notice whenever it feels compelled to praise him.

The very notion of a revolutionary tradition is elusive and requires an act of faith. That is not a point against it. For if it opens the way to self-fulfilling prophecy that some interpret as scientific prediction, it also provides an estimate upon which to base a hard politics. And perhaps more important, it fuels militant partisanship in struggle in a way that is hard for the alternatives. As Aptheker knows, a tradition is not something static, something inherited, something to be applied; it is a living cultural force that can only remain living if developed in constant struggle. Hence, no ultimate empirical test will ever be possible and the quarrel will continue.

I would not belabor this point if there were not embedded within it two radically different historical psychologies that bear directly upon our understanding of the slave experience and much else. According to the first, which Marx professed and Lenin proclaimed unambiguously in various writings and which I believe informs Aptheker's work, the destruction of class exploitation will lead to the destruction of racial and gender oppression, not as an automatic reflex— only simpletons have ever believed that—but as a result of a historically inevitable victory in struggle. The Marxist-Leninist theory of the withering away of the state and of a free communist society devoid of coercion rests on the psychological premise that the destruction of class exploitation will liberate human beings to relate to each other naturally—where the view of what is natural is one of intrinsic goodness and harmony with others. I see no scientific, much less historical, basis for such a view, although I wish I did. If, to the contrary, one regards human beings as a historical product of intrapsychic struggle—if, that is, one posits an inherent and ultimately irreconcilable antagonism between self and society—radically different expectations follow, including rejection of the withering away of the state under communism. And indeed, there are other problems, such as overcoming the social division of labor, which Marx insisted upon and Lenin made the foundation of the ideological edifice he built, but which has little to recommend it today and has increasingly poor prospects.

If I am correct in this sketchy criticism, which I recently discussed at some length elsewhere, then the Leninist development of Marxism, to which Aptheker and Hobsbawm have contributed much that is rich and powerful, remains flawed and, at the least, requires extensive comradely discussion. I raise this question here, not because this is an appropriate forum for that discussion, but because I want to illustrate what has become a serious weakness in American Marxism as a whole—a weakness that Aptheker has himself always tried to combat.

For too long American Marxists have been forced to respond to questions posed by bourgeois historians. Up to a point, we have had no choice. Even Aptheker, who obviously saw the trap early in his career, had to devote much time and energy to demolishing racist arguments and clearing away ideological rubbish before he could get on with the task of posing fresh questions. Even now, we collectively suffer in this way, although with less and less excuse. It is time to compel our bourgeois colleagues to respond to our questions, and especially to address those larger questions of historical process, in both its objective and subjective aspect, to which I have alluded. Rereading Aptheker's work makes clear that throughout his life he has fought to do just that.

Let me elaborate by reference to one of Aptheker's principal themes. He ends his book by saying that discontent and rebelliousness were characteristic of American Negro slaves. In a simple, straightforward reading, I would certainly agree, but his statement is in fact much more subtle and multileveled than it might appear. I would also agree with Aptheker that "passivity" and "docility" did not characterize the slaves in any historically meaningful sense—and those are the terms that he employs as opposites, since they were the terms introduced by previous historians. But Aptheker, like most Leninists, might not accept my own formulation in response to what I perceive as the deeper and more nuanced meaning of his concluding statement. I would add that all people, including the slaves of the Old South, combine a will to rebel with a will to submit; that the claims of individual freedom or expression run counter to the claims of submission to authority, which are also deeply internalized; and that throughout history, as a function of the human condition, the latter claims have, on balance, manifested themselves regularly and the former espisodically. It was from this point of view, the Freudian cast of which will elude no one, that I wrote *Roll, Jordan, Roll* and *From Rebellion to Revolution* as complementary books; in fact these were originally intended to form a single volume.

It may not matter much whether Aptheker's viewpoint or mine or someone else's prevails. Obviously, they cannot all be right, but they all could turn out to be wrong: There are other possibilities. What does matter is that Aptheker has always met his responsibility to bring these problems to the forefront of discussion and to try to force a confrontation with the political implications of his work and that of others. In meeting our own responsibility to connect, without ideological superimpositions and wish fulfillments, our historical work to our politics, we have Aptheker's work, thought, and political action to build on. In the end, our willingness and ability to build well will constitute the most appropriate tribute we can pay him and the only way we can render permanent what he has done for us.

4

Resistance in Africa: From Nationalist Revolt to Agrarian Protest

TERENCE RANGER

Introduction

I emerged from my formal education as a historian—six years in Oxford—totally unequipped to handle *any* of the topics or regions covered in this book. I went to teach at an African university in 1957 without having read a single book on African history. In 1969, having turned myself into some sort of historian of Africa, I went to teach at an American university without having read a single book on American history. I indulge in this brief bit of autobiography in order to highlight the importance in my own intellectual career of Aptheker's *American Negro Slave Revolts*: Quite simply, in its New World Paperback (1969) edition, it was the first book on American history I had ever bought and the first I had ever read. I still possess that copy, dogeared, underlined, and with exclamation marks and N.B.'s liberally scattered about.

Coming to it in this way, of course, I considered the book important, not as a corrective to formal white American historiography, of which I was still ignorant, but as a way into American history for an Africanist. In the two years before 1969 I had myself published a book and several articles on African resistance—the book describing and assessing the Ndebele and Shona risings against the Rhodesian whites in 1896, and the articles arguing a case for the continuous "traditions" of protest that I believed link such early armed resistance to modern movements of mass nationalism.[1] I found Aptheker's book, and in particular the preface written for the 1969 edition, enormously reassuring, since it seemed to be saying for black America just what I had myself been trying to say for Africa. (I didn't adequately appreciate then that Aptheker had said it all over twenty years earlier.)

I too had been writing about rebellion as "the highest form of protest"; I too had been seeking to give the lie "to the basic chauvinist stereotype concerning the allegedly meek, docile, passive black"; I too had been trying to prove "a tie of continuity," to show that "the present generations of [black] men and women now shaking the very foundations of racism . . . [were] the inheritors and continuers of a great tradition of militancy." And I too might have ended my book with the words Aptheker used to end his.

> The data herein presented make necessary the revision of the generally accepted notion that [the black] response was one of passivity and docility. The evidence, on the contrary, points to the conclusion that discontent and rebelliousness were not only exceedingly common, but, indeed, characteristic.[2]

I think now, after a rereading of Aptheker's book, that these were not its only significant propositions. But they were the propositions that I embraced with ardor in 1969.

Developments in African Resistance Historiography

I am only imperfectly aware of what has happened since 1969 in the historiography of Afro-American resistance. But two things have happened to my own book and articles. One is that as the Zimbabwean struggle assumed more and more the character of a guerrilla war in the years after 1969, so the relevance of the 1896 risings became more and more apparent and asserted. When I was able to revisit Zimbabwe after the triumph of the Zimbabwe African National Union–Patriotic Front (ZANU/PF) in the 1980 elections, I found myself generously hailed as a contributor to that victory because I had written *Revolt in Southern Rhodesia*. At the same time, though, the book and articles, as well as the whole historiography of which they were representative, had come under increasing academic criticism—and much of that criticism I had come to accept. Thus I found myself in September 1982, when I visited Zimbabwe for a historiographical conference, repenting my bourgeois nationalist errors in the conference chamber and unrepentantly enjoying popular esteem as a "nationalist" historian outside it!

The academic and radical criticisms of "resistance historiography" were that it had been concerned to document a continuity with the nationalist parties of the 1950s and 1960s, ignoring the ambiguities and contradictions within nationalism; resistance historiography had thereby delivered the tradition of past "mass" resistance into the hands of petit-bourgeois regimes, which could then make use of that resistance tradition to legitimate themselves. Moreover, the critics alleged, a focus on *resistance* to whites meant a focus on mere *reaction* rather than a focus on true African agency; alternatively, the critics asserted, an emphasis on African agency itself constituted merely a starting point for African historiography, and once accepted and taken for granted, there did not seem much point in making such a fuss about it. In any case, it was argued, an emphasis upon either resistance or agency obscured the extent to which Africans had been and remained unable to strike at the *real* structures of their oppression, which were located, not in the hierarchies of colonial administration or in the clusters of white settler enterprise, but in the metropolitan nuclei of international capital. Thus, would-be historians of African resistance were told either that they must make a rigorous class analysis of the movements they were describing, or that they should regard them as epiphenomena of the penetration of international capitalism.

As Donald Crummey writes in his introduction to a forthcoming collection entitled *Rebellion and Social Protest in Africa,*

> Developments in Africa and in African studies during the 1970s . . . called into question some of the framework and assumptions [of resistance historiography]. In retrospect . . . Rotberg and Mazrui's *Protest and Power in Black Africa* [a collection of essays on resistance published in 1970] seems the crest of the nationalist wave in the study of Africa. . . . Yet in the late 1960s new challenges to African nationalism emerged . . . direct challenges came to the legitimacy of postcolonial regimes, in the form of revolts, dissident religious movements and coups. . . . Meanwhile, nationalists in Guinea-Bissau, Angola and Mozambique developed the guerrilla movements which overthrew Portuguese rule and brought revolutionary regimes to West and Central Africa. . . .
>
> Frustrations in the development process called for new concepts and themes of interpretation. Accordingly underdevelopment studies and class analysis flourished, while historians began to look to radical social history. . . . These tendencies reflect . . . a distinct intellectual tradition with its own integrity; attempts to grapple with the new mood and problems in Africa itself; and the opening of the field to new comparative perspectives. Such perspectives have come from the economic history of Latin America, from attempts to understand world history and economic development as a single process, from peasant studies in Latin America

and Asia, and from the social history of Europe in the early modern period. In short the field has grown towards maturity.[3]

So far as studies of *resistance* have been concerned, however, this maturation has not been an easy one. Indeed, a general paradox bedeviled resistance studies in the last decade. It has been radical historians, influenced by Marxist formulations, who have set out the desirability of a class analysis of African protest. But the two succeeding dominant radical formulations of the 1970s have not in fact allowed much room for resistance studies.

The first of these formulations was underdevelopment historiography. The thrust of this, and its incapacity to handle rural protest, is well brought out by Allen Isaacman et al.

> During the past decade historians have increasingly come to recognize the dominant role that capitalism has played in shaping the twentieth-century history of Africa. They have given particular attention to the mechanisms of capital accumulation and the related process of underdevelopment. What has often been overlooked or understated has been the struggle of workers and especially peasants against the appropriation of their labor. As Colin Leys has noted, "in one critical respect underdevelopment theory tends to resemble development theory—it concentrates on what happens *to* the underdeveloped countries at the hands of imperialism and colonialism, rather than on the total historical process involved, including the various forms of struggle against imperialism and colonialism which grew out of the condition of underdevelopment."
>
> In its most extreme form this economist tendency has had the effect of reducing the subordinate classes to mere producers of surplus value whose own history lacked any meaning or significance within the colonial-capitalist context. It denied them the dignity of historical agents who played a role in shaping their own destinies and instead cast them as either impotent or impassive victims.[4]

I have myself leveled similar criticisms at the most effective collection of historical underdevelopment studies of colonial rural Africa, Palmer and Parsons's *The Roots of Rural Poverty*, which appeared in 1977.[5] The book argues that the needs of colonial capitalism first created African peasantries throughout southern, Central, and East Africa; and then, when they were no longer needed, destroyed them. It is a book that states more clearly than had hitherto been stated how important a role African peasantries played in the early colonial political economy, at a time when they were needed to produce food for mining and industrial work forces. But it is also a book that fails to discuss how African cultivators themselves took up this peasant option, or how they resisted the successive attempts to proletarianize them.[6]

I suggested in my review of *Roots* that the second radical formulation of the 1970s might offer a more flexible and sensitive context for studies of African rural agency and resistance. This was the idea of distinct and successive modes of production and of the articulation between them, which social historians of twentieth-century Africa were taking up from the work of French Marxist anthropologists. If *Roots* constitutes the major underdevelopment collection, Martin Klein's *Peasants in Africa: Historical and Contemporary Perspectives*, which appeared in 1980, contains the most effective collection of studies on the rural mode of production.[7] Alas, these and other studies on mode of production have turned out to be all too inflexible, describing ideal and abstracted structures rather than the contradictions and struggles of reality. In a review article of April 1981, Frederick Cooper comments justly on both dominant radical formulations.

> The "underdevelopment of the peasantry" . . . has lately become the focus of attention, but current analyses have found its logic at the level of the world market and thus leave a major question: can the dynamics or the blockages of agricultural production be understood without penetrating into the logic and contradictions of the productive systems themselves? . . . Another currently fashionable point of view at least specifies how one might take a more complex perspective: the capitalist mode of production "articulates" with precapitalist modes of production, reshaping but not eliminating them. In practice, however, many writers have left the modes of production with which capitalism has articulated vague and overgeneralized, while the process of articulation itself is often conceived in functionalist terms, as a way in which precapitalist forms of agriculture paid the costs of reproduction for the capitalist mode.

Underdevelopment theory, writes Cooper, "leaves the struggles of cultivators, peasants and workers against capital as little more than transitory and futile gestures in the face of the inevitable course of the world economy." But mode of production theory, though promising to illuminate "the production process and the class struggle," in reality fails to do so: All too often "labelling structures . . . substitutes for analyzing their basic nature."[8]

Thus, throughout most of the 1970s it was hard for radical historians to reach to the realities of rural resistance in Africa through the folds of dominant theory. But at least the resisters were being implicitly redefined: They were no longer "the masses," instinctively protonationalist; they were *peasants*. Now, I shall argue that the concept of *agrarian* protest does indeed contain within it the prospects of advance and maturation for African resistance studies. But the mere proclamation that the objects of study were peasants and peasant resistance did nothing in itself to resolve the dilemmas of the 1970s. For one thing, there was the problem of defining what one meant by the word *peasants*.

An excellent example of the difficulties of defining *peasant* is provided by a recent paper by the distinguished French radical Africanist Catherine Coquery Vidrovitch, who *has* maintained a continuous interest in African resistance. At a conference on agrarian unrest in July 1982 she pointed out that in their determination to show that "resistance to conquest was . . . ferocious and nearly universal," African historians have "insisted especially on the last great struggles of precolonial Africa." Yet these "most spectacular episodes" were not the most significant. Such resistances usually had "more of a State and political character than a national and popular one"; they were short-lived, moreover, as African political elites moved into collaboration with the colonizers. More significant were the subsequent waves of popular protest. These she proposed to consider "movements of *peasant* unrest."

But Vidrovitch's "peasant" categorization does not take us far to a differentiated analysis of early and mid colonial protest. She gets rid of "statists" but of hardly anyone else:

The problem, obviously, is to find out what we mean by "peasants." The term risks being very broad, especially if we include not only sedentary farmers but more or less nomadic cattle-breeders also. . . . We should remember that as a general rule the country dwellers, both crop-growers and cattle-breeders, indeed, in certain cases, hunters and gatherers, constituted until very recent times . . . the quasi-totality of the entire population.

Yet Vidrovitch takes the risk of being "very broad," rejecting any formal definition of peasants that would distinguish them from other types of cultivator. In the end *her* definition of *peasant* is "the country-dweller as opposed to the city-dweller."[9]

So broad a definition allows Vidrovitch to generalize on overall "rural" attitudes, underlying endemic rural protest.

If local aristocracies have sought through time to preserve what privileges they could through accepting one way or another a place in the new cadres offered them . . . the depths of rural Africa have never accepted colonization. At most rural Africa submitted to colonization, as before-hand to numerous other dominations . . . more or less despotic.[10]

Yet this profound "rural" resistance could not take "modern" forms: It was always "rural," "ethnic," localized, folkloric.

Religious protest was . . . the sole unifying bond possible. It permitted peasants with a dispersed social organization and non-existent political structures, to form a body in the name of a common ideology. . . . But the millenarian temptation . . . while finding its strength in the rural masses' tradition of resistance, was capable also in the name of respect for the past of deviating, even aborting, protest movements of a more modernizing inspiration. [11]

These formulations *do* constitute a way of giving resistance history back to the people, but they do so at the cost of evident overgeneralization. Her broad definition of *peasant* obscures the fact that peasants more narrowly defined could not so unequivocally reject colonialism: The peasant option in Central and southern Africa was a choice by Africans of one way of relating *to* colonialism, and peasant viability depended on colonial markets. Hence much "peasant" protest arose as a defense of the peasant option against proletarianization, or an attempt to preserve opportunities to sell to competing traders, or an effort to retain autonomy to make their own production decisions as peasants rather than to have to produce according to colonial command. Thus one of the key jobs for historians of resistance is to chart how people *became* peasants rather than "traditional" cultivators, and what were the implications for protest of particular paths to peasanthood or of particular forms of expropriation of the peasantry. Similarly "peasant" religion can often be shown not to be backward-looking folklorism at all, but rather to constitute an aspect of the development of a specifically peasant consciousness. It seems essential, therefore, to define peasant status rigorously rather than broadly. [12]

But even when more rigorous definitions of peasant status *have* been attempted, difficulties have remained. Many radical historians have had difficulty in coming to terms with peasant protest as a significant phenomenon in the modern world. There has been a good deal of the classic Marxist incredulity of the peasantry as a potentially revolutionary force: Analysis after analysis has insisted that only an African proletariat can mount an effective challenge to colonial capitalism; that the peasantry is a transitional class, locked in backward-looking particularisms and ideologies. And even those scholars who have supported the Lusophone "people's wars," in which peasantries have been mobilized to support guerrilla armies, have insisted on the crucial need to transform peasant consciousness. In their eyes, peasants can only be mobilized into effective resistance by intellectuals committing class suicide, by animators drawing peasants beyond rural superstition.

The burden of the scholar seeking to document peasant protest in, shall we say, northern Mozambique is a heavy one under the pressure of all these con-

descensions. Thus Allen Isaacman confesses that even the reductionist "econo-
mist tendency"

> acquires a certain logic in the context of peasant resistance because of the
> weak competitive position of the peasantry *vis à vis* the union of the colo-
> nial state and capital. Peasants divided from each other by space, ethnicity,
> religion, primordial kinship affiliations, the tyranny of their work sched-
> ule and a host of other factors were relatively powerless and generally
> failed to mount large-scale opposition which lends itself to detailed his-
> torical analysis. Instead peasant protests tended to be isolated, covert and
> often passive, their limited aims and systematic importance hard to mea-
> sure and easy to ignore.
>
> The nature of the sources available to historians reinforces the tendency
> to neglect peasant resistance in the literature. Colonial officials . . . were
> often unaware of the hidden forms of protest. . . . Oral data is often re-
> plete with examples of peasant protest, but these accounts do not tend to
> be situated precisely in time or space.[13]

In view of all this, it is not surprising that even those historians who have
focused on the peasantry have been reluctant to take up the apparently dis-
credited resistance problematic. The best chapter in the Klein collection is by
William Beinart and Colin Bundy and deals with peasant protest. They explain,
however, that they did not set out to examine the topic as an exercise in resistance historiography. It just became obvious that it was a topic crucial to studying the peasantry.

> Peasant movements tend to be localized, limited in aims and achievements
> and deficient in organization and execution—and the same is frequently
> true of their academic investigation. South African historians have paid
> insufficient attention to the incidence and nature of rural resistance. . . .
> It should not be thought that the presentation of the empirical data in the
> form of a series of separate episodes betokens an episodic view of resis-
> tance; what follows is not a history of the spectacular, nor a search for a
> lineage of militancy. The brief case studies of resistance are intended as an
> aid to an analysis of process and structure, not as an alternative. Nor does
> the focus on acts of resistance suggest that all other forms of political and
> social activity entered into during this time-span are necessarily "passive"
> or "collaborationist."[14]

I am not sure that I would want to apply to the study of the African peasantry the exhortation memorably voiced by a member of the audience during a
conference discussion: "You should look at resistance to illuminate resistance;

heaven forfend that we look at it to illuminate *slavery.*" Still, I am glad to note that the last three or four years have seen much more focused and much less apologetic studies of peasant resistance. Two developments account for this. First, as historians begin to study *peasants,* as distinct from the exploitation or underdevelopment or articulation of peasants—or better, to study peasants *as well* as their exploitation, underdevelopment, and articulation—they find that resistances incomparably reveal process, structure, and contradiction. They frequently also find that peasant resistances have been significant in themselves. Second, there is in progress a further redefinition of the radical formulation. As underdevelopment theory and mode of production analysis have revealed their limitations, so more and more emphasis has been given to rural class struggle as a determinant in agrarian change.

As we have seen, Donald Crummey remarked on the perspectives that Africanists were deriving from "the social history of Europe in the early modern period." And it is the work of Robert Brenner on agrarian class structure and economic development in preindustrial Europe, together with his devastating critique of underdevelopment and world-system theory, that has given recent students of African peasant resistance their text. I cited Brenner at some length in my 1978 critique of *The Roots of Rural Poverty*,[15] bringing out his emphasis upon "the degree to which patterns of development of underdevelopment for an entire epoch might hinge upon the outcome of specific processes of class formation, of class struggle." I cited his emphasis on the "bloody and violent confrontations" that "ultimately assured peasant victory" in Catalonia, and on the "protracted struggle on a piece-meal village-by-village basis" by which in western Germany peasants forced lords to grant rights to common land, fixed rents, rights of inheritance, and so on in "countless village charters." And I asked for a study of "the internal, village-by-village dynamics of African peasant response."

I did so with some diffidence.

It might be questioned whether one can or should seek to apply a Brenner-style approach to the agrarian history of Central and Southern Africa. Brenner, after all, was dealing with a situation in which capitalist agriculture could not have been consciously aimed at; the point of his analysis is that it emerged as the unplanned consequence of particular class struggles. By the time of Central and Southern African colonialism, of course, the situation was very different. A mature, self-conscious and powerful capitalism could deliberately set out to manipulate African agricultural production in its own interests. Again, Brenner was dealing with a situation in which the ruling classes did not dispose of overwhelming force; in which a peasant victory in the class struggle over land was possible. It could be argued that in Africa the ruling classes had established themselves by a conquest which had dramatized their monopoly of frightening military and technological power. Less even than in eastern Europe, it might be argued, could the African peasantry draw on the strength of its own institutions to resist colonial might. . . . It is, of course, perfectly true that one cannot seek to apply Brenner to Central and Southern Africa as though there could be a replay of early modern European agrarian change; one cannot see European landowners as the equivalent of early modern aristocrats, or African cultivators as the equivalent of early modern peasantries. Still, I do not believe that the might of colonial capitalism was so overwhelming that African cultivators could not at all affect what was happening to them. . . . In some circumstances there were peasant victories to be won even in colonial Africa.[16]

Since then others have cited Brenner's authority less diffidently. Ian Phimister, in the draft chapters of his forthcoming social and economic history of Southern Rhodesia, adopts a frankly Brenner-style line.

The attacks unleashed by the state and capital [on African peasants] after 1907 were made on increasingly uneven and broken social terrain. They did not simply roll across a smooth and featureless African landscape. On the contrary, their impact depended on . . . the balance of class forces located in [each district]. . . . Each district followed its own more or less distinctive path towards proletarianization . . . because the very pace and extent of that process varied according to the local importance of classes and social categories whose collective capacity to absorb the demands of capital and the state differed enormously. . . . Fragmented by difference between and within social classes and social categories . . . rural struggle against capital and the state took a variety of forms.

Phimister goes on to discuss peasants withholding crops from unfavorable markets; boycotts of traders; explicit criticisms of the Native Affairs Department and white farmers; and "hidden and silent" tactics, such as withdrawal of labor by a movement away from white-owned land, evasion of taxes, and so on.[17]

In April 1983 Belinda Bozzoli drew upon Brenner in her consideration of Marxism, feminism, and South African studies: she repudiated "the collapsing of female oppression into the capitalist mode of production" and set out to escape from "the hegemony which structuralism has exerted over South African studies in the past few years."

The approach tentatively put forward here rather than being based on the notion of structure, is based upon that of struggle. What is Marxist about this approach is that it remains a materialist, dialectical and historical focus. It posits that social change is based upon the results of contradictory and opposing forces, rooted in material reality, confronting one another, coming to a temporary resolution, and yet further contradictory and opposing forces emerging from that resolution. What is feminist about it is that it posits that the relevant conflicts and contradictory forces for our purposes are located in the "domestic sphere." . . .

. . . Brenner has argued that the failure of capitalism to destroy non-capitalism should not be attributed, as it has been by "underdevelopment" theorists, to the particular needs and whims of capital in the third world, but to the strength of those social and economic systems and the *incapacity* of capitalism to destroy them. The resilience of particular systems and indeed the struggle of the people within them to retain them, are accorded a central place in Brenner's analysis, which overturns much of the functionalism and reductionism implicit in underdevelopment theory.

Capitalism does not "articulate" with non-capitalist systems . . . but conflicts with them, often in brutal and bloody fashion. And that conflict takes place, in periods of proletarianisation, around the domestic economy. . . .

Following Brenner, but injecting his approach with a feminist concern, two forms of struggle need to be identified then. The first is struggle *within* the domestic system; the second is struggle *between* the domestic sphere and the capitalist one.[18]

One could hardly have a more explicit pronouncement that struggle, conflict, and resistance are central to radical history. And one could hardly have a more suggestive article, as Bozzoli goes on to develop it, for identifying issues central to struggle within peasant domestic systems in Africa and between them and colonial capitalism.

The Developing Historiography of Agrarian Resistance

It seems to me, then, that we have reached a point of agreement. A good many African historians have concluded, in Crummey's words, that

the themes of resistance, protest and rebellion are far from exhausted and that rich prospects await those who seek further to work this vein of African social and political development.[19]

Moreover, most of these historians have also concluded that the most profitable direction in which to orient resistance historiography is toward the now thriving historiography of the variant experiences of African peasantries. They seek to define those peasantries much more rigorously than did Catherine Vidrovitch. They seek to draw on comparative work in European and American peasant studies. It is no accident that of the two conferences held last year on African resistance one included many papers on peasant protest, and the other was entirely directed toward a comparative study of "agrarian unrest in British and French Africa, British India, and French Indo-China."[20] And I have just finished giving eight lectures, at the University of Cambridge, that are to be published under the title "Peasant Consciousness and Guerrilla War in Zimbabwe: A Comparative Study," in which I seek to compare and contrast the experience of Kenyan, Mozambiquan, and Zimbabwean peasantries under colonialism and to show how these differences conditioned peasant modes of protest and their relationship in each territory to nationalism and to guerrilla war.[21] Allen Isaacman et al., in a series of papers on rural Mozambique, has sought to show that

> neither the data problem nor the dominance of capital is sufficient reason to ignore the struggles of peasants. Acting within the serious constraints imposed by the colonial-capitalist system they were, to varying degrees, able to alter their living conditions and in some cases the outcome of their history.

William Beinart and Colin Bundy have produced a series of district studies of South African rural protest that have transformed our understanding of peasant "traditionalism," peasant religion, peasant political consciousness, and peasant ethnicity.[22]

It was in the context of all this—and there is much more afoot—that I came to reread *American Negro Slave Revolts* for this conference. I found that it had indeed done all the things I remembered from 1969. But I found to my surprise that it had done more. After all, as Aptheker points out, the slave South was a "predominantly agrarian" society—and there emerge from the book all kinds of linkages with current African studies of agrarian protest. Aptheker's account of the work process on a Southern plantation in cotton-picking time reminded me of the elaborate account of task hierarchy on the sugar estates of Mozambique in Leroy Vail and Landeg White's *Capitalism and Colonialism in Mozambique*, published in 1980.[23] His emphasis on the working conditions in cotton as a cause for revolt reminds me of the 1981 paper by Allen Isaacman et al. on peasant resistance to forced cotton production in Mozambique, with its reminders of peasant resistance to coerced cotton cultivation elsewhere in colonial Africa.

> Clearly the rural population had few possibilities to influence the supply and organization of capital and only slightly greater opportunity to affect the availability of land. They could and did, however, contest the amount of time they would put into the cotton system. . . . The central arena of

struggle focused on the appropriation of labor—there the peasants sought continuously to minimize their involvement and, simultaneously, improve their working conditions.[24]

And after having described flight, withdrawal into banditry, and so on, Isaacman et al. turn to an Afro-American parallel in order to assess the cumulative effect of peasant resistance to the cotton regime.

> In the final analysis, these protests did narrow the freedom of action of the concessionary companies. Their overriding objective of increasing the number of bonded peasants and the amount of time they had to devote to cotton production was clearly frustrated. While none of these gains altered the system as a whole, they had far-reaching implications for a large number of peasants. Genovese's discussion of similar slave protests in the American South is very much to the point.
>
> Their actions did not challenge slavery *per se*, nor were they often meant to, any more than striking workers mean to challenge the capitalist system. Yet in an important sense the slowdowns and resistance to work contributed more to the slaves' struggle for survival than did many bolder individual acts that may have reflected a willingness to attack slavery itself. The slaves did make gains in their daily living conditions . . . which often meant the difference between agony and a chance to live with at least a minimum of decency.[25]

Yet other themes of the new African agrarian historiography are there in Aptheker. In Africa it is plain that a crisis for peasant production and peasant consciousness came with the Great Depression of the 1930s, which emerges more and more as the turning point in colonial history.[26] So Africanists can certainly respond to Aptheker's emphasis on "the disastrous effect of economic depression within a slave society upon the workers"; indeed, if we substitute *peasants* for *slaves*, his citation of Senator Robert Hayne's plaint of 1832 constitutes an admirable account of rural Africa in the early 1930s.

> If we fly from the city to the country, what do we behold? Fields abandoned; agriculture drooping; our slaves, like their masters, working harder, and faring worse; the planter striving with unavailing efforts to avert the ruin which is before him.[27]

In peasant Central Africa in the early 1930s "the planter's" efforts were not quite so unavailing: They were able to use state intervention and the fixing of discriminatory prices for African and European crops, to skim off the results of peasants "working harder" in order to subsidize white production.

Once again, Aptheker tells us of black "Robin Hoods" in North Carolina, whose activities in 1821 "assumed the proportions of rebellion." A whole section of Crummey's collection on resistance is devoted to bandits and social bandits. Ralph Austin's paper will surely resonate with Afro-Americanists.

[Austin] finds five types of "heroic criminals" in Africa: the self-helping frontiersman; the populist redistributor; the professional underworld; the picaro; and the urban guerrilla. . . . He believes that picaresque figures of deep moral ambiguity are keys to understanding twentieth-century Africa.[28]

And, finally, Aptheker summons up the figure of the guerrilla—"runaway negroes" who, in the words of John K. Jackson in August 1864, organized "bands for the purpose of committing depredations upon the plantations and crops of loyal citizens." The activities of what the *Daily Examiner* (Richmond) called "this present theatre of guerrilla warfare" sound strikingly like those of the Zimbabwean guerrillas whose interaction with the peasantry is the subject of my current research. They too had their origins in "runaways," young men and women who went over the frontiers into Mozambique and Botswana; they too organized peasants in the war zone to "commit depredations" on white farms and plantations. Indeed, in the Zimbabwean case, it was these peasant attacks on white-owned cattle and white-produced crops that did the most deadly damage to white agriculture and effectively won the war in many districts. Once the guerrillas were on the scene, Ian Phimister's district-by-district balance of class forces took on a different pattern.[29]

Analysis of varying patterns of work by peasants and agricultural laborers; passive and active resistance to compulsory growing of cash crops;[30] the impact on peasant production and peasant differentiation of the Great Depression;[31] the place of "heroic criminals" in peasant lore; the coming together of local peasant radicalisms and guerrilla representatives of radical liberation movements— these are, indeed, some of the major themes of the new historiography of peasant resistance. So the study of Afro-American resistance can still interact fruitfully with the study of African resistance, no longer, perhaps, at the level of specifically *black* responses, but certainly at the level of *agrarian* revolt.

I can even glean some comfort from rereading my own book and articles, since I was very much dealing with the "mass" constituent in mass nationalism and was at least beginning to explore the rural issues that agitated the "masses." Indeed, I am pleased to find in what was probably the first collection of articles on peasant rebellion, the *Pan-African Journal* special issue of fall 1974, a remark by Nzongola Ntalaja that "historians such as Ranger, Iliffe and Lonsdale are making a needed correction to the historiography of African nationalism" by emphasizing "the whole complex situation known as *agrarian unrest*, and the desperation that this unrest is likely to promote." [32]

Still, it must be admitted that whatever may be true for Afro-American protest, the new work on African peasant resistance does not sustain the continuist view for which I argued in 1968 and which Ntalaja seconded in 1974. For some situations I would still think Ntalaja's formulation accurate.

> Communications between the rural and urban areas made it possible for migrants and visitors from the rural milieu to bring to the cities the newest revelations of prophets and charismatic leaders, and for the lumpen proletariat . . . to transmit revolutionary ideas to the countryside. And the two way diffusion process was rendered easier by the discontent among the urban masses and the peasants. These masses played a decisive role in the African independence movement. [33]

But to say that mass discontent came together and coincided with the formation of nationalist parties is not the same as saying that the former flowed into the latter. Work that focuses specifically on *agrarian* protest shows, on the contrary, how difficult and problematic has been the articulation of peasant protest with national movements.

In a number of papers William Beinart and Colin Bundy have explored the difficulty in the South African case of putting together formal nationalist aspirations and peasant radicalism. National movements, they argue, often fail to make convincing approaches to peasantries because they cannot understand either the idioms of the class solidarities or peasant radicalism. According to Bundy,

> The available evidence suggests that from the 1920s to the 1950s the various organs of the national liberation movement linked only fitfully and unsystematically with a wide range of localized rural movements. Without political leadership, without any class alliance, peasant unrest (in South Africa, as elsewhere) was unlikely to transcend its "isolated and sporadic" nature and to pose an effective political threat. [34]

By means of case studies Beinart and Bundy have explored the failure of articulation. In the Herschel District of the northeastern Cape, for example, there *was* a connection made in the 1920s between the African National Congress and the "local popular alliance." But this

> proved short-lived. The ANC leadership had, since its inception, been drawn from the African super-elite. . . . The Herschel branch, for example, was dominated by headmen, priests and teachers, who favored the

state's council system. . . . These were the very people against whom the popular movement was aimed.

In Herschel local "progressives" constituted a prosperous entrepreneurial class and explicitly aimed at the modernizing transformation of the rural economy; it was they who made natural allies for the Congress. Even the more radical of Congress leaders "could not come to terms with the separatist elements in the thinking of the popular movement. . . . No ANC leaders found a way to represent the ideology and demands that emerged from the peasant communities." [35]

In another case study of the "deep Reserve area" of Pondoland, Beinart explores further the nature of the "separatist elements" in peasant protest. In Pondoland "the chiefs were the symbols around which communal rights were defined. People were not fighting for a restoration of tributary forms, but for the local political processes which they could control." Rural political leaders "tended to espouse localized causes and develop separatist and communalist religious and political ideologies." Beinart continues:

> In the 1940s and 1950s . . . state intervention with land and cattle aroused deep suspicion and intense opposition from the vast bulk of the rural population. . . . The chiefs were placed in a difficult position. . . . Few could manage to sit on the fence, and many had to topple into the state's camp. It was such issues . . . which lay behind the widespread rural protest movements. . . . But it would be wrong to assume that because chiefs were rejected the institution of chieftaincy was no longer of importance. Indeed . . . rural rebels were often fighting for the version of chieftaincy which they thought they had won in earlier years. . . . Nationalist movements did, sometimes belatedly, involve themselves in this phase of rural struggle and attempted to instill more overarching ideologies. . . . But for the various reasons they had limited success. They could not yet fully cater for the communalist and separatist elements in rural thinking. [36]

I said above that I found Catherine Coquery Vidrovitch's emphasis on the "inevitable recourse to the supernatural" and the consequent archaic and irrational character of rural mass protest a misleading one, but she makes interesting points about the uneasy relationship of African peasants to the state and hence to nationalism.

> There is one thing constant in these peasant movements which has lasted until this very day. The rural community . . . is organized "against" something. Once against the chief, formerly against the "commandant," today against the bureaucrat. Whatever the encompassing superior power, the "state" is, it is always manifested by its imperatives, rarely by its gifts

or immediate benefits. . . . Peasant resistance, no more today than yester-day, is not the bearer of political revolution, if we understand by that the substitution of a new State, regardless of how just, corrupt, socialist or otherwise it may be, for an existing state is evil by virtue of its mere exis-tence. Abused for at least a century . . . by the continuously increasing demands of succeeding powers, African peasants often at the very limits of survival aspire today as yesterday, and perhaps more than yesterday, not to *change* power but to *reject* it. That means, lacking a better method, to ignore it. We have here the entire problem of peasant "consciousness rais-ing" whose absence revolutionary intellectuals stubbornly deplore. To try to change the state would mean changing masters. What good would that do?

The very acceleration in the historic process in this domain would tend to prove them right. . . . The dialogue which puts face to face in numer-ous African prisons the revolutionary intellectual and the rebellious peas-ant happens with difficulty when it happens at all.[37]

Catherine Coquery Vidrovitch concedes that such a dialogue *can* take place in situations where the peasantry perceive the oppressive machinery of the colonial state so clearly that they come to realize that it must be replaced by another. This leads to the kind of fusion between peasant and guerrilla pro-grams that I have found in Zimbabwe. She finds fascinating the few attempts by revolutionary movements to sustain such fusion after independence or after revolution.

In its time the populist, rural and decentralized conception of an insurrec-tion in Bissau Guinea aroused so many hopes. Amilcar Cabral had under-stood—and put into practice—the need to give priority to the rural com-mune, center of struggle but center as well of decision and formation. In the same way the Ethiopian peasant insurrection had, for a brief period at least, succeeded with its agrarian reforms because it did them in itself and by itself, putting aside for the moment all initiatives of central power.[38]

Yet these attempts are bound to be few and bound to fail.

The economic and political context . . . is such that power teams, what-ever their ideological (configuration), do not have the option, or at least judge that they do not have it. . . . This is the drama of a country like Mozambique which along its 1,500 miles . . . faces both the South Af-rican threat and the Soviet African strategy. It sees itself as constrained to impose uniformly on its rural masses the national language of the former colonizer, the rejection of ancestral customs, and the centralized generalization of a system of communal villages. It would be naive in these conditions to believe in the "massive adherence" of the rural masses to the revolutionary state.[39]

I hope that these examples demonstrate the value of the new historiography of rural resistance not only to illuminate structure and process but also to enrich resistance historiography as such. The old notions of "mass" and "elite" begin to break down into a subtle analysis of rural differentiations and nationalist class interests: The old generalizations of continuity of "resistance emotion" give way to a complex picture of contradictions and more or less clumsy, imperfect, and impermanent articulations. All this does not reduce the significance of resistance as a theme in modern African history. Rather it increases it. The old continuist version had difficulty in conceptualizing the nature of resistance *after* the overthrow of colonial racist institutions. The newer historiography lays the foundations for understanding not only resistance to colonialism but also rural resistance to postcolonial states.

Conclusion

In this form African resistance historiography has not only recovered its morale and justification but also makes an essential contribution to our understanding of Africa's history and of its relationship with the world.

African resistance historiography is an exemplary historiography, by which I do not mean a historiography of ideal achievement but a historiography that raises issues that ought to be taken into account by students of "black rebellion" everywhere. It has become evident that historians and activists of the Afro-American protest movement have not been so exercised about the implausibilities and dangers inherent in a "continuist" argument as have historians of African resistance. No doubt this is largely because state power has never fallen into the hands of Afro-American elites. And yet the question *is* relevant: The idea of Afro-American resistance over time as a single stream *is* implausible. A call for "a class approach" to black resistance and rebellion seems limited to the demand that we appreciate the distinction between the necessities and potentialities of protest for slave societies dependent upon whether they existed within tributary or feudal or mercantile capitalist or industrial capitalist social formations. While this is certainly an important emphasis, and a caution against free-ranging comparison of slave protest everywhere and anywhere, the African historiography of resistance suggests that a class approach needs to be taken further. "Slave-owners as a class" and even "slaves as a class" do not sound like very convincing categories. Africans in the rural areas in the twen-

tieth century have shared blackness and colonial subordination, and very many
of them have shared peasant status, but we cannot understand rural protest unless we study the processes of differentiation within African rural communities.
Manifestly slave communities in the Americas give less scope for differentiation but they give some; particularly in Central and South America I would
assume that identification as *slaves* and identification in terms of class position
have been crosscutting rather than mutually reinforcing.

These comments call for a breaking down of generalization. But it also seems
that the historiography of African resistance *is* relevant to the way in which we
seek to generalize African history, seek to make it part of the general process of
world history. If Aptheker's book was the first I had ever bought in America, the
book I most recently bought and read there in the period before a conference on
Aptheker's work and black resistance was Eric Wolf's ambitious attempt to write
an account of the processes that have led to the modern world, *Europe and the
People without History.*[40] As I read this magisterial bringing together of the
history of Europe, of Africa, of Asia, of the Americas, with its very welcome
attention to and respect for African historiography, I was aware of a nagging
sense of incompleteness. At last I realized that Wolf of all people had left out
rural resistance. His Africans were linked to the history of the rest of the world
by their participation in and their sufferings from the penetration of international capitalism: The African historiography upon which he drew was the
classic one of long-distance trade, state formation, labor migration, rather than
the historiography of rural production and consciousness. Wolf's book is a
strikingly sensitive and subtle version of underdevelopment theory, but it is a
version of it nevertheless. What was needed was for Wolf to fuse these perspectives with the stress on peasant resistance that characterizes so many of his own
earlier works.[41] And in doing this, Wolf could now draw not only on the data for
peasant revolt in Mexico, China, Vietnam, and Cuba but also on the increasingly sophisticated historiography of African rural resistance.

Notes

1 T. O. Ranger, *Revolt in Southern Rhodesia, 1896–1897: A Study in African Resistance,* London, 1967; "Connexions between 'Primary Resistance' Movements and Modern Mass Nationalism in East and Central Africa," *Journal of African History,* 9 : 3 and 4 (1968), 437–453,
  631–641. For subsequent reflections on these works and a review of resistance historiography
  as it stood in the late 1970s see T. O. Ranger, "The People in African Resistance: A Review,"
  Journal of Southern African Studies, 4 : 1 (October 1977), 125–146.
2 Herbert Aptheker, *American Negro Slave Revolts,* New York, 1969, 3–5, 374.
3 Donald Crummey, "Introduction: The Great Beast," in Donald Crummey (ed.), *Rebellion and
  Social Protest in Africa* (forthcoming). The reference is to R. Rotberg and A. Mazrui (eds.),
  Protest and Power in Black Africa, New York, 1970.

4 Allen Isaacman, Michael Stephen, Yussuf Adam, Maria Joao Homen, Eugenio Macamo, and Augustinho Pillilao, "Cotton Is the Mother of Poverty: Peasant Resistance to Forced Cotton Production in Mozambique, 1938–61," *International Journal of African Historical Studies*, 14:1 (1981), 1–2.

5 Robin Palmer and Neil Parsons (eds.), *The Roots of Rural Poverty in Central and Southern Africa*, London, 1977.

6 T. O. Ranger, "Growing from the Roots: Reflections on Peasant Research in Central and Southern Africa," *Journal of Southern African Studies*, 5:1 (October 1978), 99–133.

7 Martin Klein (ed.), *Peasants in Africa: Historical and Contemporary Perspectives*, Beverly Hills, 1980.

8 Frederick Cooper, "Peasants, Capitalists and Historians: A Review Article," *Journal of Southern African Studies*, 7:2 (April 1981), 286.

9 Catherine Coquery Vidrovitch, "Peasant Unrest in Black Africa," presented at the Past and Present conference titled "Agrarian Unrest in British and French Africa, British India, and French Indo-China," held at Oxford University, July 1982, 1, 3–4.

10 Ibid., 29–30.

11 Ibid., 22.

12 Two remarkable studies explore central African religion from very different perspectives: W. M. J. Van Binsbergen, *Religious Change in Zambia: Exploratory Studies*, London, 1981, seeks to relate religious innovation to the emergence of peasant and proletarian consciousness and to the articulation of modes of production. Karen Fields in her forthcoming book seeks to show that peasant religion was the most effective challenge to the ideological structures that sustained colonialism.

13 Isaacman et al., "Cotton Is the Mother."

14 William Beinart and Colin Bundy, "State Intervention and Rural Resistance: The Transkei, 1900–1965," in Klein (ed.), *Peasants in Africa*, 272–273.

15 Robert Brenner, "Agrarian Class Structure and Economic Development in Pre-industrial Europe," *Past and Present*, 70 (1976), 30–75; and "The Origins of Capitalist Development: A Critique of Neo-Smithian Marxism," *New Left Review*, 104 (1977), 25–92.

16 Ranger, "Growing from the Roots," 127–128.

17 Ian Phimister, "Reconstruction and the Rise of Domestic Capital, 1903–22," draft chapter in a forthcoming history of colonial Zimbabwe by Phimister, 121.

18 Belinda Bozzoli, "Marxism, Feminism, and South African Studies," *Journal of Southern African Studies*, 9:2 (April 1983), 144–146.

19 Crummey, "Introduction," 1.

20 Crummey (ed.), *Rebellion and Social Protest.*

21 These lectures are to be published by Heinemann Education Books and by the Zimbabwe Publishing House.

22 Isaacman et al., "Cotton Is the Mother"; William Beinart, "Conflict in Qumbu: Rural Consciousness, Ethnicity, and Violence," *Journal of Southern African Studies*, 8:1 (October 1981), 94–122; "Elites Old and New," conference paper, Paris, 1982; "Amafela *ndawo enye* (the Diehards): Rural Popular Protest and Women's Movements in Herschel District, South Africa, in the 1920s" (typescript); and with Colin Bundy, "Rural Political Movements in South Africa: Transkei and Eastern Cape, 1890–1930," conference paper, Oxford, 1982; and Colin Bundy, "Dissidents, Detectives, and the Dipping Revolt: Social Control and Collaboration in East Griqualand in 1914," in Anne V. Akeroyd and Christopher R. Hall (eds.), *Southern African Research in Progress*, 5, University of York, 1980, 111; and "The Agrarian Question and Rural Resistance in South Africa" (typescript).

23 Leroy Vail and Landeg White, *Capitalism and Colonialism in Mozambique*, London, 1980.

24 Isaacman et al., "Cotton Is the Mother," 14.

25 Ibid., 33, citing Eugene Genovese, *Roll, Jordan, Roll: The World the Slaves Made*, New York, 1974, 261.

26 John Iliffe, *A Modern History of Tanganyika*, Cambridge, 1979; Gavin Kitching, *Class and Economic Change in Kenya*, New Haven, 1980; Terence Ranger, "The Great Depression and the Zimbabwean Peasantry," in *Peasant Consciousness and Guerrilla War in Zimbabwe* (forthcoming); K. J. McCracken, "Planters, Peasants, and the Colonial State in Malawi," *Journal of Southern African Studies*, 9:2 (April 1983), 172–192; and John Miles, "Rural Protest in the Gold Coast," in C. Dewey and A. G. Hopkins (eds.), *The Imperial Impact*, London, 1978.

27 Aptheker, *Negro Slave Revolts*, 121.

28 Crummey, citing Ralph Austin, "Social Bandits and Other Heroic Criminals: History, Myth, and Early Modernization in Africa and the West," in Crummey (ed.), *Rebellion and Social Protest*.

29 T. O. Ranger, "Guerrilla War and Peasant Violence: Makoni District, Zimbabwe, 1890–1980," in *Political Violence*, London, 1982; and "Peasant Nationalism and Guerrilla War: Makoni District, 1960–1980," in Crummey (ed.), *Rebellion and Social Protest*.

30 Isaacman et al., "Cotton Is the Mother"; Leroy Vail and Landeg White, "'Tawani Machambero': Forced Cotton and Rice Growing on the Zambezi," *Journal of African History*, 19:2 (1978), 239–263; Bogumil Jewsieswicki, "Unequal Development: Capitalism and the Katanga Economy, 1919–1940," in Palmer and Parsons (eds.), *Roots of Rural Poverty*; Jane I. Guyer, "The Food Economy and French Colonial Rule in Central Cameroun," *Journal of African History*, 19:4 (1978), 577–597; and A. L. Asiwaju, "Migrations as Revolt: The Example of the Ivory Coast and the Upper Volta before 1945," *Journal of African History*, 17:4 (1976), 577–594.

31 Kitching, *Class and Economic Change*.

32 Nzongola Ntalaja, "Peasants and Nationalism: An African Overview," *Pan-African Journal*, 7:3 (Fall 1974), 264.

33 Ibid., 266–267.

34 Colin Bundy, "Land and Liberation: A Survey of Perspectives on the Agrarian Question in South Africa" (typescript).

35 Beinart and Bundy, "Rural Political Movements."

36 Beinart, "Elites Old and New."

37 Vidrovitch, "Peasant Unrest," 34.

38 Ibid.

39 Ibid., 35.

40 Eric Wolf, *Europe and the People without History*, California, 1982.

41 Eric Wolf, *Peasant Wars of the Twentieth Century*, London, 1970.

5

Kikuyu Women in the "Mau Mau" Rebellion

CORA ANN PRESLEY

Studies on African independence movements seldom give evidence of an active participation by women. Indeed, in the major works on Kenyan nationalism, few authors place at the core of the anticolonial movement a growing involvement by women; instead, a minimal role is assigned to the activities of women.[1] Such references, attenuated as they are, fail to show the historical development of women's involvement in the key issues and events of nationalist movements, and neglect to mention the achievements and sacrifices of those women. Evidence that would lead to a reassessment of the nature of female participation, of the range of activities women engaged in, and of the value of their contributions derives from two sources. First, the British colonial government was quite aware of the potential power of women. District commissioners in their annual reports frequently chronicled individual female activity and their perception of the political mood of Kikuyu women, often commenting on the impact women had in sustaining nationalist ideas and activity. Second, through the collection of oral data, it has become evident that there was a nucleus of women who took as their task the organization of rural resistance to colonialism in the Central Province of Kenya.[2]

It is important to study the positions women held in the struggle for independence for several reasons: First, any investigation of the dynamics of nationalism in Africa, and in Kenya in particular, is incomplete without a consideration of women if it can be demonstrated that women played pivotal roles in either the organization of anticolonial activities or the dissemination of nationalist ideas. Centering the nationalist movement on male figures and, moreover, on those who were trained in the English language inaccurately focuses nationalism on urban areas, ignoring the equally powerful impetus for African control that originated within the reserves and rural areas. Second, investigating the role of women as major activists in the nationalist movement raises the question of a transformation of ideas about the nature of activities that were considered suitable for women. Investigations into women's roles in the "Mau Mau" movement reveal a far greater degree of sexual parity within the movement than previous scholarship on the subject has indicated. Women were active in every aspect of the movement and performed vital tasks for the continuance of the struggle, whether as members of "gangs" in the forests or as participants in the rural network of information and supplies. Further, women, like men, were incarcerated in detention camps and jails, processed through "pipelines," and forced into barbed-wire enclosed villages during the "Mau Mau" emergency. Finally, when one considers the legacy of "Mau Mau," the pride with which many Kenyans view the struggle in retrospect, it is absolutely essential that women's contributions be accounted for. Increasingly in the postcolonial era, African women have been seeking legitimacy within Kenyan politics. The women leaders often look back to the untold story of female participation in the most widely known anticolonial struggle in East Africa as a justification for a greater voice in the independent government of Kenya and in government development plans.

The story of the participation of women in "Mau Mau" can be divided into five sections: (a) the growth of political consciousness among women; (b) the role of women in the formation and spread of nationalist parties and "Mau Mau"; (c) the identification of pivotal women who were imprisoned as "Mau Mau" terrorists; (d) conditions in the Kamiti Prison, which housed women; and (e) women's roles in the Land and Freedom Army in the forests.

Kikuyu women did not suddenly in 1947, when the colonial government became aware of "Mau Mau," develop a world view that included anticolonial sentiments. The growth of women's involvement in the anticolonial struggle began early in the twentieth century. At first political activism among women was not focused primarily on associational politics, although it is true that the earliest political associations, specifically the East African Association (EAA), did include as part of their demands of the colonial government certain issues that affected women. In the early years of the colonial state, women's political activities were highly localized, directed mainly toward rural issues. Women were not formally part of the membership of the association. The issues that women were concerned with, in Kiambu District, were the forced labor of women and children on the coffee estates and on government road projects. Thus we see women in the years from 1912 through 1930 protesting labor policies of the colonial government. This protest took two forms: The first was support for the petition of the East African Association at the Dagoretti meeting in 1919, and the second was the use of political protest songs by women.

The Dagoretti meeting was held between government officials, missionaries who were interested in promoting more liberal policies toward affiliated Africans, the moderate Kikuyu Association, and the more militant EAA, headed by Harry Thuku. One of the issues at this meeting was women's labor. In a government policy statement known as Labour Circular No. 1, district commissioners and African chiefs had been asked by the government to seek out women to work on settler-owned coffee estates. Disastrous practices stemmed from this. Women were beaten, detained away from their homes, and sexually molested by tribal retainers.[3] The protest of the East African Association and Europeans, especially missionaries stationed in East Africa, resulted in the moderation of this labor practice and the Native Women's Protection Act (1923), aimed at eliminating the worst of the offenses committed against women under the labor laws.

The informal action of women during this period included vocal protest. Women sang scurrilous songs about chiefs, retainers who were forcibly obtaining them for labor, and the government's policies. These songs—some in praise of Harry Thuku, the leader of the EAA who was later deported for seven years to the coast because of his political activities in the Central Province—were the precursors of political songs known as *muthirigo*, which were later used as a vehicle for criticism of the policies of the missions and their African supporters over the issue of female circumcision from 1929 to 1945.

In the late 1920s the issue of female circumcision, the operation whereby Kikuyu girls had their genitalia altered, tore asunder the fabric of missionary activities, divided the Kikuyu deeply, and added fuel to a growing nationalism among the Kikuyu. The controversy between the missions and the Kikuyu revolved around whether it was "heathen" and medically unsound to perform a clitoredectomy. The missions, under the leadership of Dr. John S. Arthur, maintained that female circumcision was immoral and unhealthy. Three missionary societies in Kenya, the Africa Inland Mission, the Church of Scotland Mission, and the Church Missionary Society of the Church of England, issued an ultimatum to the Kikuyu to cease allowing their girls to be circumcised and to sign a declaration that they abhorred the practice. Failure to declare their opposition to circumcision resulted in expulsion from the church. Church after church in the Central Province lost significant numbers of its congregation. In the first two years of the controversy, the Kiambu District commissioner estimated that 80 to 90 percent of the Kikuyu left the church and formed their own independent churches and schools.[4]

Women strongly identified with the issue of female circumcision. Many older women in particular saw it as a legitimation of their passage from minor status to full adult status. Many of the women also interpreted the attack on this custom as an attempt by the European missionaries to destroy the integrity of Kikuyu culture. Kikuyu women along with the men left the churches, withheld their children from the mission schools, and established independent primary schools for their children. At the height of this move toward independence in education and religion was the founding of the Githunguri School in the northern part of the district. Women played a significant role in the building and funding of this school. Women activists, committed as they were to education for the young, raised money for and built a girls' wing to the Githunguri School.[5] This wing, called *kiriri*, was conceived and built by women who were the most visible in associational politics; they sometimes taught in the school and maintained an ongoing interest in the selection of female candidates for admission to the school. Many of these women had been political activists as early as 1930. They were the first generation of Kiambu women to seek entrance into the protonationalist organizations and to attempt to be recognized as initiators rather than observers of the political conflict between Africans and Europeans over the issue of land, labor, education, and taxation.

The Kikuyu Central Association (KCA) had been founded after the prohibition of the EAA and the deportation of Harry Thuku. The leaders of the new KCA, many of whom had been members of the EAA, were primarily men.[6] Founded in the Fort Hall District of Central Province in the late 1920s with a strong base in Nairobi, the KCA used as its main issue of contention grievances over the alienation of land from the Kikuyu, the sale and gift of that land to European settlers, and the failure of the government to provide education for the Kikuyu and to eliminate such practices as the *kipande*, or pass system. Questions on the hut and poll taxes were also part of the program of the KCA.[7]

The KCA expanded into the rural areas by organizing meetings at the homes of individuals. At these meetings, issues were discussed and new members were recruited. These early meetings were open only to men; no women were allowed to be present, though they prepared the food that was served. As soon as the meeting was opened to serious talk—discussion of the issues and tactics for recruitment policies—the women were told to leave the room.[8] During this period (1925–1930) women had already demonstrated their deep concern over the issues of forced labor, circumcision, the expropriation of Kikuyu lands, and the detention of Harry Thuku. They felt that they, too, should have a voice in politics and a role in the political parties. They wanted to be included and to be recognized as more than mere providers of food for the men's meetings. A growing number of women began to resent the membership policies of the

KCA and in 1930 they split from the KCA and formed their own association, the Mumbi Central Association.[9]

One of the women organizers of the Mumbi Central Organization described the decision to leave the men's organization and form a women's association.

> Starting in 1930, the women were angry because of the cooking and be-
> cause we were not allowed into meetings. . . . Women of the village
> known as Rugigi cooked *jahe, uji,* and killed a goat. Then we went to dif-
> ferent villages and started to give oaths; this was in 1930. . . . We went to
> the villages and organized in each place. . . . Then starting in 1933 we
> joined the men again. . . . The women told the men we should join to-
> gether. We killed a goat, made *jahe, uji,* and we prepared the thing. We
> called the men. By 2:00 we took the oath: We will not sell our soil. Don't
> report a Kikuyu to a European.[10]

This move away from the male-dominated association had two important aspects: First, the tactics the women adopted were similar to those that the men's
association had used, organizing on a local level in small units, and the issues
the women chose to address were identical ones; second, the women were not
seeking to detract from the nationalist movement, but rather they were seeking
inclusion as concerned, politicized Kikuyu. In no recountings of this movement
did the women express a concern with establishing themselves as a perma-
nently autonomous female-oriented body; they were not seeking liberation
from male control but a recognition of the potential value of women's organizational abilities and spheres of influence.[11] These women initiated the separation
from the male-dominated organization because they felt that the nationalist
movement was seriously hampered by not taking advantage of women's talent
and commitment. These women saw the break as a way to make their point, not
as a goal of female ambition. After the return of the women to the KCA in
1933, women increasingly assumed positions of leadership in rural politics.

With the outbreak of World War II, the colonial government in Kenya moved
to proscribe all African political parties out of a fear that these organizations
could nurture subversive, anti-European ideas and activities. The threat of invasion from Italy seemed to many in the colonial government to be a strong
possibility and because the KCA had from 1925 through 1940 sent a stream of
petitions to the government headquartered in both Nairobi and London, European officials were anxious to eliminate from the Kenya scene those Africans
who had been responsible for voicing African dissatisfactions.[12] African leaders,
who were considered by many in the government to be "adept liars and past
masters in sowing the seeds of false rumours,"[13] had been credited with constantly stirring up African discontent over land policies, the lack of significant

government funding for African education, and the pivotal issue of the imbalance of political power between Africans and Europeans.

During the years 1940 to 1945, therefore, the colonial government concentrated its energies on the war, and the stage for African political activity was severely limited. In the postwar era, African political activity surged to the forefront of the country's attention. A new political association, the Kenya African Union (KAU), which included many of the members of the defunct KCA, was formed in the Central Province in 1944. By 1950 the Kenya government had convinced itself that KAU had created a dangerous climate. KAU's membership had reportedly grown to a fantastic figure of one hundred thousand members.[14] In 1950, the Native Affairs Department in Kenya noted that there had emerged a violent organization that it called Mau Mau and the government took prompt action to curtail and eliminate the activities and influence of the movement. The annual report for that year noted:

> [Mau Mau] first came to light in Nyeri and Kiambu, when it was found that secret meetings were being held at which an illegal oath, accompanied by appropriately horrid ritual, was being administered to initiates binding them to treat all Government servants as enemies, to disobey Government orders and eventually to evict all Europeans from the country.[15]

The government reacted to the threat of "Mau Mau" by arresting the oath takers and declaring the association illegal. Despite this prohibition, the society grew over the next two years. Hundreds of thousands of Kikuyu took the oath of this new, aggressive party, fled to the forests to conduct a guerrilla war against the Europeans, and conducted what amounted to a civil war against those Kikuyu who remained loyal to the British government or allowed themselves to be co-opted into the Homeguard forces.

Kikuyu women participated in significant numbers in nearly every aspect of the war waged by "Mau Mau" adherents. Women who had been instrumental in the formation of the Mumbi Central Association were first among the thousands of women who were identified by the government as "Mau Mau" subversives.[16] Those Kikuyu women who were recognized rural leaders in Kiambu District, who in many cases had given and taken the oaths, were among the first Kikuyu to be jailed under the Emergency Orders of October 1952. Two of the women leaders recounted their experiences:

> [At] the starting of Mau Mau . . . the leaders were taken to Kapenguria. Mzee [Kenyatta] was caught and jailed. All the leaders were jailed, even I and my husband were jailed on the same day.[17]
> . . . and the woman who was the leader was Wambui [Wagarama]. There were many women [in this group] but I don't know how many since

we didn't count them. Up until 1952 I was a leader. I was jailed in 1952 in Githunguri . . . because of being a politician. . . . I stayed in jail for one month and two weeks. The second time I was taken to Kamiti; that was in 1953. I was released in November of 1957. They said that I was organizing the women and put me in jail.[18]

The politically prominent rural women in the district were jailed almost immediately after the enactment of the Emergency Orders: Rebecca Njeri Kairi, Wambui Wagarama, Priscilla Wambaki, Mary Wanjiko, and Nduta wa Kore are a few of the many women activists who were singled out by the colonial government as subversive influences.[19] The district officials pinpointed what appears to have been the top layer of a hierarchy of a network of women leaders created during the 1930s. From oral interviews conducted in the Kiambu District, it has been possible to reproduce the chain of command for the women's network; responsibility for the dissemination of information and for the organization of women was divided according to the six divisions in the district. This hierarchy of authority and responsibility appears as follows:

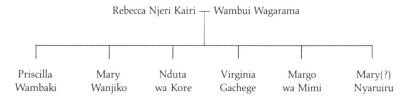

Rebecca Njeri Kairi — Wambui Wagarama

Priscilla Wambaki	Mary Wanjiko	Nduta wa Kore	Virginia Gachege	Margo wa Mimi	Mary(?) Nyaruiru

Rebecca Njeri merited special mention in the district annual reports as the "ex-woman's leader of Mau Mau, close associate of Kinyatta [*sic*] vitriolic tongue, friend of Kiano and Mboya, stirring up all the hate she can."[20] This description of Rebecca, colorful as it is, shows that women activists were not invisible to local officials. Accordingly, officials were as adept at identifying women leaders as they were male politicians. The women organized themselves into an ever-widening network. Wambui Wagarama estimated that by the outbreak of "Mau Mau" one in every four women in the district was to a greater or lesser extent influenced by women politicians to cooperate in some manner with KAU.[21]

The intent of the 1952 actions of the government was to decapitate the movement, to eliminate the leaders, and thus, from the outset, thwart the growth of the resistance. The arresting of women as "Mau Mau" adherents was not the result of ignorance or whim. British officials and Western observers in Kenya during the Emergency and shortly thereafter frequently noted that women were active in two important phases of the secret network: oath ceremonies and the supply of materials to the forest fighters.[22] In the first instance, women were highly visible at the ceremonies. The oath was a declaration of allegiance to the Kikuyu, a desire to obtain the return of Kikuyu land, and to expel Europeans from Kenya. In traditional Kikuyu society, women and children never took an oath, but the Mumbi Central Association and KAU bound women by the oath. Later, "Mau Mau" used the oath irrespective of age and sex to bind the Kikuyu together.[23] There were six oaths; the first, known as A oath, and the second, the B-*batuni* oath, were given to all initiates after a goat had been slaughtered and its blood drunk by the oath takers.

> (A) Even if we are cut,
>   We will not leave our soil.
>   If anyone asks about the soil and the oath,
>   We will not tell.

> (B) If I become a freedom fighter,
>   I will not tell.
>   Even if my mother is guilty of
>   betraying the Mau Mau,
>   I will tell it.[24]

These oaths were often given to large groups of men, women, and children.[25] The later oaths, according to informants, were administered on the basis of the degree of involvement of the individual in the rebellion. The leaders took the most advanced oaths, and those only minimally involved took only the first oath of secrecy.[26]

Mass oath ceremonies originated in the first few years of the founding and spread of the KAU, when people had to take an oath to demonstrate their loyalty to the party. The ceremonies were performed by both men and women.[27] Nduta wa Kore, a women's wing leader who was responsible for the area from Ndumberi to Tingang'a, frequently performed oath ceremonies for mixed groups of men, women, and children outside the *shamba* (homestead farm) near her home.[28] The usual procedure was for a woman to contact friends, relatives, and neighbors and to ask them to join the KAU. Before the declaration of the Emergency in October 1952, this was rather openly done. After the arrests in October of the most visible leaders and the proscription of the KAU, there was more secrecy in the recruiting of members. In 1954, when a massive military operation known as Operation Anvil was launched by the British against the freedom fighters, even greater caution entered the recruitment process. During Operation Anvil, thousands of Kiambu Kikuyu were imprisoned under detention orders, over 375 from the Gatundu location alone.[29] In the course of the operation to separate the "Mau Mau" adherents from the loyal and uninvolved Kikuyu, nearly eight thousand women were detained in the jails of Nairobi and at the detention camp established at Kamiti Prison, which had a special facility for women prisoners.[30]

When the Emergency officially ended in 1956, of the 27,841 Kikuyu who were still in the detention camps (many of them not to be released until 1960), 3,103 were women.[31] Former women prisoners in the Kamiti camp described conditions of terror, physical punishment, and forced labor, as well as a lack of adequate food and clothing. Muthoni Gichege spent four and one-half years in detention.

> They came to my house to get me because I was a leader. They took me to Tingang'a and I was beaten there. Then I was taken to Kiambu the next day and I stayed there for three days. After that I was taken in a lorry to Kamiti. I still have the manacles they put on me. My number in prison was 800. . . . We were doing heavy work, being beaten, and punished. We had to carry stones on our heads.[32]

Mary Wanjiko, who was detained in the first months of the Emergency described the conditions in the prisons for women in the same way: "We were punished, beaten, forced to carry stones and doing all kinds of work. We were guarded by the police."[33]

Other women were only arrested for periods of one week to three months, but they too described beatings during the course of their relatively brief internment, and were constantly questioned about their adherence to "Mau Mau" and asked whether they had taken any oaths. Women who were detained from one to nine years reported much harsher treatment than those who were briefly detained and released. In the prisons, they claim to have lived with torture and near starvation. Frequently, they said, they were only given water and a few beans a day. Milk, meat, and even maize meal were withheld from them. According to these survivors, women and young girls had to work on road-building projects in the vicinity of the prison, without tools and under guard. Some of the women reported that they gave birth to children while in prison and that many of the children died from lack of nourishment and adequate care. The following excerpt from one former prisoner's testimony about her experiences gives the flavor of the kind of treatment the "Mau Mau" women received:

> I was released in 1958 and all those years I was being questioned. All this time I was questioned, I was beaten, some had teeth broken, some were made lame and some were badly wounded. We were all women and when we were taken to jail we were examined by the doctor. If you were pregnant then it would be written down so it would be known if you were expecting

before you came in. It would be known if you had it in prison. If not, we would know who from. We took care of the children in prison—those who were born there and brought there. We built nurseries for them.[34]

During 1956, Eileen Fletcher, a Quaker who had worked for one year among the women in Kamiti Prison, stunned the House of Commons in London with information about the treatment of women in the prison. In an interview with the London *Tribune* in late May of 1956, Miss Fletcher described the conditions for women and girls of eleven and twelve in Kamiti Prison that was purportedly designed to rehabilitate them.

> Girl prisoners who sang Mau Mau hymns were sentenced to 16 days solitary confinement. . . . I saw girls come out and I can tell you that even now it sometimes keeps me awake at night when I remember the look of stark terror on their faces. Not only were children aged eleven and twelve given life sentences, but young girl prisoners had to work at stone labour. In one prison, women who only had one blanket to wear asked "What would your Queen think if she saw us wearing blankets?"[35]

Eileen Fletcher charged the prison administrators with being too severe in their punishment; she also asserted that several young girls were being illegally held in the prison camp, since they had been underage when they were arrested.

> I have seen African children in British gaols sentenced to life imprisonment for consorting with armed persons and unlawful possession of ammunition. . . . In a woman's prison less than a year ago I saw 21 young people—including 11 and 12 year olds—who were all condemned to this inhuman punishment for supposed Mau Mau offences.[36]

According to Miss Fletcher, the young girls' cases only came up for review every four years and the commandant of the prison expected these young girls to serve a minimum of eight years in prison.[37]

In the face of such suffering and possible death, women activists showed a depth of commitment to the movement and exhibited genuine courage. Perhaps the most crucial area of women's involvement in "Mau Mau" was in helping to maintain the supply line of the organization. The rebellion could not have lasted for seven years without information, food, medicine, and guns, which flowed from the towns and reserve areas into the forests. Early in the rebellion, women had been recognized as a primary source of those items. The district commissioner of Kiambu noted this.

> In September, the Chura location appeared to become a centre of the Mau Mau central committee, and every Itura had its own sub-committee, nor

did they lack a women's section. The latter throughout may well be described as the "eyes and ears of Mau Mau."[38]

The Native Affairs Department's annual report of 1953 recognized both the importance and diversity of female participation in the continuation of the struggle. It noted that women, in addition to supplying food to the fighters when they were in the vicinity of their homesteads, carried food to the forces in the forests, and some were caught dressed as "Mau Mau" *askaris* (soldiers).[39] Imbued with notions of women as submissive and docile, European male officials of the government were frequently shocked by the "truculence" of Kikuyu women. The Native Affairs report for 1953 commented on women's activism.

> The attitudes of the women of the tribe towards the Emergency was, in general, particularly distressing. Perhaps owing to the divergences in educational standards between the sexes, the primitive and indigenous cult of Mau Mau has had for many a powerful appeal. There have been instances of female relatives being privy to the murder of their loyal menfolk.[40]

The 1955 Handing Over Report for Githunguri Division, Kiambu, said the area had "a reputation for particularly tough women who are certainly the backbone of the sub-location. Their truculent attitude is most noticeable at barazas [public meetings where government policies were explained]."[41]

The women did, indeed, provide a backbone for the "Mau Mau" movement. In the early years of the KAU a chain of command had been established for the dissemination of information and the collection of party dues. As noted above, attached to each division of the KAU central committee was a women's wing and leader. That leader knew the degree of commitment to the KAU and later "Mau Mau" of nearly every woman in her division. When the freedom-fighting forces took to the forests, the network for funneling supplies into the forests were already in place. Each district had a central committee responsible for the supply and storage of food and information. The woman in charge of the coordination of the rural women's activities would be contacted by the central committee and informed when supplies were needed. The women's division leader would then seek out "Mau Mau" sympathizers and obtain the needed goods or services. During an interview, one of the women in the network described her role in the supply line.

Q: Did you help the forest fighters?
A: Yes.
Q: How did you help?
A: I gave food and money, everything.
Q: Where were the fighters you helped located?

A: They were in Ndeiya Forest, they came from Ndeiya to Muguga, from Muguga they went to the [Abedares] forest. People from all these areas cooked for them.

Q: How would you know when to prepare the food?

A: They would send one of the fighters from the forest to say that they would be there at a certain hour and that we should prepare.

Q: How long did you cook for the fighters?

A: I stayed in the place I was living for five months and helped the Mau Mau while I was there.

Q: Were you ever caught?

A: No, I was never caught.[42]

Food was of course the easiest of goods for women to supply to the freedom fighters. Rarer goods such as medicine and doctor's services, guns, and ammunition were also needed. Women were the primary procurers of these goods, too. Some women who did not consider themselves to be formal "Mau Mau" members but who felt an identification with the aims of the movement, because of their relatively special place within the colonial regime, could, on crucial occasions smuggle the scarce goods from European facilities to members of the supply network. During the Emergency, for example, a woman who worked at the Kiambu Hospital as a nurse's aide often smuggled medicine out of the hospital and delivered it to a woman who was known to her as a "Mau Mau" woman.

Q: Where did you live at the time of the Emergency?

A: I lived in the hospital.

Q: Why was this?

A: I was a nurse at the Kiambu Hospital.

Q: How long were you there?

A: I was there from 1950 until 1957.

Q: Did you ever cook for the Mau Mau?

A: No, but I gave them medicines.

Q: Were you ever caught giving medicines?

A: No. I was giving them secretly.

Q: How did you get the medicine to the fighters?

A: The fighters came secretly at night to get the medicines and then they would go back to their camps.

Q: Did you ever go to the camps yourself?

A: No.

Q: Do you think that the Mau Mau resulted in independence?

A: We knew that if only ten people kept fighting we would be free.[43]

These are a few of the experiences of the thousands of women who made up what the British termed the "passive wing of Mau Mau."

There were, in addition, many women who were more directly involved by going into the forests. While in the forests, women performed two kinds of duties: caring for the communities in exile or fighting as "Mau Mau" *askaris*. Life in the forests was precarious at the best of times. It was particularly tenuous for women who were "homemakers" after the British began to send forces into the forested areas to "flush out" the "Mau Mau." The King's African Rifles, the Homeguard forces, and gangs dressed to appear as "Mau Mau" sometimes stumbled upon groups of women and children in the forest while the fighting units were on a mission. Some women, despite that danger, reared their families in the camps. In the once heavily forested area just outside Nairobi, now named the Nairobi City Park, a forest camp was established in the first few years of the rebellion. Elizabeth Wanjiko spent part of the Emergency in this forest.

Q: What did you do during the Emergency?
A: I helped by cooking and staying in the forest.
Q: Where was this forest?
A: This was at City Faka where Aga Kahn [hospital] is now.
Q: How long did you stay in the forest?
A: One year.
Q: Were there other women there?
A: There were other women but I don't know them now.
Q: Did these women actually fight?
A: I didn't carry a gun because I cooked and I was pregnant but others were carrying guns. I just cooked for the group.
Q: Were you married then?
A: Yes, I had four children.
Q: Did your husband know you were in the forest?
A: Yes, he was with me and the children were left with their grandmother.
Q: Was it a large group in the forest?
A: Yes, there were very many of us and I left the forest at the time my husband was jailed.
Q: Where did you get the food for cooking?
A: The other fighters brought the food, we even went out to steal food.
Q: Was the camp ever attacked by the Europeans?
A: The Europeans kept searching to see how they could destroy us. They stopped coming to the forest at the time my husband was detained.
Q: Did you live in the forest after he was detained?
A: My husband was taken during the night, the following morning I

went home. I never returned to the forest but the fighters continued to help me.

Q: What kind of help did they give you?

A: They brought me money so that I could educate my children.

Q: How long was your husband detained?

A: Seven years. He was caught at the beginning, that was just after Mzee was detained.

Q: How was it that your husband was taken?

A: He was taken in the forest, he was not alone. There were very many men with him. The women were hiding in another place and the women were the ones who knew what was going on.

Q: Were all the men taken?

A: No, we were not all together.

Q: Did other women leave after that or did they stay in the forest?

A: Because the men were detained, the wives went each to their own homes.

Q: Did the camp continue?

A: It moved from the forest when the war ended.

Q: How did you get new members to come and live in the forest?

A: For example, if now you ask me where I am going, I would say "to the forest" and you could accompany me.

Q: What was life like in the forest?

A: The houses were just huts that we built out of junk so that if you saw a policeman coming you could leave it. We were just putting rubbish together. There were no *shambas* [homestead farms]. Food came from the homes [in the villages]. We washed and hung clothes near the streams, the camp was built near the stream but if not then the fighters would bring water in their cars. [44]

The recognized leader of the camp during Elizabeth Wanjiko's year in the forest was John Diuni. The camp followed the traditional Kikuyu male-female division of labor. One man was delegated the authority over the women's activities. According to the information given by Elizabeth Wanjiko, the forest camp had developed an efficient network for obtaining supplies. Medicines were regularly smuggled into the camp and sympathetic doctors even ventured into the forest regularly to treat the ill. Former camp dwellers frequently continued their ties with the resisters in the forest. When Elizabeth Wanjiko, for example, left the forest after the capture and detention of her husband, she joined the "passive wing" of "Mau Mau" and participated in the communication network that had been established to transmit information, food, medicine, and guns into the forest.

Other women joined armed fighting forces. The number of women who bore arms in the rebellion is impossible to estimate. There must have been more than a random one or two, since the district reports make special mention of female *askaris*. The capture of a "Mau Mau" fighter who was female, though rare, did occur. One such captured woman, Wangui wa Gikuhi, described herself as a freedom fighter. Wangui first took the oath in 1951. In 1952 she was betrayed by fellow villagers and was given a three-month jail sentence. She and thirty-five others were sent to Nairobi prison. The sentences given to the other women ranged from three months to three years. After her release, Wangui wa Gikuhi joined one of the established forest camps in the Nyandura Forest. Wangui, like other women in the forest, cooked and smuggled food, though she claimed that in her particular camp, no strict division of male-female labor existed. Elizabeth Gachika, with male fighters, participated in the military operations of the camp. She recounted her experiences.

Q: How long did you stay in the forest?

A: About two years until 1955.

Q: Why did you come out?

A: Because I was shot. . . . The first [bullet] hit me in the side and the second one which was in my thigh had already hit someone else and killed them. . . . When they were fighting us with the airplanes, that was harder. There was an airplane known as "Fighter." It was the tough one. It shot from a machine gun. The airplane was only sent to the forest, not to the Reserves. We were there with the elephants but they did not bother us because we were also afraid. Even animals like elephants would run away when we heard the sound of the plane.

Q: Did the women take part in the actual fighting?

A: We were doing just like men. We could shoot and so forth. If the Europeans came into the forest, they would be beaten even by two fighters and then removed because the Europeans could not see the ones who were not fighting.

Q: Did you shoot anyone?

A: How could you stay in the forest without shooting?

Q: Did you personally shoot anyone?

A: I shot many, even when Virginia's son was with me I was shooting.

Q: I asked because other women I have talked to told me that they were only involved in the cooking.

A: . . . I was not cooking, only the old women cooked. I went with the men on raids. The man with me refused to shoot. I took the gun and shot and then we ran away. Another woman who was with me would go to look for Europeans and if they yelled we would shoot them. We were the ones who fought for freedom, not the ones who told you about the cooking.

Q: Did the men feel resentment because of your shooting?

A: Men were the ones who were giving us strength to fight; it was the men who wanted us to continue to ask [for freedom].[45]

Kikuyu women's involvement in political protest in Kenya began relatively soon after the extension of colonial control over the rural areas and over Kikuyu women. The women protested and organized, albeit gradually, a concerted resistance to government policies on land alienation, the dismantling of traditional culture, and the co-optation of women into the wage labor force. As women's protest grew from reactive forms to ongoing resistance, women sought inclusion in the African male-dominated political arena. Women who had been involved in local issues, such as intermittent strikes against individual planters, began to create formalized structures for their resistance in the 1930s. This formalization involved the creation of a women's network, which was first a corollary to male protest and later, as attempts at negotiation through associational politics failed, constituted an aspect of Kikuyu rebellion itself. That network included one-fourth of the adult female population in Kiambu District and permeated every aspect of the "Mau Mau" rebellion. The network channeled food, medicine, guns, and information between the villages and the forest groups. Finally, women served as soldiers in the rebellion. The strength and determination of women's opposition to colonialism was demonstrated by their courage during their brutalizing imprisonment for "Mau Mau" offenses.

Despite their documented participation in the resistance to European colonialism, women have been ignored in the historiography of the "Mau Mau" rebellion. Perhaps that neglect can be attributed to the research proclivities of analysts of the rebellion and the nature of their historical evidence, and to their cross-cultural assumption about male-female political roles in Kikuyu society. Accounts of "Mau Mau" have generally sought to establish a correlation between political activism, as exhibited in the rebellion and African nationalism generally, and Western education. That focus excludes women because Western education and urbanization were largely confined to men. Oral history among rural women thus broadens the analysis to include both men and women, and the urban and rural sectors.

The cross-cultural view of previous authors holds that decision making on the public scale and the handling of intergroup conflict, for example, in wars, was almost exclusively men's role. Kikuyu women, except for membership in traditional women's councils dealing with "women's matters," were largely excluded from the public arena and relegated to informal networking. But that assumption fails to account for the possibility of change. Colonialism, by its very nature, disrupted established political and economic relationships, and led to an almost total alienation of the Kikuyu male's control over the decision-making process. Because the British colonial government opposed the return of the public arena to the Kikuyu, African resistance assumed an extreme and eventually violent form. Women, in the radicalization of nationalist politics, gained entry to the previously male-dominated sphere. As the importance of women's involvement in the resistance movement increased, their political roles in Kikuyu society also grew. "Mau Mau," when viewed either through stereotypic assumptions of roles in Kikuyu society or through accepted Western ideas of the role of women, can only be misinterpreted. Women substantially contributed to the rebellion's success; in turn, the rebellion led to the transformation of women's roles in Kikuyu society.

Notes

1 See Carl G. Rosberg and John Nottingham, *The Myth of "Mau Mau": Nationalism in Kenya*, Stanford, 1966; Robert Tignor, *The Colonial Transformation of Kenya*, London, 1974; and Martin Kilson, "Land and the Kikuyu," *Journal of Negro History*, 40:2 (1956), 105–153.

2 Cora Presley, Kikuyu Women's Texts, oral interviews collected in Kiambu District, Kenya, October 1978–July 1979.

3 See W. Ross McGregor, *Kenya from Within*, London, 1968; and Cora Presley "The Transformation of Kikuyu Women and Their Nationalism," Ph.D. dissertation in progress at Stanford University; and "Labor Unrest among Kikuyu Women," paper published in the *African Studies Association Conference Papers* (December 1981).

4 Kenya National Archives, AR/301/KBU/22/3–4.

5 See Jeremy Murray-Brown, *Kenyatta*, London, 1972, 231–232; and Cora Presley, "Transformation of Kikuyu Women," for a full discussion of the founding of the Githunguri School.

6 George Bennett, "The Development of Political Organizations in Kenya," *Political Studies*, 2 (1957), 120–125; and Marshall Clough, "Chiefs and Politicians," Ph.D. dissertation, Stanford University, 1978.

7 See the discussion of land alienation in M. P. K. Sorrenson, *Land Reform in Kikuyu Country*, London, 1967.

8 Cora Presley, "Kikuyu Women, Culture, and Nationalism," *African Studies Journal*, 6 (1981), 1–9.

9 Mumbi is the name of the legendary female progenitor of the Kikuyu.

10 Kikuyu Women's Texts, Wambui Wagarama, April 29, 1979.

11 Ibid., Nduta wa Kore, January 13, 1979.

12 Bennett, "Development," 93.

13 Kenya National Archives, HOR/KBU/22/23.

14 Bennett, "Development," 128.

15 Kenya National Archives, Native Affairs Department, AR/1950/2.

16 Kikuyu Women's Texts, Nduta wa Kore, January 13, 1979.

17 Ibid., Wambui Wagarama, April 29, 1979.

18 Ibid., Nduta wa Kore, January 13, 1979.

19 All of these women were identified through the colonial archives and by men and women in Kiambu District during the period of research as being in the forefront of the political movement. All of them except for Rebecca Njeri Kairi and Mary Nyaruiru were interviewed. Mary Nyaruiru could not be located during the research period and Rebecca Kairi unfortunately went insane just weeks before the author's scheduled interview with her.

20 Kenya National Archives, HOR/KBU/50/8.

21 Kikuyu Women's Texts, Wambui Wagarama, April 29, 1979.

22 L. S. B. Leakey, *Mau Mau and the Kikuyu*, London, 1952, ix; and T. F. C. Bewes, *Kikuyu Conflict*, London, 1953, 56.

23 Greet Kershaw, "Confidential Report on Migrant Labor and Connected Matters in Four Villages in Kiambu Reserve of Kenya," 73–82, Kenya National Archives, AR/333/KBU/45/3.

24 Kikuyu Women's Texts, Sarah Wambui, October 20, 1978.

25 Information on the widespread giving of the oath is blurred. Some women maintain that everyone was given the oath, others claim that only those who could understand the meaning of the words had the oath administered to them.

26 Kikuyu Women's Texts, Margo wa Mimi, December 20, 1978.

27 Ibid., Margo wa Mimi, December 20, 1978; Priscilla Wambaki, May 16, 1979; and Mary Wanjiko, November 22, 1978.

28 Ibid., Nduta wa Kore, January 13, 1979; and Muthoni Gichege, January 4, 1979.

29 The total number arrested under Operation Anvil was 27,000.

30 Kikuyu Women's Texts, Wangui wa Gikuhi, May 13, 1979.

31 *Daily Chronicle* (Nairobi), September 7, 1956, 1.

32 Kikuyu Women's Texts, Muthoni Gichege, January 4, 1979.

33 Ibid., Mary Wanjiko, November 22, 1978.

34 Ibid., Tabitha Mumbi, May 24, 1979.

35 *Daily Chronicle* (Nairobi), May 31, 1956, 1.

36 *Tribune* (London), May 25, 1956, 1.

37 Ibid., Eileen Fletcher's allegations prompted a series of countercharges, government investigations, and parliamentary debate. See Presley, "Transformation of Kikuyu Women."

38 Kenya National Archives, AR/326/KBU/44/1.

39 Ibid., Native Affairs Department, AR/1953/25.

40 Ibid.

41 Kenya National Archives, HOR/KBU/50/8.

42 Kikuyu Women's Texts, Hannah Wandia, May 24, 1979.

43 Ibid., Elizabeth Warimu, October 18, 1978.

44 Ibid., Elizabeth Wanjiko, December 29, 1978.

45 Ibid., Elizabeth Gachika, January 7, 1979.

6

Fugitive Slaves: Resistance to Slavery in the Sokoto Caliphate

PAUL E. LOVEJOY

Resistance and Property

The contradictions inherent in slavery offered slaves the opportunity to resist their subjugation; foremost of these contradictions was that slaves were both chattel and human.* In theory slaves lacked control over their selves; they were exposed to coercion that could be used at will; their labor was at the complete disposal of their masters; they were denied the right to their own sexuality (and by extension, to their own reproductive capacities). Orlando Patterson has characterized this powerlessness of slaves as a form of "social death"[1]—slaves were outsiders, aliens by definition. Masters could grant their slaves limited rights, which could provide a semblance of choice, individuality, or privilege for particular slaves in specific situations (hence slaves could be generals, court officials, concubines who were exempt from most household work, and so on), but the underlying characteristic of slavery remained the same. In most places and at most times, slaves were property: They could be bought and sold, bequeathed, inherited, used as collateral or otherwise exploited for their monetary value.

The property nexus was so fundamental to slavery that slaves discovered that they could use their chattel state as a weapon against their masters. Resistance,

---

* I would like to thank Russell Chace, Martin Klein, Robert Ross, Richard Roberts, and Joseph Ernst for their comments on an earlier draft of this paper.

in whatever form, reduced the worth of slaves to their master. Slaves could work more slowly than their masters wanted; they could feign sickness, misunderstand directions, cheat, lie, and steal. In all these ways, slaves thwarted the ability of masters to realize the full value of their property. Slaves bargained over the terms of bondage and thereby forced masters to temper their theoretical power. Because slaves were human too—not just property—they could and did transform slavery from a situation of powerlessness and "social death" into a struggle for individuality and personal rights. In practice, slavery involved a give-and-take between master and slave over how far the slave could be pushed and how much the slave could resist exploitation.

The incompatibility of the two dimensions of slavery—slaves as property and slaves as human beings able to struggle with their bonds—has long been recognized by students of slavery, although in recent years some scholars have begun to challenge the importance of property as a fundamental component of slavery. Igor Kopytoff and Suzanne Miers, for example, examine the institution in terms of "rights in persons," not property, which they consider a concept inapplicable to many societies.[2] Their approach, most recently adapted and expanded upon by Patterson, has emphasized the marginal status of slaves, whose benefits for masters are realized through the exercise of power. The present analysis, which focuses on a particular form of resistance to slavery (flight), reinserts the property element into the equation. As will become evident, some of the ways by which slaves struggled against their bondage struck at their identity as things, thereby reinforcing their existence as people, and it was precisely because of the challenge to proprietary rights that their resistance had effect.

As property, slaves often constituted the major investment of their masters, but as humans they could reduce the value of themselves as property. This chapter draws attention to this dimension of struggle through an analysis of slavery in the Sokoto Caliphate, the largest state in nineteenth-century West Africa, where slaves undermined the wealth and authority of their masters through flight. It is argued that flight was an effective means of destroying property because flight struck directly and thoroughly at the property element of slavery. Escape represented an absolute loss of property, and even if slaves were recaptured, their worth could be reduced because they had been fugitives. Slaves thereby could destroy value merely by removing their own persons from the control of their masters.

This point may seem obvious, but it is one that is frequently overlooked in the study of slavery, especially in the Americas. The more dramatic examples of slave revolt and sabotage are sought after, and it is thought that the absence or the infrequency of revolt and armed confrontation can be used as a gauge of the relative mildness of slavery in a particular setting. One reason that Herbert Aptheker sought to document the prevalence of slave revolts in the United

States was to counter this bias.[3] He reasoned that if slave revolts and conspiracies could be documented in large numbers—which he succeeded in doing—then he could demonstrate that slavery was indeed harsh, and even more to the point he could prove that slaves acted in their own defense. Where revolts were missing, the corollary would have it, slavery was somehow different, more benign, more acceptable to slaves themselves. Slavery in Africa would seem to confirm this interpretation. Relatively few slave uprisings have been recorded; yet the importance of flight has been largely overlooked. The evidence from the Sokoto Caliphate shows that fugitive slaves were a major problem. Consequently, this study challenges—indeed offers a startling revision—of interpretations of slavery by Africanist scholars. For students of slavery in the Americas, it serves as a warning that the study of slavery in Africa must be taken seriously for its comparative insights. Flight could be—and was in Africa—a major form of resistance, largely unconnected with the violence of armed struggle.

Slaves could sabotage property in ways other than running away; they could burn fields, break equipment, and steal crops and other valuables.[4] But whenever they undermined or destroyed their own value, they successfully twisted the fundamental contradiction of slavery around the necks of their masters. By manipulating their value as commodities, slaves invariably asserted their identity as human beings, even if they suffered as a consequence. Slaves carried out this attack on the property of their masters through abortion and other forms of birth control, suicide, and revolt, as well as through flight, but masters did not always want the expense of raising slave children and suicide appears to have been always less frequent than flight. Hence neither birth control nor suicide was as effective as flight, except perhaps on the personal level. Revolts were more dramatic than simple flight, but they were relatively rare and often involved escape too. Certainly in the Sokoto Caliphate and probably in many other slave societies too, flight was perhaps the most effective form of resistance against slavery.

Slaves did not flee because escape undermined their master's property, even though flight had that impact. Slaves fled because they wanted freedom from their bondage, and flight—desperate as such action often was—offered some hope that freedom, however tenuous, might be attained. Suicide, abortion, and infanticide, though even more desperate, also demonstrated the extent of the struggle involved in slavery. Although as effective in destroying the property of their masters, these more extreme acts registered the futility some slaves felt at the prospects of successful escape. The intention of slaves, no matter what the form of their resistance, must be distinguished from the impact of their actions on their masters. The most effective form of resistance attacked property, but slaves were not necessarily motivated by a desire to destroy property. Despite the level of awareness of the effectiveness of their actions, slaves were involved in a struggle. They were active agents in the attempt to undermine their bondage.

Slave fugitives were an ever-present phenomenon in most slave societies, but their numbers became much greater during moments of political crisis, precisely when the control of the masters was at a low ebb. At such moments, slaves found it easier to escape, and masters were less able to attack fugitive sanctuaries. This opportunity presented itself whether the refuge areas were the Ningi Hills of Northern Nigeria, the Guyana backlands, the Florida swamps, or, for that matter, Canada or New York City. If masters could not pursue their slaves, then it was worth the slaves' while to attempt to reach safe territory. Even on small islands—Barbados in the West Indies or Pemba on the East African coast—slaves could flee by boat or raft. Perhaps there were areas in the southern United States where the degree of control made long-distance flight a difficult proposition, but the places where flight was almost impossible were certainly few. For virtually all places, the borderlands of slave societies were almost always an attraction to slaves.[5]

The geographical and spatial dimension of slave flight obviously has to be separated from a consideration of political collapse, whether the breakdown occurred during the French Revolution in St. Domingue or during the British conquest of Nigeria. In the Americas, both political and geographical factors have been in evidence though not always clearly delineated. A comparison with the African data helps to distinguish the relative importance of these variables. Despite the relative paucity of source material for the study of slavery in Africa—or perhaps because of that relative lack—students of Africa have to approach the topic of resistance from a different angle. It is easier to start with an appreciation of political collapse or the geographical potential on the possibilities for flight, rather than from an internal analysis of slavery itself. One result of this necessary, but different, approach is a greater understanding of the dynamics of the relationship between slaves and masters as one involving struggle. In the African context, resistance to slavery demonstrates that the oft-repeated claim of a benign institution—which is implicitly contrasted with the harsh regime of the Americas—is a gross oversimplification. Slavery in Africa certainly differed from slavery in the Americas, but the forms of resistance establish quite clearly that the similarities were far more important than is usually thought.

Slave Flight and the Colonial Conquest of Africa

The importance of resistance in Africa first became apparent in the identification of the fugitive slave crisis that accompanied the colonial conquest of Africa.

Political upheaval facilitated the escape of slaves. E. A. Oroge and Philip A. Igbafe, in separate studies of British penetration of Southern Nigeria, discovered that slaves seized the opportunity presented by the defeat of their masters to run. Oroge documented the flight of slaves from their Yoruba masters in the last four decades of the nineteenth century.[6] The exodus, which followed the British occupation of Lagos in the 1850s, was associated with European commercial expansion, Christian missionary activity, and the rivalry between the various Yoruba states in the struggle to establish political hegemony. Oroge's work is all the more significant because he has established what will surely remain a dominant theme in the study of resistance—the correlation between the abolition movement and the independent actions of slaves themselves to end slavery. Igbafe has examined the impact of the British conquest on neighboring Benin, where colonial forces occupied the capital city in 1897, only to find it deserted. In order to encourage its resettlement, Resident Alfred Turner offered slaves their freedom should they reach the city before their masters.[7] In this case, expedience removed the necessity of catering to the wishes of slave masters. The resistance of the slaves was used to bring the masters, with whom the British eventually cooperated, into line. Both the Yoruba and Benin cases demonstrate, nonetheless, that political collapse provided opportunities for mass escapes.

Richard Roberts and Martin Klein have identified an even larger exodus in their study of the massive desertion of slaves in the western Sudan from 1895 to 1908.[8] Indeed the scale of slave escapes was so great that by 1908 at least two hundred thousand slaves—perhaps many more—had left. Although Roberts and Klein do not do so, we may characterize this slave exodus as a gigantic slave revolt, probably one of the largest in history. Flight in itself cannot be classified as revolt, but the scale of this exodus indicates a social movement of a different order than simple escape or even marronage. As Roberts and Klein note, "slave labour could no longer be the basis of a productive economy," for "the departures weakened the power and destroyed the wealth of the richest families in the colonial empire."[9] Whether or not the exodus is characterized as a revolt, Roberts and Klein have correctly identified a major social upheaval at the time the French consolidated colonial rule. The full implications of their discovery remain to be studied in detail, but in the meantime it is important to examine other areas for a similar exodus.

Gerald McSheffrey has undertaken just such a search in his study of the fugitive slave problem on the Gold Coast after 1874, although he too falls short of labeling the exodus of slaves a revolt.[10] Again, the formal occupation of the Gold Coast by a colonial power—in this case the British after their defeat of Asante—set the stage for the turmoil on the coast. Despite British efforts to contain the exodus, slaves took the initiative in undermining slavery in those areas closest to British outposts. Missionaries were a catalyst in this movement, and Christian communities received large numbers of fugitives—both slaves and pawns.

Frederick Cooper has provided the fullest analysis of slave resistance during the period of colonial conquest in his study of the transition from slavery to other forms of labor on the Kenyan coast and the islands of Zanzibar and Pemba from the 1890s through the 1920s.[11] Cooper demonstrates that slaves were active participants in the redefinition of labor relations on Zanzibar after the termination of slavery. Slaves became squatters, and the terms of their obligations shifted in their favor. Where once masters and slaves had struggled to define their relationship, now landlords attempted to meet their labor requirements through a combination of migrant workers from the mainland and former slaves who continued to live on the island. On the Kenyan coast, slaves deserted into the interior in large numbers; there it was necessary to encourage the settlement and migration of people who had lived immediately beyond the frontier of coastal, plantation society.

Finally, I have discussed other examples of resistance to slavery—many of these scattered in the literature—to establish a preliminary survey for various parts of Africa.[12] It is clear that in other places where the concentration of slaves was particularly high (the Niger Delta and Cross River area, the lakes region of Central Africa, elsewhere on the East African coast, and the central Sudan), slave escapes accompanied European penetration.

This survey has identified the imposition of colonial rule as one of the crucial points at which slave resistance exploded. Established authority was in abeyance; the new regimes, though not fully in place, were publicly opposed to slavery and the slave trade. Despite European ambivalence over the slavery issue, colonial officials were still committed (no matter how lukewarm that commitment) to liberal ideals that were incompatible with the political economy of precolonial Africa. Both the British and the French tinkered with the foundation of the old order, thereby eroding the basis of authority under slavery. Antislavery ideology was certainly not introduced uniformly or fully consciously; nor were its consequences even, but the collapse of the political order provided an opportunity for slaves to escape. Too little is known about the actual thinking of slaves themselves, but enough is known about their actions to assess the probable impact of events on slave motivation. Slaves knew the system was in disarray, and they ran. The correlation between the colonial conquest and the flight of slaves is clearly established as a major theme in the demise of slavery in Africa, although local studies will surely demonstrate the extent of the exodus and identify variables in the response of slaves.

The study of resistance has barely ventured beyond a recognition of the exodus accompanying colonial occupation, however. With the exception of Robert

Ross's study of slave resistance in the Dutch colony of Cape Town in the eighteenth and the early nineteenth centuries, there are virtually no studies of resistance in Africa before the era of European conquest.[13] Even Ross's excellent analysis belongs to the literature on European slave regimes, despite the African setting. Nonetheless, Ross adds to our understanding of slave resistance in a way that is applicable to black Africa as well as to the Americas. Through a careful analysis of court cases and other documents, primarily from the eighteenth and the early nineteenth centuries, he is able to demonstrate that flight was a common response among slaves at the Cape. It is instructive that the geographical conditions at the Cape facilitated escape; the large interior offered sanctuary even though hostile Khoi tried to intercept fugitives. Slaves at the Cape could flee by land because of the terrain—and also by stowing away on ships—far more easily than could slaves in many parts of the Americas. Ross is to be credited with the clearest statement of the physical and geographical factors in slave escapes.

The flight of slaves during the chaotic days of transition to colonial rule demonstrates that mass resistance can erupt when the political order collapses. It stands to reason that other periods of disorder provided opportunities as well. Invasion, civil war, dynastic struggle, drought, and famine could facilitate escape on a large scale, just as these same crises also resulted in the enslavement or reenslavement of people. Warfare and raiding were the most common means of acquiring slaves; economic dislocation associated with drought and famine frequently contributed to the slave supply too. In short the conditions for enslavement were often identical to those in which slaves could escape.

The Fugitive Problem in the Sokoto Caliphate

The problem, therefore, is to identify periods of rapid political change when resistance to slavery could have blossomed. Such an exercise must involve an examination of a specific historical context, in this case the nineteenth-century Sokoto Caliphate. All of the potential situations for mass escape were present: The *jihad* of 1804–1808 initiated a revolution in government throughout the central Sudan as every major political unit was overthrown; periodic unrest, including rebellion and civil war, shook the new empire, particularly Zamfara in 1817–1818; Hadejia in 1848–1863; Bauchi in 1881–1882; and Kano in 1893–1894; and droughts and famine, although not as serious as in the middle of the eighteenth century, nonetheless undermined the ability of masters to hold slaves. Finally, the colonial conquest, which began in 1897 near the confluence of the Niger and Benue rivers and lasted until 1903, was a period of particularly severe political instability.

As in most parts of Islamic Africa, slavery in the Sokoto Caliphate was a complex institution that shared many similarities with slavery in the Americas but nonetheless had many features that were not found in the Americas.[14] These similarities and differences must be taken into account in understanding how slaves struggled with their bondage. First, most slaves were employed in agriculture, either on small farms in which they worked alongside their masters or on plantations of varying sizes, from those with a dozen slaves to huge estates with hundreds, even as many as a thousand slaves. Clearly the relationship between slave and master differed in these contexts. More slaves appear to have escaped from large holdings, partly because they were more impersonal and partly because the problems of control were often greater. Second, slaves were employed in craft production and trade on a large scale, sometimes working alongside their masters in spinning thread or weaving cloth but often working on their own, in exchange for providing a regular payment to their masters. Because of the seasonal nature of work, slaves usually pursued a craft or participated in trade in addition to farming. The acquisition of craft or commercial skills was an important factor in flight; on the one hand slaves were tied more closely to the local economy and society and thereby had reasons not to escape, but on the other hand acquired skills could allow fugitives to melt into distant communities along the many trade routes that crisscrossed the caliphate and its neighbors.

Third, slaves participated in government; they were soldiers, tax collectors, messengers, retainers, and administrators at all levels, from the closest advisers and high officials to the lowest stable boy. These officials included eunuchs and slave generals, whose identification with the far more numerous field slaves was minimal, to say the least. Many palace slaves had more loyalty to the aristocracy and the perpetuation of slave society than to the struggles of the majority of slaves. Fourth, many slave women were concubines, sometimes in large harems of as many as one hundred women. Prosperous men—merchants and government officials alike—took concubines, who were almost always slaves. Sometimes men married slave women, but more often than not slaves were confined to the inferior status of a concubine. Caliphate law, based on Islamic precedent, held that the children of concubines were free, and indeed many important caliphate officials, including several caliphs, were the sons of concubines.[15]

Clearly, therefore, resistance to slavery could not be a concerted attack on the institution by a conscious class. There was no *class* of slaves; the plight of concubines and their struggle against bondage had more similarities with the general condition of women in society than to the condition of the rural slave population, which included men and women. Field slaves, men and women, had some problems that overlapped with the free peasantry, and their interests often conflicted with those of palace slaves as well as concubines. In most cases, therefore, a concentration on flight focuses on the agricultural, craft, and petty-trade sectors, not on the slaves in the palaces and large households of officials. Concubines represented an ambiguous category, for concubines ran away, despite their attachment to palace households.

This brief overview of caliphate slavery hardly does justice to the institution—how it developed in the course of the nineteenth century, its relative importance with respect to other sectors of the population, the crucial role of enslavement and slave trading in the regeneration of the slave population, and the extent to which slaves contributed to the economy and the consolidation of aristocratic government. Despite the superficiality of this overview, a number of features still stand out. First, caliphate slavery must be understood in the context of Islamic society as it developed after the *jihad* of 1804–1808. This slave system was based on the hegemonic function of religion, in contrast to the southern United States, which Genovese has so aptly characterized in terms of the legal structures that dominated the ideological foundations of slavery there. Second, lineage structures and kinship played a relatively unimportant role in the caliphate, unlike many other parts of West and Central Africa. This slave system contained a clearly defined distinction between slave and free; emancipation was a recognized legal act based on ancient codes. Third, the status of women was far different from the plight of women under slavery in the Americas. Polygyny and concubinage, both recognized under Islamic law and widely practiced, protected women from the often unacknowledged sexual exploitation that existed in the Americas. The exploitation of women in the caliphate assumed different forms: much labor, especially spinning and carding and tasks related to cooking and child rearing, were based on gender. Women's world was much more separated from male-dominated society in the caliphate than in the Americas.

Resistance by means of flight can be examined in the context of three stages in the history of the Sokoto Caliphate. First, escape was common during the *jihad*, which spread to new areas after the initial phase ended in 1808, lasting in some places as late as midcentury. Second, slaves fled on a smaller scale during the period of caliphate ascendancy, especially during the last half of the century. There were at least two revolts in this period. Finally, a massive exodus—comparable to those identified by Roberts and Klein for the western Sudan and McSheffrey for the Gold Coast—occurred immediately following the conquest of the central caliphate by Great Britain between 1897 and 1903. This exodus lasted until about 1910. The slaves who escaped appear to have acted for different reasons in these three situations, although in each it is clear that slaves effectively challenged the authority of their masters and consciously or not undermined their wealth.

Usman dan Fodio, the Muslim scholar who founded the caliphate, appealed to the slave population of the various Hausa states that were overthrown in the course of the *jihad*. He accepted fugitive slaves in his ranks; flight was recognized as sufficient adherence to Islam to justify freedom. In his call for his supporters to join the Muslim camp—known as the *hijra* (emigration)—Usman issued a series of regulations that included

> the law concerning giving freedom to slaves of unbelieving Belligerents if they flee to us; . . . the law concerning one who has been found as a slave in the hands of unbelievers and claims to be a freeborn Muslim but has not emigrated: And the law concerning one who has been brought from a land where the selling of free men is commonplace and claims to be a freeborn Muslim.[16]

At least one settlement, Gimbana, appears to have become a center for ex-slaves who heeded Usman's appeal.[17] It is likely that many fugitives merely joined the armies of individual leaders and hence cannot be identified further; at least they are lost to the historical record in the central emirates of the new caliphate.

In Liptako, Oyo, and Nupe—three emirates to the west and south of Sokoto—slaves were a significant factor in the success of the *jihad*. Yobi Katar, a fugitive who joined the Muslim faction in Liptako, led an armed force that appears to have been composed almost entirely of escaped slaves.[18] In Oyo, a revolt among Muslim slave soldiers was responsible for the final destruction of the Oyo Empire, which had been a major exporter of slaves to the Americas since the last half of the seventeenth century.[19] When the rebels entered the capital of Oyo, sometime in the early 1820s, they gave "liberty to all the Mahometen slaves, and encouraged others to kill their pagan masters and join them."[20] Fugitives were also a factor in the *jihad* in Nupe, where in 1831 it was reported that "all runaway slaves are encouraged to join the ranks on condition of receiving their freedom; and they are joined by a vast number from the surrounding country."[21]

The link between the *jihad* and resistance to slavery demonstrates a departure from previous conditions in which escape was possible. Usually slaves had not been part of political struggles, although it can be assumed that war and dynastic dispute enabled slaves to escape. Indeed slaves had to flee, for they were seized as booty. Reenslavement had long been a problem for slaves who sought accommodation with their masters' society. By appealing directly to slaves, asking them to join the Muslim cause, Usman dan Fodio introduced ideology into slave resistance, perhaps for the first time. Now slaves could flee because they were Muslims; not to flee left slaves open for reenslavement, as before. Adherence to Islam, as defined in terms of political support for *jihad*, became a basic loyalty in the new regime. The corollary—opposition to *jihad* and unbelief—became the justification for enslavement. Conversion to Islam was not sufficient grounds for emancipation in the new state, but it was a necessary condition. Moreover, escape from slavery during the *jihad* on the claim of Islamic belief was sufficient reason to be accepted as a free person.

Non-Muslim slaves had to resolve the contradiction between accommodation via conversion and resistance through flight. While it became more difficult for slaves to assume the status of free Muslims through flight, slaves could improve their status if they became Muslims, even if they were not recognized as being as good Muslims as their masters. But slaves could also shun Islam, seeking to rejoin their home communities or to establish a new relationship with a community in active resistance to the political hegemony of the Sokoto Caliphate. In either case, slaves had to adapt their strategies to an Islamic context, one that was propagated by the dominant class of the caliphate.

Caliphate society lost a steady stream of slaves through flight. The geography of the central Sudan facilitated such escapes: The open savanna stretched outward, offering few natural barriers that could contain slaves. Even the Niger and Benue rivers were not serious obstacles to slaves who wanted to cross over to reach home country. As Hugh Clapperton noted in 1827, "Those who are taken when grown-up men or women, and even boys and girls, run whenever an opportunity offers, and, whenever they can, they take their owner's goods or cattle to assist them on their journey. Instances of this kind happened every night."[22] Clapperton's observations were made at Kulfu, in northern Nupe, which in the 1820s was the principal market town between the Hausa cities and the Niger River. The major problem for slaves was distance itself. It was not always possible to return to one's village, even if the village was known to exist. Journeys for new captives were often long, and it was difficult for recent captives to retrace their steps, even if they knew the way. Nonetheless, large expanses of territory were underpopulated, and it was possible to become lost from caliphate authorities. It was more difficult to attach oneself to a functioning community, although one can assume it was not impossible.

In at least two situations, fugitives joined dissident Muslim clerics who were attempting to organize broadly based movements against the caliphate. In the late 1840s, Hamza, a popular Muslim mystic from Tsakuwa, located in southeastern Kano emirate, had to flee to the nearby Ningi Hills after attacking the tax collectors of the central government. From a base in the hills, Hamza and his successors—known as Isawa, a millennial sect awaiting the second coming of Isa (Jesus)—raided the neighboring emirates (Kano, Bauchi, Zaria, Katagum) in search of slaves and other booty, but they also provided sanctuary for escaped slaves who were willing to join their cause.[23]

A similar movement, although apparently not with millennial overtones, erupted in Liptako in the 1860s. Seeku Diagourou, another Muslim cleric, acquired a local following, including slaves, that proved an embarrassment to the Liptako authorities, especially when he disagreed with their interpretation of Islamic law. Perhaps because Diagourou may have had political ambitions as well, he was forced to leave Liptako in 1869–1870. The group sought refuge with the traditional enemies of Liptako, Koala, and Tera, which had been sanctuaries for escaped slaves for several decades; hence Diagourou's collection of fugitives and other dissidents received a ready welcome.[24]

In both Ningi and Liptako, slaves received their freedom because they joined a Muslim cause. Caliphate authorities did not consider the Isawa and the Diagourou group legitimate—indeed the Kano government persecuted the Isawa (adherents were impaled in the Kano market in the 1850s) and Liptako attacked Diagourou's community in 1876–1877.[25] Nonetheless, fugitive slaves took advantage of a political situation that was reinforced by ideology in the same way that earlier slaves had responded to Usman's call for *jihad*. Slaves claimed that they deserved their freedom because of their adherence to Islam, and both the Isawa and Diagourou accepted these confessions as sufficient.

Open revolt broke out in the Bauchi emirate twice in the second half of the nineteenth century. At Wase, a dependent town to the south of Bauchi, an estimated three thousand slaves rebelled in the 1850s or 1860s. They retreated west into the hills of the Jos Plateau, where they found sanctuary first with the Yergam and then with the Shendam, both of whom were hostile to Wase. Eventually, these fugitives established their own town at Yelwa.[26] The second revolt occurred about 1870, when an estimated seven hundred slaves rose near Bauchi, about half of whom fled to Duguri, where they founded the village of Yuli.[27] In both cases, the revolts were little more than mass escapes; the aim was to reach safe territory beyond the borders of Bauchi emirate. Although neither band of fugitives appears to have had millennial or Islamic interests, their struggle had ideological overtones, nonetheless. Resistance against the caliphate had to be based on opposition to its Islamic ideology; repeated attacks on these refugee communities demonstrate that the caliphate, at least, considered the presence of fugitive sanctuaries a danger. Yelwa and Yuli were not isolated maroon settlements that had to come to terms with slave society. Because fugitive settlements could find allies among local enemies of the caliphate, they could enter into larger patterns of resistance.

The Colonial Exodus

The introduction of the colonial factor altered the scale of resistance, but even more important the nature of that resistance changed. As was the case in the western Sudan and along the West African coast, the European advance offered an opportunity for escape at least on the same scale as in any similar period of political instability in the past, and probably on a greater scale. Unlike earlier cases, the Europeans were not enslaving people as they advanced. Slaves did not have to fear reenslavement, which may have helped to keep some slaves in place, but when slaves realized that their flight could not be stopped, many simply left. The ideology of abolition reinforced the exodus, even though Europeans were far from committed to that ideology. A careful distinction was made between enslavement, slave trading, and "domestic" slavery. Enslavement was rigorously suppressed, for the colonial regimes—British, French, and German— could not tolerate the indiscriminate use of power by the newly subjugated population. Slave trading, considered less of a sin, was abolished because the elimination of a distributional system would discourage enslavement, since slavers would find it difficult to dispose of their wares. It was also thought that slavery would gradually disappear if the source of slaves was removed. As for slavery itself, the effort (especially in the British sphere, which encompassed most of the caliphate) was directed at reform, not emancipation. Although colonial officers were marginally committed to an ideology opposed to slavery, the actual struggle to end slavery rested on the shoulders of the slaves themselves. The new colonial regimes became the final defense of the dying institution.[28]

The exodus began near the confluence of the Niger and Benue rivers, particularly in Nupe, and spread to neighboring areas. By late 1898, after the conquest of Nupe, the British received complaints that "all our slaves are running away to the other side of the river."[29] By 1902 all the southern emirates were experiencing a similar exodus. In the small emirates of Agaie and Lapai, along the Niger, the situation was so bad that "farms were being deserted by the slaves and such was the state of unrest that cultivation had almost ceased."[30] In Keffi there was a "constant stream of complaints . . . of slaves running away," and similar reports came from Zaria, Ilorin, Nassarawa, and elsewhere. Many of these slaves were able to reach their home countries; the slaves from Nupe generally came from south of the Niger and it was easy to cross the river and escape from their masters, who were politically powerless in the wake of the British conquest.[31] Slaves in Keffi and Abuja were also able to return home, because, as Resident G. W. Webster explained, "in both these towns the greater number of slaves have been seized from the surrounding country and most of them too recently to have forgotten their old ties so that they are naturally inclined to take advantage of our advent to run to their old homes."[32]

The most seriously affected province in the central emirates of the caliphate was Sokoto, which had received a steady stream of slaves as tribute from the eastern emirates throughout the nineteenth century. Although exact figures are not possible to obtain, Lord F. L. Lugard, the first governor of Northern Nigeria, estimated that tens of thousands of slaves escaped from Sokoto Province.[33] Some were reported roaming the countryside as petty traders selling sheep and cloth, but most must have fled beyond the borders of the province.[34] It may well be that fewer slaves actually made their way home, in contrast to slaves in the southern emirates, for slaves who had been brought to Sokoto as tribute came from much greater distances—some from southern Adamawa, a thousand kilometers away—than was the case in Nupe and Keffi.

The size of the exodus was so great that the colonial crisis represented a new stage in the evolution of slave resistance. Previously, slaves fled in relatively small numbers, except in the revolts in Bauchi emirate and the evacuation of Diagourou's community. Now slaves traveled in groups; some reports refer to whole "tribes" on the move.[35] Plantations, such as the one studied by J. S. Hogendorn near Zaria, lost as much as half their population at once when slaves decided that they were leaving and dared their masters to stop them.[36] More often, reports only mention that "a large number of slaves ran away," as was the case in Nassarawa in 1901.[37]

Fugitives swelled existing communities or founded new settlements, usually in hill country where their new-found freedom could be protected. Pategi, a small town on the Niger, suddenly found itself with a population of ten thousand as a result of the exodus from Nupe.[38] The Mada Hills, east of Keffi, also proved to be an attractive sanctuary; fugitives founded "a regular city of refuge."[39] Some two hundred slaves flocked into one Bassa town near the Benue River. In certain parts of Zaria Province there were "whole towns peopled by ex-slaves freed by the Fulani."[40] Whether or not these slaves had been actually freed or had fled is not clear, but it seems probable that these places too were centers of refuge.

The colonial exodus also differed from earlier resistance because women—particularly concubines—left in large numbers. Scattered information suggests that women were among the fugitive population of earlier times, but the incidence of escapes appears to have increased dramatically after 1897.[41] According to how concubines were supposed to be treated, there should have been little reason for women to run; at least proponents of Islamic tradition and students of slavery in Muslim societies have often argued as much. Concubines were protected from sale, and once they gave birth to children, who were born free, they were guaranteed emancipation on the death of their master. Concubines were not free to leave their masters or marry, but their status provided more safeguards than most slaves had. That escape suddenly became more attractive to concubines indicates that the transformation caused by the fugitive crisis represented a serious dislocation in caliphate society.

The British regime tried to contain the exodus by instituting reforms that, it was hoped, would lighten the yoke of slavery. Whereas it had been possible for slaves to buy their own freedom if a master agreed to a price, it now became a slave's right to have the courts set a price. This arrangement (*murgu*) was the cornerstone of the reformed slave edifice; by 1917 fifty-five thousand slaves had gained their freedom through court intervention, many, perhaps most, as a result of *murgu* cases.[42] Another "reform" was the reclassification of concubines as wives, thereby letting the British ignore the problems associated with the treatment of women. Unlike the British policy on *murgu*, however, it is unlikely that this legalism had much impact. Islamic law recognized the right of men to four wives and an unlimited number of concubines, depending upon ability to support them. This distinction enabled a separation of free women from slave concubines, which the tinkering of the British could not disguise.[43] Otherwise the British tried to contain the exodus through vagrancy laws, manipulation of the legal system, and other heavy-handed practices.

Despite the reforms and the determination of the colonial regime to maintain the existing class structure, slaves successfully challenged their masters and the British at the crucial moment. The attitude of slaves in the early years of colonial rule has been captured in a poem written by Imam Imoru, the learned scholar and jurist who wrote extensively on caliphate society between 1890 and the First World War. According to Imoru,

> The slaves became free with Joy,
> They were saying "We refuse to be slaves
> because the Christians are here."
> They all regained their freedom;
> They were boasting because of the Christians.[44]

Not only did many slaves leave and others avail themselves of the new opportunities under the reformed slave system, but others still pushed against their bonds in order to work out a new arrangement with their masters within slavery. Slaves refused to work; they threatened to leave; and they demanded more material incentives for the work they did do. Such actions demonstrate that the terms of servility were being renegotiated.[45] It was possible, in ways that almost certainly had never been possible before, to alter the balance between what masters demanded and what slaves were willing to give.

The Colonial Reform of Slavery: Alternative to Rebellion

Genovese has identified a sharp distinction between rebellion and revolution in the slave systems of the Americas.[46] Rebellion, escape, and marronage characterized the period before the abolition movement and the St. Domingue revolution influenced the actions of slaves. Revolution became possible when slavery itself was challenged. This distinction offers a useful comparison for the history of slave resistance in the Sokoto Caliphate, and perhaps other parts of Africa too. The central Sudan also underwent a transition in the nature of resistance to slavery. When slavery was recognized in the Islamic ideology of the caliphate, it became possible for slaves to justify resistance on the basis of adherence to Islam. Ideology influenced the actions of slaves in a manner that was different from earlier periods in the northern savanna. Escape to the ranks of Muslims—whether in the *jihad* or in subsequent millennial movements that challenged the caliphate—became an acceptable response to slavery, acceptable, that is, to those encouraging such flight. Muslim slaves who responded to Usman dan Fodio's appeal, the Liptako slave soldiers who were promised their freedom, and the Isawa converts in Ningi had a common grievance. Their loyalty to Islam, as they defined it, was a legitimate reason for their freedom, and flight enabled them to realize that freedom.

Fugitives often joined existing communities that were opposed to the caliphate, in some cases old ethnic groups that had to defend themselves against slave raids and in other cases new polities that had regrouped after the dislocations of the *jihad*. The fugitive phenomenon did not result in maroon settlements, in the sense that the term is used in the Americas. Rather, escaped slaves took advantage of the state of belligerency prevailing in a land wracked by holy war. By fleeing, slaves were choosing sides, but they were not opposing the institution of slavery as such. Very often their host societies were actively involved in slave raiding on their own, usually against the caliphate but often against other opponents too. Although the maroons of the Americas also raided plantations, sometimes seizing slaves, especially women, these raids were a survival tactic, not part of institutionalized enslavement for purposes of economic exploitation. Plantation America obtained its slaves through trade with Africa, whereas the caliphate generated its own slave supply within the central Sudan. Fugitives in Africa found themselves caught up in the larger political issues concerning enslavement, and throughout the nineteenth century—indeed earlier too—raiding, war, and kidnapping begat raiding, war, and kidnapping as reprisals. Maroons attempted to maintain their independence *from* the larger slave society; fugitives in Africa had to join communities that were trapped in a larger web of enslavement. The justification of escape on the basis of religious belief introduced a new dimension that was not fundamentally different from the older pattern. Slaves could claim that they deserved to be free as Muslims, but such legitimization of action did not threaten a social order based on slavery.

A second, more profound change came with the spread of abolitionist doctrines, and because this change challenged slavery itself, it represented a potentially revolutionary situation similar to the one Genovese has identified for the

Americas during the abolition era. The introduction of antislavery ideas can be traced to Hugh Clapperton, whose visit to the caliphate in the 1820s was partly designed to secure an antislave trade treaty.[47] This early mission had little effect; the caliphate was opposed to the sale of slaves to Christians anyway.[48] But later European missions, as well as contacts with other states in West Africa, North Africa, and the Middle East demonstrated to caliphate officials, if not to some slaves too, that hostility to slavery was a European trait. Still the encouragement of desertion must have been minor, despite the flight of some slaves to the model farm at the Niger-Benue confluence in 1841. The Mahdist revolt in the Turko-Egyptian Sudan during the early 1880s, which was a local reaction to the abolition movement and foreign intervention, may have alerted caliphate officials to the potential danger, but this uprising and antislavery agitation among Christian Africans in West Africa probably had only a marginal, if any, effect on thinking among slaves in the caliphate.[49] Real change only came in the 1890s, as the British, French, and Germans advanced inland, and the reaction in the caliphate came slightly later than in the western Sudan because the conquest of the caliphate proceeded later.

The imposition of colonialism created a revolutionary situation that slaves were quick to exploit, but the slaves were unable to transform their actions into a successful revolutionary movement. Massive flight, both by concubines and farm laborers, altered the nature of resistance, so that it is possible to talk about a "revolt," but despite the threat to the old regime and severe dislocation in the social order, caliphate society survived the transition to colonial rule. Because slaves could reestablish ethnic ties with existing communities, flight was a logical means of attacking the slave system without the necessity of much armed confrontation. The return of slaves to their homes and the recreation of ethnic communities by the Yagba and others dissipated the revolutionary potential of the revolt; the fugitives looked to the past for models of the life to come rather than seeking a new society that transcended their experience. The movement was ultimately restorationist, not revolutionary, which thereby facilitated colonial aims. Only when masters attempted to stop the flight or to recover fugitives did slaves react violently. Otherwise, the political vacuum neutralized the masters, thereby eliminating the necessity of fighting. Nonetheless, the social and economic structure of caliphate society was severely shaken. It took the concerted action of the British (and the French and Germans in their spheres) and the Fulbe aristocracy to prevent the complete destruction of the caliphate.

The fugitive crisis differed considerably from previous conditions of revolt and escape. Earlier actions had not threatened the institution of slavery as such. Whether rebellious slaves rose against the caliphate or whether they joined existing enemies of the caliphate, their actions only benefited themselves if they were successful, and only they suffered if they failed. After 1897, the exodus enabled even those slaves who did not flee to improve their condition. Lugard's reforms tried to contain this struggle, but not without dramatically altering the terms of servility. It is difficult to assess the relative importance of slave initiative and administrative pressure in this process, for both were instrumental in the development of a new social order. Nonetheless, slavery was transformed.

The colonial regime and the caliphate officials who accommodated themselves to British overrule were terrified that the slave exodus might get out of hand. Fears were centered on millennial uprisings, particularly Mahdism, a popular ideology that was prevalent at the time of Usman dan Fodio's *jihad* and continued to attract adherents throughout the nineteenth century. Sultan Attahiru's flight eastward after the British march on Sokoto in 1903 was perceived in Mahdist terms, and it appears that slaves, as well as disaffected aristocrats and many peasants, joined the movement.[50] But this resistance to the colonial conquest only involved slaves indirectly and incidentally. The real threat came from other Mahdist preachings that condemned submission to colonialism *and* renounced allegiance to the caliphate government. Clerics with Mahdist sympathies were reported in a variety of places, and in at least three cases—near Garoua in northern Adamawa, in Djerma country to the west of Sokoto, and at Satiru, twenty kilometers south of Sokoto—Mahdism directly challenged the colonial occupation (German, French, and British rule, respectively).[51] Of these uprisings, the one at Satiru bears closer analysis, because fugitive slaves played a major role in the revolt.

The Satiru community was founded in about 1894 on the borders of four fiefs, and thereby beyond the effective administration of caliphate officials.[52] Its leaders were poor Muslim scholars engaged in farming and teaching. In preaching Mahdism, they implicitly challenged caliphate authority; soon they attracted poor peasants and fugitive slaves; some reports indicate that the community, which numbered an estimated ten thousand in 1905, was "nearly all run away slaves."[53] The ethnic composition of the community reflected this social background; there were virtually no people associated with the aristocracy (Fulbe). Instead the fugitives identified with humble origins (Zamfarawa, Gobirawa, Gimbanawa, Kabawa, Azbinawa, Arawa, and Katsinawa). According to Sokoto Muhammad, the Satiru leaders "encouraged the emigration of slaves."[54] Local tradition has it that "the leaders of Satiru abolished slavery and as a consequence of which slaves flocked to them. The freedom of these fugitives was effectively and strenuously guarded."[55]

The community refused to pay taxes to the caliphate, even after the British conquest, and because of the disturbed political climate in the early years of colonial rule, the Sultan did not dare even to try to collect taxes there. By 1905 the community was causing considerable unrest; neighboring villages were harassed, robbery was common, and Satiru agents were infiltrating the countryside. The only recourse was a frontal attack by colonial troops, with the open support of the caliphate aristocracy. Thousands of people were killed, and the captured women and children were distributed among the aristocracy in a thinly disguised measure designed to re-establish the authority of masters over their slaves. [56]

The incidence of escape—whether in its revolutionary form at Satiru or its restorationist form elsewhere—serves as an indicator of the progress of this revolt, just as the success of the reforms introduced by Lugard demonstrates the extent to which the British regime was able to prevent the revolt from becoming a revolution. The colonial forces served as a catalyst for the revolt; it is no coincidence that the exodus of slaves increased immediately after the conquest. Although colonial officials realized that "the inauguration of British rule has had the unavoidable effect of disorganizing to some extent the social relations previously existing," [57] resistance itself was largely an internal affair between slaves and masters. The British knew that many slaves would run; indeed it was "inevitable that large numbers should have done so." [58] The fifty-five thousand slaves freed through the courts by 1917 represented the success of the containment policy; this was clearly a major factor in preventing the spread of revolutionary doctrines. The many more slaves who actually fled were isolated from those who stayed behind. Except at Satiru, there was little possibility of concerted action, and hence the evolution of class consciousness was undermined. In the end the British outlasted the revolt and thereby prevented more radical change; millennialism was curtailed and the aristocracy was kept in power. Colonialism had established itself as a paternalistic force, albeit dictatorial and repressive, and those slaves who did not flee had to endure more gradual change.

The colonial state assumed an ambiguous role in the events surrounding the collapse of slavery. The commitment to end judicial and political restrictions on the economy, particularly in the play of market forces, which would allow entry of European commercial interests, and the elimination of warfare as a means of resolving disputes and recruiting labor and clients instituted different principles of adjudication and power that invariably weakened the foundations of the precolonial political economy. The colonial state could not stop slaves from leaving their masters, despite efforts to contain the exodus, but the very attitude of the colonial regime toward the slavery issue was consistent with the generally passive intention of colonial ideology. European notions of social engineering were concerned with removing restrictions on access to markets, resources, and property—preferably without causing unnecessary social dislocation. [59]

This ideological orientation differed sharply from the setting for revolution in St. Domingue one hundred years earlier. As Genovese has argued, the St. Domingue revolution marked the turning point in the history of slave resistance in the Americas. For the first time slaves articulated the ideology of a new social order, and to that extent they participated in the implementation of the principles of the French Revolution. Liberal ideals of freedom, equality, and liberty motivated slaves in a frontal attack on slavery as an institution. By the end of the nineteenth century in Africa, by contrast, these ideals had lost much of their revolutionary significance and instead were harnessed to imperialism as a means of justifying conquest and political subordination. Slaves seized the moment but not Western ideology, stripped as it was of its revolutionary clothing. The leaders of the Satiru movement consciously tried to establish a new revolutionary society based on an Islamic millennial vision that incorporated abolitionism. But it was easily crushed and most slaves moved to communities based on past relationships, or they demanded limits on the extent of their exploitation. Despite the restorationist quality of slave resistance, the exodus and the alteration in the status of slaves who did not flee contributed to the evolution of a new society, one that looked like the product of a revolution and counterrevolution. Only the revolution had been destroyed in embryo. Colonial society was indeed different, but slaves and former slaves were largely ineffectual in helping to shape resistance to foreign control and capitalist domination.

The experience of 1897–1910 in Northern Nigeria sheds new light on the collapse of slavery in Africa during the period when European regimes imposed colonial rule. The exodus of slaves in the western Sudan, analyzed by Roberts and Klein, and the turmoil on the Gold Coast after the British defeat of Asante in 1874, discussed by McSheffrey, had certain similarities to the exodus from the Sokoto Caliphate.[60] The revolutionary potential in each of these crises did not result in an organized and sustained challenge to the old order on the part of slaves, even though flight helped to undermine the authority and wealth of the former masters. The colonial regimes were able to resurrect the weakened ruling class, removing individuals from power but permitting the existing class structure to survive. The fugitives chose to reestablish old ties with kin and ethnic groups whenever possible, with the result that ethnicity rather than class was reinforced. In many cases, this choice restricted the possibilities that fugitives would benefit from the limited opportunities of the colonial regime. More often than not the homes to which fugitives returned were far from the centers of power and economic development. Yagba country, the Mada Hills, and other such refuges from the caliphate became backwaters in the tide of colonial change. Fugitives in the western Sudan also fled to peripheral areas and subsequently found it necessary to migrate to seek employment in the colonial sector. On the Gold Coast, the fugitives were closer to areas of economic growth, but because they did not own land, they too were confined to a marginal status in the colonial economy.[61] These limitations on the opportunities for fugitives were important in setting the stage for a later act—the emergence of a working class and the expansion of the peasantry—but the revolutionary script that might have been presented in the early colonial era had a short season. After Satiru, the colonialists were left center stage to manipulate the ruling class, like puppeteers directing their puppets.

As the African data demonstrate, massive flight worked against the formation of a revolutionary movement; revolt too was similarly discouraged, unless, as is argued here, a large-scale exodus can be characterized as a type of revolt. Understandably, historians have sought out the highly visible revolts and revolutions, not the less-spectacular forms of resistance, including flight, because these actions are more difficult to document. Only when fugitives have created maroon communities has flight received the attention given to rebellions. All these acts of resistance shared a common characteristic—the destruction of the master's property, most dramatically displayed when slaves denied their master their own persons through the removal of themselves from their master's control. Flight constituted a sudden loss of property for slaveowners. Burned fields, broken equipment, and stolen goods could be restored, and even escaped or dead slaves could be replaced, but because slaves constituted such a major portion of the property of masters the acts of resistance that reduced these holdings were the most serious challenge to the authority and power of the masters. Flight increased during periods of political unrest or collapse, but, above all, topography probably played the most important role in determining the frequency and success of escapes. It may well be that there is a correlation between ease of flight and frequency of revolt; where flight was difficult because of the topography or the political power of the masters, the tensions that could lead to revolt probably increased. The extent of this correlation needs to be tested; all that is claimed here is that there probably was *some* correlation. The African data only establish that flight was more common than has often been thought; when flight was on a large and steady scale, organized rebellion was less likely and revolution was virtually impossible.

Notes

1 Orlando Patterson, *Slavery and Social Death: A Comparative Study*, Cambridge, 1982.
2 Igor Kopytoff and Suzanne Miers, "African 'Slavery' as an Institution of Marginality," in Miers and Kopytoff (eds.), *Slavery in Africa: Historical and Anthropological Perspectives*, Madison, 1977, 7–12.
3 Herbert Aptheker, *American Negro Slave Revolts*, New York, 1983.
4 Eugene Genovese, *From Rebellion to Revolution: Afro-American Slave Revolts in the Making*

of the Modern World, Baton Rouge, 1979; and *Roll, Jordan, Roll: The World the Slaves Made,* New York, 1974.

5 I am aware that many slaves who ran away in the Americas stayed in the vicinity of their home plantations. In studying the fugitive phenomenon in the Americas, this factor must be taken into account. Less is known about the ultimate destination of fugitives in Africa, but it seems that most fugitives attempted to get as far away from their place of captivity as possible.

6 E. Adeniyi Oroge, "The Fugitive Slave Crisis of 1859: A Factor in the Growth of Anti-British Feelings among the Yoruba," *Odu,* 12 (1975), 40–53; and "The Fugitive Slave Question in Anglo-Egba Relations, 1861–1886," *Journal of the Historical Society of Nigeria,* 8 (1975), 61–80. Also see B. A. Agiri, "Slavery in Yoruba Society in the Nineteenth Century," in Paul E. Lovejoy (ed.), *The Ideology of Slavery in Africa,* Beverly Hills, 1981.

7 Philip A. Igbafe, "Slavery and Emancipation in Benin, 1897–1945," *Journal of African History,* 16:3 (1975), 417–424.

8 Richard Roberts and Martin Klein, "The Banamba Slave Exodus of 1905 and the Decline of Slavery in the Western Sudan," *Journal of African History,* 21:3 (1980), 375–394.

9 Ibid., 393.

10 G. M. McSheffrey, "Slavery, Indentured Servitude, Legitimate Trade, and the Impact of Abolition in the Gold Coast: 1874–1901," *Journal of African History,* 24:3 (1983), 349–368.

11 Frederick Cooper, *From Slaves to Squatters,* New Haven, 1982. Also see Roger Frederic Morton, "Slaves, Fugitives, and Freedmen on the Kenya Coast, 1873–1907," Ph.D. dissertation, Syracuse University, 1976.

12 See Paul E. Lovejoy, *Transformations in Slavery: A History of Slavery in Africa,* Cambridge, 1983, 246–268. Also see W. G. Clarence-Smith, "Slaves, Commoners, and Landlords in Bulozi, c. 1875 to 1906," *Journal of African History,* 20:2 (1979), 228, 231.

13 Robert Ross, *Cape of Torments: Slavery and Resistance in South Africa,* London, 1983. Also see Peter Delius and Stanley Trapido, "*Inboekselings* and *Oorlams*: The Creation and Transformation of a Servile Class," *Journal of Southern African Studies,* 8:2 (April 1982), 232–235, 238, although Delius and Trapido describe resistance to a modified form of slavery.

14 A full study of slavery in the Sokoto Caliphate is being undertaken, but for a preliminary overview see my "Slavery in the Sokoto Caliphate," in Lovejoy (ed.), *Ideology and Slavery,* 200–243, and "The Characteristics of Plantations in the Nineteenth-Century Sokoto Caliphate (Islamic West Africa)," *American Historical Review,* 84:4 (1979), 1267–1292.

15 Paul E. Lovejoy, "Problems in Slave Control in the Sokoto Caliphate," in Lovejoy (ed.), *Africans in Bondage: Studies in Slavery and the Slave Trade,* Madison, 1986.

16 See *Bayān wujūb al hijra ʿala 'l-ʿibād* (The exposition of the obligation of emigration upon the servants of God), where Usman dan Fodio cites numerous Muslim authorities to support his ruling that fugitive slaves were free if they fled to the side of *jihad,* and that free Muslims who had wrongly been enslaved could also claim their liberty. See the edited and translated version by F. H. El Masri, Khartoum, 1978, 117–120.

17 Murray Last, *The Sokoto Caliphate,* London, 1967, 14n.

18 Paul Irwin, "An Emirate of the Niger Bend: A Political History of Liptako in the Nineteenth Century," Ph.D. dissertation, University of Wisconsin, 1973, 155.

19 Robin Law, *The Oyo Empire, c. 1600–c. 1836: A West African Imperialism in the Era of the Atlantic Slave Trade,* Oxford, 1977, 258; also see pp. 255–256.

20 Hugh Clapperton, *Journal of a Second Expedition into the Interior of Africa,* London, 1829, 204.

21 Richard Lander and John Lander, *Journal of an Expedition to Explore the Course and Termination of the Niger,* New York, 1832, II, 71.

22 Clapperton, *Second Expedition*, 143–144.

23 Adell Patton, Jr., "The Ningi Chiefdom and the African Frontier: Mountaineers and Resistance to the Sokoto Caliphate, ca. 1800–1908," Ph.D. dissertation, University of Wisconsin, 1975; and "Ningi Raids and Slavery in Nineteenth-Century Sokoto Caliphate," *Slavery and Abolition*, 2 (1981), 114–145.

24 Joseph Paul Irwin, *Liptako Speaks: History from Oral Tradition in Africa*, Princeton, 1981, 159–160.

25 Ian Lindin, "Between Two Religions of the Book: The Children of the Israelites (c. 1846–c. 1920)," in Elizabeth Isichei (ed.), *Varieties of Christian Experience in Nigeria*, London, 1982, 79–98; and Irwin, *Liptako Speaks*, 159–160.

26 I am indebted to M. B. Duffill, who examined the Hausa text of *Asalin Mutanen Yelwa Kasar Chandam* in the Nigerian National Archives at Kaduna for this information.

27 Nigeria National Archives, Foulkes, Bornu Report, 1902, SNP 15/1 Acc 18.

28 J. S. Hogendorn and I are examining the end of slavery in Northern Nigeria, 1897–1912; a preliminary summary will appear in a forthcoming volume edited by Suzanne Miers, Richard Roberts, and Igor Kopytoff, and a full-scale treatment will follow. In the meantime, see Louise Lennihan, "Rights in Men and Rights in Land: Slavery, Labor, and Smallholder Agriculture in Northern Nigeria," *Slavery and Abolition*, 3:2 (1982), 111–139, although it should be noted that Lennihan considerably underestimates the importance of slavery in the Sokoto Caliphate at the end of the nineteenth century.

29 Michael Mason, *The Foundations of the Bida Kingdom*, Zaria, 1983, chap. 7; and "The Nupe Kingdom in the Nineteenth Century: A Political History," Ph.D. dissertation, University of Birmingham, 1970, 394–395; "Report of Sir George Goldie," encl. in Morley to Salisbury, 29 April 1899, C.O. 147/124, as quoted in Mason, "Captive and Client Labour and the Economy of the Bida Emirate: 1857–1901," *Journal of African History*, 14:3 (1973), 464n.

30 BIDANA 6, B 655, as quoted in Dirk Kohnert, *Klassenbildung im Landlichen Nigeria. Das Beispiel der Savannenbauern in Nupeland*, Hamburg, 1982, 91.

31 Ade Obayemi, "The Sokoto Jihad and the 'O-Kun' Yoruba: A Review," *Journal of the Historical Society of Nigeria*, 9 (1978), 81–82, 85; and Michael Mason, "Population Density and 'Slave Raiding'–The Case of the Middle Belt of Nigeria," *Journal of African History*, 10:4 (1969), 551–564; and "The *Jihad* in the South: An Outline of the Nineteenth-Century Nupe Hegemony in North-Eastern Yorubaland and Afenmai," *Journal of the Historical Society of Nigeria*, 5 (1970), 193–208.

32 G. W. Webster, Nassarawa Provincial Report, September 1904, SNP 7/5, 285/1904.

33 F. L. Lugard, *Political Memoranda: Revision of Instructions to Political Officers on Subjects Chiefly Political and Administrative, 1913–1918*, 3d ed. by A. H. M. Kirk-Greene, London, 1970.

34 Goldsmith, Sokoto Province, Report for December 1906, SNP 7/8, 1643/1907.

35 E. C. Duff, Annual Report on the Nupe Province for 1906, SNP 7/8, 1520/1907.

36 Jan Hogendorn, "The Economics of Slave Use on Two 'Plantations' in the Zaria Emirate of the Sokoto Caliphate," *International Journal of African Historical Studies*, 10:3 (1977), 372, 382. Hogendorn's information is based on interviews conducted on May 27, 1975, with Malam Najuma and Malam Audu Goma at Biye.

37 Webster, Nassarawa Report, September 1904.

38 Mason, "Nupe Kingdom," 383n, citing A. W. Banfield, *Life among the Nupe Tribe in West Africa*, Berlin, Ont., 1905, 14.

39 Webster, Nassarawa Report, September 1904.

40 Mary Smith (ed.), *Baba of Karo: A Woman of the Moslem Hausa*, London, 1954, 67. Also see

Duff, Annual Report on Nupe, 1906; and F. L. Lugard, *Instructions to Political and Other Officers, on Subjects Chiefly Political and Administrative*, London, 1906, 308, citing Orr.

41 See, for example, Webster, Nassarawa Report, December 1904; and Lugard, *Instructions*, 145.

42 Lugard, *Political Memoranda*, 222.

43 Lugard, *Instructions*, 144–145.

44 As translated by Abubakar Sokoto Mohammad, "A Social Interpretation of the Satiru Revolt of c. 1894–1906," M.S. thesis, Ahmadu Bello University, 1983, 170.

45 W. C. Moore, Balala District, Reassessment Report, December 1917, Yolaprof G. 24, as quoted in Muhmud Madibbo Tukur, "The Imposition of British Colonial Domination on the Sokoto Caliphate, Borno, and Neighbouring States," Ph.D. dissertation, Ahmadu Bello University, 1979, 833. Also see Lugard, *Instructions*, 149.

46 Genovese, *From Rebellion to Revolution*.

47 Clapperton even told people in Kano about the slave revolt in St. Domingue (*Second Expedition*, 172). For Clapperton's diplomatic mission to secure the abolition of the slave trade, see p. 235.

48 Lovejoy, "Slavery in the Sokoto Caliphate," in Lovejoy (ed.), *Ideology of Slavery*, 213–214.

49 Gabriel R. Warburg, "Ideological and Practical Considerations regarding Slavery in the Mahdist State and the Anglo-Egyptian Sudan: 1881–1918," in Lovejoy (ed.), *Ideology of Slavery*, 245–269; and Lovejoy, *Transformations in Slavery*, 249–268.

50 For a discussion of mahdism in the caliphate, see Mohammad Ahmad Al-Hajj, "The Mahdist Tradition in Northern Nigeria," Ph.D. dissertation, Ahmadu Bello University, 1973. Also see Mohammad, "Satiru Revolt."

51 See Ahmadu Bossoro and Eldridge Mohammadou, *Traditions historiques des Foulbe de l'Adamaoua, No. 3. Histoire de Garoua, Cité Peul de XIXᵉ siècle*, Garoua, 1977; Idrissa Kimba, "Les populations du 'Niger' Occidental au XIXᵉ siècle et leurs reactions face à la colonisation," Thèse de doctorat de 3ᵉ cycle, Université de Paris, VII, 1979; and Mohammad, "Satiru Revolt."

52 Mohammad, "Satiru Revolt," 183–184.

53 Mohammad, "Satiru Revolt," 164; the quotation is from Resident Burdon, C.O. 446/53, p. 115. Mohammad provides considerable evidence from oral sources to support this claim.

54 Mohammad, "Satiru Revolt," 171.

55 Mohammad, "Satiru Revolt," 171, quoting Maidamma Mai Zari of Dutsen Assada ward, Sokoto, interviewed by Saleh Abubakar, August 14, 1975.

56 For details, see Mohammad, "Satiru Revolt."

57 S. Neely, Memorandum on Cotton, Lokoja, 25 May 1904, in F. Lugard to Lyttelton, 28 July 1904, F.O. 879/84, Public Record Office, London.

58 Neely, Memorandum on Cotton. It should be noted, however, that two earlier studies of the decline of slavery in the central parts of the caliphate minimize the importance of slave resistance. Polly Hill in "From Slavery to Freedom: The Case of Farm-Slavery in Nigerian Hausaland," *Comparative Studies in Society and History*, 18 (1976), 408–409, underestimates the fugitive question, whereas M. G. Smith in "Slavery and Emancipation in Two Societies," in *The Plural Society in the British West Indies*, Berkeley, 1965, 150–156, emphasizes the ease of transition from slavery to freedom. Neither Hill nor Smith explores the fugitive crisis, and neither scholar attempts to understand the evolving relationship between slave and master after British occupation as a continuing struggle over the terms of servility.

59 I am particularly grateful to Richard Roberts for his assistance in elaborating these ideas.

60 Roberts and Klein, "Banamba Slave Exodus," 375–394; and McSheffrey, "Abolition in the Gold Coast."

61 The Yoruba case is slightly different; Oroge concentrates on the flight of fugitives to Lagos, not elsewhere in the interior, and consequently it is not possible to trace the subsequent history of these people until further research is done (see his "Fugitive Slave Crisis," 40–53, and "Fugitive Slave Question," 61–80). Similarly, Igbafe explores the fugitive crisis in the context of British military policy, not Benin society as such ("Emancipation in Benin," 417–424).

7

From Caribs to Black Caribs: The Amerindian Roots of Servile Resistance in the Caribbean

MICHAEL CRATON

Of all the distilled wisdom Herbert Aptheker has disseminated during his long and distinguished career, perhaps the most thrilling revisionary remark is the simple statement that "resistance not acquiescence is the core of history."[1] These eight words soar beyond the mere concern for the oppressed and neglected masses—which itself was a revisionary notion a short while ago—to assert not only that resistance has always been far more common than usually described but that anything other than resistance is scarcely history at all.

Even more follows. If resistance has been endemic whenever class relations have existed—that is, throughout the history of the world—there must have been continuities between the manifestations of resistance under different conditions. Indeed, once we are wearing Aptheker's magic spectacles, it is the allegedly different conditions—the preoccupations of traditional historiography—that must now be disregarded in favor of the continuities newly revealed.

This was the inspiration for this essay, which is an expansion of a few paragraphs in the introduction to my recently published study of resistance to slavery in the British Caribbean, called *Testing the Chains*.[2] Where book and essay, perhaps, veer from the pure Aptheker line is in defining *resistance* more broadly, to include manifestations far short of armed rebellion, including even apparent collaboration where such behavior was designed to frustrate the absolute domination by the master class. I also visualize the word *continuities* in a double sense: structural similarities in the patterns of oppression and response, as well as direct linkages such as that signified by the mutation of Caribs into Black Caribs.

In contrast to the later exploitation by the colonizers of imported peoples, whose social dislocation had been initiated by the process of enslavement or indentureship in other continents, the Amerindians had an indigenous social order doomed to disruption by European domination. In this respect, the Spanish impact upon Amerindian society more closely paralleled the general effect of European imperialism upon African peoples—in Africa and the slave diaspora together—than the special effects of European colonialism upon transported Africans in the Americas. Later slaves and indentured servants were treated as an undifferentiated class, whereas the different segments of the Amerindian class structure were bound to be treated by, and to respond to, the Europeans differentially. Thus—though the details are cloudy and require much more work—Spanish behavior toward Amerindian caciques and the *nitaino* aristocracy might find parallels in European behavior toward African "kings and caboceers," whereas that toward the indigenous helot class, the *naborias*, might approximate that toward Africans bought as slaves in Africa.

Nonetheless, in a more general sense, the relationship between the Amerindians and the Spaniards during the initial phase of contact set a pattern that was to be replicated—with other Europeans, other Amerindians, African slaves, and indentured Asians—throughout the period of European colonialism. Some Amerindians collaborated for the advantages they hoped would accrue, or appeared to collaborate, or collaborated for a time; some fled from the Spaniards in the forlorn hope of preserving their social system and way of life in isolation; and some, from realistic calculation, pride, disappointment, or desperation, offered armed resistance. This range of general responses was to be repeated or continued (even if not directly copied) by later subjects.

Amerindian behavior and motivation were, of course, far more complex than the simple description given above, varying from group to group—even within each group—and changing with time. Motives that brought people together could subsequently tear them apart, and attitudes regarded as antithetical could sometimes turn out to be complementary. Miscegenation was inevitable, given the shortage of women among the newcomers and the relaxed attitude toward sexuality of the Amerindians, and some Christianization was bound to occur given the missionary zeal of the Catholics and the curiosity of the natives. Yet the attractions of miscegenation soon faded, producing enmity in the disadvantaged males, social dislocation, and a mestizo class that was despised by the second generation of Spaniards and by the Amerindian survivors alike. Catholic Christianity offered the parlous attractions of partial assimilation, and some clergy strove, largely in vain, to provide a mitigating influence; but though the cross was closely allied to the sword and scepter, it gained few converts among the more resistant tribes. Only, in the longer run, where the native peoples were able to reshape the faith to their own uses and traditional beliefs did the church make spectacular, if somewhat illusory, progress.

The initial trading of foodstuffs, gold, cotton, and tobacco for European goods also offered reciprocal advantages. But the trade proved unequal and short-lived. The Europeans always cheated on the value of the goods traded and from the start were reluctant to provide the Indians with the metals and arms that might be turned against them. At first, just as the Spaniards needed the products of Amerindian agriculture in order to survive, they did not hesitate to arm friendly natives to help defend and extend the tenuous early settlements. Yet the protection the Spaniards offered to the less-aggressive Indians against their established enemies, or the advantages offered to calculating allies ambitious to dominate their fellow tribes, proved to be as illusory as the other benefits proffered. In fact, those in closest contact with the newcomers generally suffered most, and within a short time any differences between the Amerindians were swallowed in a common cause.

From the reverse perspective, that of the self-styled conquistadors, Columbus himself began the pernicious tradition of dividing the native peoples into the good Indians, who submitted quietly to European rule, and bad Indians, who because of resistance, idolatry, or cannibalism could actually be enslaved. Of the Arawaks, who almost invariably greeted the Spaniards peaceably on their first appearance, Columbus wrote in December 1492:

> They are affectionate people and without covetousness and apt for anything. . . . I believe there is no better people or land in the world. They love their neighbors as themselves and have the sweetest speech in the world, and are always smiling. . . . They are without arms, all naked, and without skill at arms and great cowards, a thousand running away from three, and thus they are good to be ordered about, to be used to work, plant, and do whatever is wanted, to build towns and be taught to go clothed and accept our customs.[3]

Having invented the unresisting, tractable Arawaks, Columbus was predisposed to believe tales of a people who were their polar opposites. On his first return to Spain he brought lurid accounts of the cannibal Caribs, whom he had not yet seen; the tales were immediately relayed to an avid audience throughout western Europe. "Far away," he wrote in his journal,

> there were men with one eye, and others with dogs' noses who were cannibals, and . . . when they captured an enemy they beheaded him and

drank his blood, cut off his private parts. . . . Those of Cariba, whom they call Caribes . . . come to capture the natives and have bows and arrows without iron, of which there is no memory in any of these lands. . . . The Admiral said, by signs, that the Sovereigns of Castile would order the Caribes to be destroyed, and that all should be taken and placed in bonds.[4]

Though the warlike qualities of the Caribs proved to be real enough, for ideological reasons their savagery was exaggerated—as was their enmity toward the Arawaks—until Carib and cannibal almost became synonyms for unfriendly natives.

Yet even with the Arawaks the idyll was short-lived and the myth of their unequivocal acquiescence was exploded. Angered by the Spaniards' greed and licentiousness, Haitian Arawaks slaughtered the handful of settlers left behind by Columbus at Navidad on the first voyage, and as many fled into the interior as stayed to take their chance on the coast. With his naive Manichaeism, the discoverer exonerated the cacique Cuacacanagari and his people—on whom the Spaniards depended desperately for food—and blamed instead Caonabo of Managua, who in 1494 was tricked into capture and perished in Spanish chains. At much the same time, Columbus first encountered the Ciguayos of Samaná, who because they sported bows and arrows and offered resistance he erroneously labeled Caribs. As a reprisal for resisting the Spanish advance into the interior of Española and the levying of tribute in gold, sixteen hundred Ciguayos and other Arawaks were rounded up like cattle and the healthiest survivors shipped off to Spain as slaves.[5]

Worse was to come. During the anarchy of Columbus's personal rule, the followers of Francisco Roldán took the aristocratic *nitaino* women as wives and concubines, and Arawak men were armed and used as auxiliaries by both sides in the virtual civil war between the Spaniards. Whole villages were shifted for work at the mines under the system of *repartimientos*, which were grants of people rather than land. Not only was the authority of the remaining caciques virtually erased and the *nitaino* eradicated as a separate class, but familial patterns were disrupted as the people were herded into the unfamiliar interior.

Resistance was inevitable, and the result was the savage "pacification" supervised by Nicolás de Ovando, commander of the crusading Order of Alcántara. The rebels of Saona and southeastern Española were suppressed by Hernán Ponce de León and Juan de Esquivel, who later carried the sword to Puerto Rico and Jamaica, respectively. In Xaragua—the most highly developed Arawak kingdom—Diego Velázquez slaughtered more than eighty caciques, with their roldanista allies, after tricking them into coming to a feast, before subduing the rest of Española with cavalry, guns, dogs, and Indian auxiliaries. It was in pursuing the heroic cacique Hatuéy across the Windward Passage that Velázquez began a similar pacification in Cuba.[6]

When the Spaniards had suppressed the dissident Arawaks, they established townships called *villas*, where the Spaniards were to live, close by but separate from their conquered subjects. The able-bodied Arawaks were organized to work up to two-thirds of the year at the mines, the rest of the year at their *conuco* agriculture, providing cassava for themselves and the Spaniards.[7] Thus, within ten years the Arawaks had been reduced from bartering traders at the coast to tributaries and finally to forced laborers, virtually enslaved. Except for the handful of Amerindian wives of the Spaniards and their mestizo offspring, the only Arawaks to escape this process were that indeterminate minority which hid out in the mountains or who, like Enriquillo of Xaragua, revolted and fled to become the first of the *cimarrones*—named for the domestic cattle that, like them, had escaped to the wilds.[8]

In any case, within twenty years the number of Arawaks declined alarmingly; they were dying off faster than they could be "tamed." Indeed, the first expansion of the Spaniards from Española was as much because of a growing need for labor because of a lust for land and gold. As the Arawaks perished—partly by the sword and suicide, but mainly through disease, malnutrition, and the failure to reproduce—the rapacious Spaniards took to scouring the other islands for tractable recruits. Ponce de León and Velázquez, in fact, were more devoted to slave hunting than the intrepid explorers and founding fathers of legend.

By 1514, the Bahama Islands, as well as the nearer islands of Saona, Mona, Tortuga, and Gonave, had been completely depopulated, a fate soon to be shared by Barbados, Trinidad, Margarita, and "Los Gigantes" (Aruba, Bonaire, and Curacao). Yet the Spaniards were not able to concentrate into the fourteen *villas* of Española more than a fortieth of the number of Indians found in the island in 1492, and the move to import Africans as laborers had already begun.[9] Thirty years later there were only a handful of Indians left in the Spanish settlements in the Greater Antilles, many of which had consequently faded away. The maroon *palenques* in the mountains of Española, central Puerto Rico and Jamaica, and eastern Cuba now included Negro recruits, or consisted entirely of runaway slaves.[10]

In contrast to the island Arawaks, the Caribs and the fiercer mainland tribes survived and effectively blocked the Spanish advance, to the degree that one modern writer has spoken of a "poisoned arrow curtain."[11] In 1503 a license issued by Queen Isabella authorized the enslavement of Caribs on the grounds of their resistance to Christianity and their alleged proclivity for eating Christians; and in 1511 the Spanish Crown officially declared war.[12] Yet although it was expressly stated in 1503 that Arawaks were to be protected and in 1518 a commission was sent out under Rodrigo de Figueroa to ascertain which tribes were which, it was the Arawak not the Carib islands that were depopulated.[13]

The Spaniards learned by bitter experience to leave the Caribs and similar tribes alone. In 1510 Juan de la Cosa and seventy other Spaniards were killed with clubs and poisoned arrows near Cartagena by Chibcha warriors whom Herrera guessed were Caribs, and in 1520 the Caribs of Cumaná, failing to make a distinction between the "good" Dominicans and the slave-hunting *armadores*, wiped out the Christian missions hopefully promoted by Bartolomé de las Casas.[14] Although the Spaniards eventually subdued what became known as the Spanish Main, they never overcame the Caribs in the Antilles. To the consternation of their enemies the Caribs allied with the Arawaks to resist the Spanish occupation of Puerto Rico between 1509 and 1511, and though they retreated from the nearby islands of Vieques and St. Croix once Puerto Rico was lost, they were left firmly in control of the Lesser Antilles for another hundred years.[15]

Indeed, as the Spanish turned their attentions to Mexico and Peru the Caribs remained at least as great a menace to Spanish settlements as were the growing number of Dutch, French, and English corsairs, at each end of the island chain. In 1534 Francisco de Lando wrote from Puerto Rico that though the island was vulnerable to French and English pirates, for whom it was a convenient first stopping place in the Indies, "the Caribs carry off our settlers and their people without let or hindrance. If a ship should come at night with only fifty men, it would burn and kill the entire population." This was echoed in 1593 by Antonio de Berrio, who wrote from Trinidad, complaining first of marauding English ships.

> Besides these Englishmen whom I loathe and always injure, I am surrounded by Caribs who have tried to destroy this Island and have eaten a great number of [our] Indians. And since I have been here we have lost eleven Spaniards killed in two attacks and more than 100 Indians who with the few men we have, were sent with Domingo de Vera to attack them in their own lands, where they found four pirogues on the point of starting. These Caribs were all killed and none escaped; but they are so many and so wide spread and I have so few people and so little help that I cannot do what I want.[16]

What was potentially even more dangerous to the Spaniards was that the Caribs and other Indians might ally with the Protestant corsairs against them. This led to renewed dependence on friendly tribes. Throughout history, subjected people have shown more sensitivity in using conflicts between their masters to their own advantage than the masters have been prepared to recognize. Thus, in the second stage of conquest, when the conquerors fall out with each other or rival masters appear, the simple initial stereotypes become yet more richly confused. From the viewpoint of their owner or overlord, slaves and subjects who rebel are villains—all the more so when they run to the aid of a rival—compared with those who defend the master and hunt down runaways. Yet to the master's enemies the roles are completely reversed. Rebels and runaways point up the villainy of the rule from which they have escaped; whereas those who are prepared to accept or defend such a regime share in its villainy, and are fit to be killed, captured, or reenslaved. The European use of native allies was always self-serving, and the Europeans never failed to renege on native treaties as soon as it suited them and they were able to do so. Yet it was invariably the natives and subjects who, in their own interest, demonstrated a similar expediency who were labeled wily, treacherous, unreliable. Indeed, with arrogant inconsistency such alleged treachery was often used by the Europeans as justification for breaking agreements.

When they first began to challenge the monopoly in the Caribbean claimed by Spain, the English—like the Dutch and French—found useful allies among the maroons and those Indian tribes not yet overwhelmed by Spanish imperialism. The most famous case was that of the *cimarrones* of the Panama Isthmus, who provided such invaluable guidance and support for Francis Drake in his campaigns against Nombre de Dios and the Peruvian silver trains in the 1570s.[17] In the chauvinistic accounts of the school of James Anthony Froude this alliance is explained as the result of Drake's magnetic personality and the natural preference of the *cimarrones* for English Protestant leadership instead of Catholic oppression. Rather it should be viewed as a wartime alliance, by no means unequal, calculated by the *cimarrón* leaders to sustain and extend independence from all European masters.[18]

For the situation radically changed once the English themselves graduated from being anti-Spanish privateers to form settlements of their own. At first these were on the mainland, in the area between the Venezuelan Caribs and the Brazilian Portuguese; but they failed because of the climate, English ineptitude, and the opposition and noncooperation of the Amerindian natives. No settlement on that tropical shore could succeed without the support of friendly natives, and the Amerindians spurned the newcomers when they did not actively resist. Those Englishmen lusting for El Dorado were frustrated by the terrain and unfriendly natives before they realized that the gold mines did not exist. And those who expected to plant found that with such an illimitable and daunting interior they could neither round up sufficient Indians for the necessary labor nor restrain any African slaves whom they brought from running away.[19]

The solution, clearly, was to settle on islands. But the English were not yet strong enough to wrest any of the Greater Antilles from Spain, and most of the smaller islands were firmly possessed by the Caribs. Moreover, the first two English ventures were hardly auspicious. In 1605 the *Olive Branch*, working laboriously to windward with sixty-seven settlers destined for Charles Leigh's colony on the Wiapoco, put in to St. Lucia for food and recuperation. The Caribs greeted the English with fruits, chickens, and turtle meat, and sold the use of some huts for the sick. The island seemed so attractive for settlement that most of the passengers decided to stay. But as soon as the *Olive Branch* sailed away, those who stayed were set on by the Caribs, who killed most of them in a nightmare fight spread over several days. A month after landing, nineteen survivors escaped in their longboat to the Spanish Main, preferring Spanish captivity to life with the Caribs. Only four ever saw England again.[20]

Four years later five merchants of London sent out the *Diana, Penelope*, and *Endeavour* with 208 men, to settle Grenada. Despite being "often Disturbed by the Indians," and not being "Persons fitt for the settling of Plantaccons being the Greater Part the People of London, noe way inured to hardship and soe not Capeable of encountring the Difficulty that Attends new Plantations in the West Indies," the settlers were landed at Great Bay (St. George's harbor), and the ships sailed on to Trinidad to negotiate the trading arrangement with the Spanish governor without which the settlement could not be sustained. According to the picturesque contemporary account, Governor Sanches de Mendoza craftily delayed the ships while sending "some Fryers that spoke the Indian Language" to "heighten the Jealousies of the Indians." In due course the trade negotiations broke down, and when the ships returned to Great Bay they found "their Colony the greatest part Destroyed," and nothing left but to take the survivors back to England.[21]

The first successful English colonies in the Antilles were not founded until the 1620s, in St. Kitts, Barbados, and Providence Island (alias Catalina). But the first named was only established with great difficulty and the help of the French, and the other two were on uninhabited islands out of range of the Caribs.

The colony of St. Kitts was established between 1623 and 1624 by Thomas Warner, an East Anglican refugee from Roger North's settlement on the Amazon, and Sieur Pierre d'Esnambuc, a privateer from Dieppe. The accounts given by Captain John Smith, Père du Tertre, and John Hilton differ in detail and chronology, but the outlines are clear, and hardly creditable to the Europeans.[22] Warner first reconnoitered the island and established friendly relations with the Carib inhabitants through their chieftain, Tegreman, who had already given shelter to three shipwrecked Frenchmen. Warner returned on January 28, 1624, with fifteen settlers, who built "a fort of pallesadoes with flanckers &

loope holes for their defence," and planted tobacco. At this stage the support of the Caribs was vital, particularly in providing the "Cassada bread, Potatoes, Plantines, Pines, Turtels, Guanas, and fish plentie" on which the settlers subsisted. The tenuous amity between the races was both cemented and jeopardized by miscegenation between the European men and Carib women— Thomas Warner himself siring at least one half-breed son.[23]

With the arrival of the French privateers and English reinforcements relations turned sour. The Caribs showed little enthusiasm for planting more tobacco than they needed and questioned the settlers' need for elaborate fortifications. D'Esnambuc brought tales of Carib murders "in other of the *Charybee* Iles," and of a Carib war fleet planning to descend on St. Kitts, consisting of "six Peryagoes, which are huge great trees formed as your Canowes, but so laid out on the sides with boords, they will seem like a little Gally."[24] "Acting," as Hilton said, "like a wise man and a soldier," Thomas Warner authorized a massacre of Tegreman and one hundred and twenty of his people while they were at a drunken feast, on the pretext that they were plotting a rising.[25] Almost immediately the European allies had to withstand a massive Carib reprisal raid by "strange Indians," in which perhaps a hundred settlers and an unknown number of Caribs were killed.[26] The Europeans had to clear the island of independent Caribs before they could safely plant, and for several years were virtually besieged. Captain Smith reported that when a hurricane destroyed crops for a second time in September 1626, the settlers were forced to sail to other islands for provisions. On their return they were attacked by Carib pirogues in their own roadstead and eight Frenchmen killed. The settlers were forced to subsist on what they could get in the "wilde woods" until the migrating "tortels" returned in June 1627 and new crops were harvested. In November 1627 "the *Indians* set upon the *French*, for some injury about their women; and slew six and twentie *French* men, five *English*, and three [friendly] *Indians*." It was the destruction of one of the first plantings on the windward side of St. Kitts in 1628 that led Anthony Hilton to begin the settlement in neighboring Nevis. Not until 1629, when the English and French were said by Smith to number three thousand, were all Indians cleared from St. Kitts—with the exception of some women and their half-caste children.[27]

The comparatively rapid success of Barbados was as much because of its position—more than a hundred miles to windward of the true "Caribee" islands— as because of its fertility and lack of indigenous inhabitants. First settled by the English in 1627 it remained unmolested by Caribs and Spaniards alike. Within two years it was said to have nearly two thousand settlers, and by 1643 over thirty-three thousand inhabitants, nearly all whites.[28] Indians, however, did play an important part in the initial settlement. In the very first ship, Henry

Powell brought forty Englishmen and seven or eight Negroes, but these were soon augmented by thirty-two Indians, "men, women and children, of the *Arawacoes*, enemies both of the *Caribes* and the *Spanyards*," whom he persuaded to settle in Barbados to teach the English how to plant and process sweet potatoes, cassava, cotton, tobacco, and (surprisingly) sugar cane. Despite their claim to be at least equal settlers these Indians and their descendants drifted into bondage, along with others brought from the Spanish Main or North America. Some were freed by metropolitan decree in 1655, but by that time the usefulness of Indians had passed, and their numbers were insignificant compared with the Negro slaves, who formed the majority of the labor force.[29] Only in the puignant legend of Inkle and Yarico have the Barbadian Arawaks left a memorial to posterity.[30]

The tiny island of Providence—now a part of Colombia—was an English colony for only a dozen years (1629–1641), though it is still inhabited mainly by English-speaking blacks. As one can read between the lines of A. P. Newton's famous account, the colony's brief history was a classic illustration of the reconciliation of the principles of evangelical rectitude and the profit motive by such prototypical bourgeois Puritans as John Pym, certain other members of the Long Parliament, and the nouveau riche family of Rich, headed by the earl of Warwick.[31] The first colony developed wholly by a company and the first English colony to develop plantations dependent on Negro slaves, Providence had as its chief function, in fact, to serve as a privateering base, being directly athwart the route of the Spanish *galleons* bringing silver from Peru to Spain by way of the Isthmus and Havana. It was for this reason that a Spanish expedition destroyed the settlement in 1641, consigning the survivors to a more blatant phase of buccaneering from the island of Tortuga. The short-lived Providence colony was also significant, though, for being the scene of the first full-fledged Negro slave revolt in the British West Indies (1638) and for the institution of a unique and lasting relationship between the English and the Indians of the Miskito Coast.

The first Spaniards to encounter the Miskito Indians, Diego de Nicuesa and Alonso de Hojeda in 1502, found them almost as forbidding as Caribs. The tortuous and swampy coast of what is now Nicaragua and Honduras offered few attractions compared with Mexico, the Isthmus, and Peru. Yet as the Spanish Empire extended into Central America and the Miskito Indians came under pressure from the landward side, they looked for allies among the non-Iberians who came to their lagoons and islands for logwood, turtle meat, and shelter. In 1633 Captain Sussex Camock opened up trade and treaty relations at Cape Gracias a Dios, and Governor Phillip Bell encouraged the Indians to continue to visit Providence Island for fishing and trade. The Providence Island Company, through its treasurer, John Pym, gave firm instructions that no Indians were to be enslaved but that those who chose to settle in Providence should be Christianized. Further, there was to be no trade with the Indians in firearms. In the event, the Indians easily acquired whatever arms they needed, and few were ever converted. But they did remain free. Though the English colony was erased from Providence in 1641, the close connection between the Miskitos and the English continued through Jamaica after 1655. Because of the mutual advantages it offered it survived, remarkably, until the Hay-Pauncefote Treaty of 1900.[32] Unlike the Belizean shore, which the logwood cutters colonized, the English remained content with a nominal protectorate. For their part the Miskitos, though they miscegenated with African runaways, remained the least Europeanized of Caribbean Indians, practicing their ancient methods of farming and turtle fishing, and living in ecological balance with land and sea—until they became victims of the neoimperialism of the twentieth century, with its banana plantations and turtle-canning factories.

Because of the European intentions to plant the Lesser Antilles, the Caribs were bound to rely on arms rather than treaties for resistance, though the forces that determined that plantations would in due course predominate meant that eventually they too were doomed. That they lasted so long, and that they slowed and shaped the course of European imperialism, were towering achievements that deserved their own Hakluyt, Froude, or C. M. Andrews.

Even after they lost St. Kitts and the English and French spread to other islands, the Caribs continued to terrorize the infant European settlements as seaborne marauders. Some of their war pirogues were forty feet long and carried over a hundred men in the roughest seas. Besides paddles they carried up to three masts with sails and sophisticated rigging, and were capable of long and difficult voyages. "Their weapons are bowes and arrowes," reported Captain John Smith; "their bowes are never bent, but the string lies flat to the bowe; their arrowes [are] a small reed, foure or five foot long, headed some with the poysoned sting of a Stingray, some with iron, some with wood, but all so poysoned, that if they draw but bloud, the hurt is incurable."[33] Carib arrows were effective at up to a hundred yards—even small boys could split a wand at fifty paces—but for close combat the warriors carried hardwood clubs like baseball bats, three feet long and tapering from two inches at the handle to four inches at the head.

Caribs were strong and athletic, and their warriors, like Maoris, were made up to look formidable in battle, their foreheads artificially flattened, black hair braided like modern "dreadlocks," and almost naked bodies painted red and black with dyes made from annatto and guenip tree juice. In battle they were masters of camouflage and ambush. Preferring to attack at night, especially around the full moon, they often shot fire arrows into the thatched roofs of the houses, slaughtering those within as they fled from the flames and smoke. According to Père Labat, they held life in low esteem and shifted unpredictably from lethargy to fearsome violence. They were always ready to parley but extremely fond of drink, and the parleying sessions seldom ended without a murder or two, or general mayhem.[34] The Caribs' reputation as cannibals inspired terror, but the eating of enemies was mainly for ritual purposes. "They rather eat out of Mallice," wrote one reliable reporter,

> chewing only one Mouthfull and spitting it out againe, and animating one another thereby to be feirce and cruell to their Enemies, as a thing pleaseing to their Gods, and it hath been a great mistake in those that have reported the Southerne Indians eat one another as food, for it's performed rather as a Religious Injunction, although the Custome be Barberous.[35]

As the flow of planters and white "servants" increased, the English branched out modestly from their base in St. Kitts; to Nevis, Antigua, Montserrat, Tortola, and the arid islets of Barbuda and Anguilla. All settlements were subject to Carib attack, and even unprepossessing Barbuda was colonized successfully only after two groups of settlers had been wiped out. Progress southeastward was halted by Carib counterattacks that destroyed the second English colony in St. Lucia in 1640; a similar attempt was made on Marie Galante.[36] When a major colonizing expedition set out, it was in the opposite direction—resulting in the takeover of almost uninhabited Jamaica between 1655 and 1660.

Meanwhile from the same base but more slowly the French settled Martinique, Guadeloupe, and the smaller islands of Marie Galante, the Saintes, St. Croix, St. Martin, and St. Bart's, while the Dutch established mere trading bases on tiny St. Eustatius, Saba, and the half of St. Martin not taken by the French. The French in particular underwent great hardship in colonizing their major islands, which until the 1630s were the chief Carib bases in the northern Antilles. As told in honest detail by J-B. du Tertre and J-B. Labat, the gradual takeover was a sordid and bloody tale, following the pattern already familiar.[37] Initial settlements were only made on Carib sufferance after careful negotiation, with a far from peaceful coexistence between nervous settlers and allegedly friendly Carib groups. Some Carib women cohabited willingly and a few converts were made, but conflict was invariably sparked by increasing demand for land as more French settlers arrived and temporary small holdings became permanent plantations. Tensions increased with the importation of African slaves, as Negro males sought out Carib women in the nearer villages, or when slave runaways were harbored by the more distant Carib groups.

Like the Spaniards before them the French tried to divide the Indians into friendly and unfriendly groups, but found the division blurred by the close communication between all Caribs and their willingness to make joint cause whenever it suited them. On the pretext of Carib unreliability or "treachery," or the sporadic depredations of untamed Indians from other islands—nearly always provoked, as du Tertre acknowledged, by European outrages—Carib villages were cleared, with frequent massacres and outright wars, in which French victory was by no means inevitable. The climax of the conflict came in the 1650s, when the Caribs combined to resist the takeover of Grenada and St. Lucia. As French military forces were overstretched plantations became especially vulnerable to surprise attack. Moreover, Carib raids were almost invariably accompanied by slave uprisings—such as that in 1654 which ravaged Martinique, when complete disaster was averted only by the timely intervention of a Dutch naval force.[38]

It was at this time that the last unassimilated Caribs were rooted out of the eastern forests of Martinique and the western mountains of Guadeloupe. But Caribs remained numerous in Grenada and St. Lucia and fully in control of Dominica and St. Vincent, and were certainly not party to the agreement made in St. Kitts in 1659 between the French and English colonists that aimed to restrict the Caribs to the two latter islands.[39] Indeed, like the notorious Sykes-Picot Protocol of a much later era, the 1659 treaty was made in direct contravention to agreements made independently by the English and French signatories with the natives—including specific concessions and even pledges of alliance against mutual foes. As in all diplomacy, such agreements lasted only as long as they remained in the mutual interests of the signatories, and the only overriding principle was that of force. In this light, the Carib involvement in the diplomacy of the Caribbean is perhaps the best evidence that the Caribs formed—and were seen to form—a nation, in competition for land with other nations.

When need be, the Europeans made common cause against the Caribs, but the struggle between the Europeans and Caribs was increasingly complicated by the growing rivalry between the Europeans themselves. Once they had broken the Spanish monopoly and established their own plantations, each of the mercantilist nations ceased to regard Spain as the common enemy and disputed with each other for colonies, trading routes, slave-trading bases in Africa, and the trade of the Spanish Empire. The process began with the three Anglo-Dutch wars of 1652–1674 and led to the intermittent Anglo-French struggle that brought hostilities to the Caribbean for more than a third of the years between 1666 and 1815. This rivalry between the imperialists was cleverly used by the Carib nation in its slow retreat, first to postpone the loss of St.

Lucia and Grenada and their confinement to the islands of Dominica and St. Vincent, and then, a century later, to delay the takeover of the last two islands and prevent the final eradication of the surviving island Caribs.[40]

The initiation and operation of this complex triangular process is best illustrated by the almost symbolic story of Thomas "Indian" Warner, the half-caste son of the English founder of St. Kitts. Born in 1629 he was brought up in the easygoing household of his father, which must have been much more like a Brazilian *casa grande* than later, more proper English establishments. When the pioneer died in 1648, though, the young mestizo was maltreated by Warner's widow (his third wife) and fled to join a band of maroons hiding out on the wooded slopes of Mount Misery in the center of St. Kitts. Recaptured, he was put to work in the fields in chains, but was released through the intercession of his legitimate half brother Edward (son of Sir Thomas's first wife).[41] Shortly afterward he escaped from colonized St. Kitts to join his mother's family in the all-Carib island of Dominica. There over the years he became one of the most important leaders—a role determined by his imposing presence, energy, ferocity in combat, and skill in playing both ends against the middle in negotiations.

The 1659 treaty between the English and French had been pointedly silent on the fate of St. Lucia, coveted by both nations. As events in Europe brought England and France toward war in the 1660s, Lord Willoughby of Parham, the enterprising governor of Barbados and the "Caribbee Isles," drew up a third English plan to take over the island, with Indian Warner as ally and intermediary. Warner was invited to London in 1664, feted in Whitehall, and awarded the empty title of governor of Dominica.[42] In return he signed a spurious document assigning Carib rights in St. Lucia to the English, with Willoughby as proprietary governor.

Far better prepared and equipped than the two previous English attempts at settlement, Willoughby's expedition to St. Lucia included a thousand settlers, accompanied by an additional five hundred armed Englishmen in five warships and six hundred Carib warriors under Indian Warner in seventeen pirogues. The few French in St. Lucia surrendered without a fight and fled to complain to the governor of Martinique. The French blustered but it was the Caribs who put paid to the English settlement. Warner's warriors faded away and the St. Lucian Caribs were, to say the least, uncooperative. Crops were burned or stolen, outlying farms attacked from the sea, and straggling settlers killed in the woods. Within two years the bedraggled remnant of settlers retreated, bitterly complaining of French collusion with the Caribs.[43]

In the Anglo-French War of 1666–1668, during which nearly all the English Leeward Islands were captured, Indian Warner was carried by the French to St.

Kitts. But his imprisonment did not scotch later accusations of double-dealing. "For those by him protected as his freinds [*sic*] and nearest relations," declared a *Remonstrance of the Inhabitants of Antigua* in 1676,

> were chief in comitting many outrages, murders, rapes and burneings . . .
> for as often as ye men engaged ye Ffrench enemy, the said Indians were
> comitting their murders, rapes and other villainyss against ye women and
> children, and when ye Ffrench had subdued ye Island and disarmed our
> inhabitants and carried away our negroes and what else they thought fitt,
> then did these Indians prosecute all villanies imaginable against our naked
> inhabitants having nothing but the mercy of God to protect ourselves
> from their cruelties . . . and in these and like bloody practises they con-
> tinued untill a peace was proclaimed betwixt our most gracious king, ye
> Ffrench, and Dutch. All of which bloody cruelties were acted and done by
> ye Chief of Indian Warner's friends, without the least cause or provocation
> on our part.[44]

When the news of the Treaty of Breda reached the West Indies in 1668, the French returned Indian Warner to the English and he was nominally, if more warily, reinstated in Dominica. In the same year Sir William Willoughby, who had succeeded his brother on his death by drowning in 1666, made a unilateral treaty with the Caribs of St. Vincent, in which English and Caribs were re-ferred to as equals, with reciprocal rights and privileges.[45] The Caribs who signed the treaty pledged allegiance to the English king and amity toward their fellow subjects, in return for remaining unmolested in St. Vincent and St. Lu-cia. In return for the release of English subjects captured by the Indians and French and held by the Indians, all Indian slaves were to be freed. Certain runaway Negroes from Barbados were to be sent back forthwith, and all future runaways "to be secured and delivered up as soon as required." Besides this the treaty pledged aid against mutual enemies—chief of them, presumably, the French.

This imposing document, however, did not stop other Caribs from signing similar and contradictory treaties with the French. Nor did it halt Carib de-predations in Antigua and other English islands—with or without the pretext of a French alliance. Nor, for that matter, did it prevent secret English plans to renege on any treaties and to engineer a "final solution" for the Carib problem as soon as the opportunity presented itself.

The most implacable of the English colonists were those of Antigua, who complained that they were forced to keep fourteen files of men on guard every night against Carib attacks, and double the number for the period three days before and three days after each full moon.[46] In 1674, during an interval of peace with France, Sir William Stapleton, governor of the Leeward Islands, wrote to the Council of Trade and Plantations, begging,

> as one of the considerablest services which may be done to these islanders in case of breach with the French, that whilst the nations are friends, the destroying of the Caribee Indians of St. Vincent and Dominica may be represented to his Majesty, for the French drew them to their assistance in the late war, and will do again on occasion; and the islanders dread them more than any other, because they can come with 30 or 40 periagoes to windward, whilst they are at Leeward in the Trenches or opposing a landing Christian enemy, and so destroy men, women, and children, and burn all, as the people of Antigua and Montserrat have felt in the last year.[47]

Without waiting for official approval, Colonel Philip Warner, another son of Sir Thomas Warner and now lieutenant governor of Antigua, led a punitive expedition to Dominica in January 1675. Indian Warner and the Caribs were, as usual, ready to talk. But the negotiations turned into a battle in which Indian Warner was killed, reportedly by the hand of his own half brother.

To the surprise and anger of the Antiguans, Philip Warner was thrown into the Tower when he went to England on leave, and later sent for trial in Barbados. He was charged with "killing his half brother, an Indian, and several other Indians, at an entertainment, after they had, as friends to the English, assisted them against other Indians that were enemies. The reason alleged, that he had a pique against his brother."[48] Defending his lieutenant's actions, Stapleton wrote to London that Indian Warner had fallen "among his fellow Heathens" and "though he had an English Commission, yet was a great villain and took a French Commission." Far from falling suddenly on the Indians at a feast, Colonel Warner was said to have "twice fought the Indians out of pallisadoed trenches," pursued them from one side of Dominica to the other, and obtained unequivocal evidence of the duplicity of Indian Warner. Stapleton also denied both that Indian Warner had been killed by Philip Warner in person and that the two were half brothers, claiming that "the son pretended to be killed is at St. Christophers."[49]

For his part Philip Warner remained suspiciously silent on his relationship to Indian Warner, but claimed that the chief prosecution witness, one William Hamlin, was a perjured renegade whose evidence conveniently skipped over the interval of a fortnight between the parley-feast and the main battle with the Indians. He also pleaded superior orders: a commission issued by Sir William Stapleton on a petition of all the planters of Antigua, specifically instructing him to attack the Indians by surprise, "it not being otherwise to be done."[50] Predictably, Colonel Philip Warner was found innocent by the grand jury in

Barbados in September 1676, though he was "put out of the government of Antigua and any other employment of trust in the King's service," by an imperial Order-in-Council in May 1677.[51]

The Carib raids continued, especially at times of war between the English and French. As late as 1700 Governor Codrington of Antigua wrote that the windward part of that island was

> very thinly if at all settled, by reason of the frequent attempts of the Indians from Dominique and Sta. Lucie, who have so often landed there and carried off the negroes and sometimes whole families which have lain too distant from others, that no Planters are now willing to venture themselves or their stocks there.[52]

Yet by 1700 the tide had definitely turned against the Caribs. It was now the internal threat of the resistance and rebellion of their "stocks"—the African slaves—that chiefly concerned most planters. Instead of roaming freely up and down the archipelago, the Caribs were now cut off from their mainland cousins and effectively restricted to two mountainous islands that in aboriginal times had been barely inhabited by them.[53] More seriously, this had drastically changed their life style. From being a people who lived almost peripatetically on the flatter islands and coastal plains, they had become just as much a mountain and forest people. Such a restrictive habitat alone would have reduced the population, quite apart from the ravages of new diseases and warfare with the whites. The island Carib population may have fallen by as much as 90 percent in the two hundred years after 1500, and was to suffer an equally severe reduction in the following century.

Perhaps the most significant trend, though, lay in the changed attitude of the Caribs to the African slaves. Previously they had regarded the blacks as intruders like the whites, fit to be slaughtered or enslaved like the ancient Arawaks. Even those runaway slaves who were harbored by the Caribs had been treated virtually as slaves. Now, as Père Labat noticed in his visits to the Carib islands in 1700, the Caribs welcomed blacks as allies. They actively encouraged runaways to settle with them and make common cause, even to intermarry—thus mingling the life and fighting styles of Africa and America.[54] Such reinforcement helped to hold back the colonial tide for almost another century, if at the risk of ethnic submergence. In the precipitous jungles of Dominica the bands remained distinctly Amerindian, as did the partially miscegenated Miskitos and the Florida Seminoles.[55] But in St. Vincent, where the indigenous Caribs were augmented by a shipwrecked cargo of African captives and a steady stream of black slave runaways from other islands, the African element in time became completely dominant. These were the famous Black Caribs who, as Sir William

Young and all those who fought against them testified, were even more formidable in battle than their "yellow" predecessors.[56]

The Black Caribs resisted the British takeover of St. Vincent in whatever way they could, including two bitterly contested wars in the 1770s and 1790s, and it was not until they were deported to Central America in 1797 that the colonization of the island could be completed. This heroic tale, which, needless to say, has hitherto been slighted in the literature, requires at least a paper to itself.[57] We can only conclude here by suggesting that the passionate resistance of the Black Caribs more than symbolically represents not just the Amerindian roots of Caribbean slave resistance but the continuities of resistance to European and capitalistic exploitation of the Caribbean and its peoples that have run from the coming of Columbus to the present day.

Notes

1 Recorded first at the conference of the New York Academy of Sciences entitled "Comparative Perspectives on Slavery in New World Plantation Societies," in New York on May 6, 1976, this apothegm was heard again at the special Aptheker symposium at the Organization of American Historians conference in Cincinnati on April 8, 1983.

2 Michael Craton, *Testing the Chains: Resistance to Slavery in the British West Indies*, Ithaca, 1982, 19–23.

3 Journal of the first voyage of Christopher Columbus, 1492–1493, entries for December 16 and 25, 1492. Quoted in Carl Ortwin Sauer, *The Early Spanish Main*, Berkeley, 1966, 32.

4 Columbus's journal entries for November 4, December 26, 1492, quoted in Eric Williams (ed.), *Documents of West Indian History, 1492–1655*, Port-of-Spain, 1963, 47–50.

5 Sauer, *Spanish Main*, 70–88; and Troy S. Floyd, *The Columbian Dynasty in the Caribbean, 1492–1526*, Albuquerque, 1973, 20–28.

6 Floyd, *Columbian Dynasty*, 51–56, 112–122; and Sauer, *Spanish Main*, 147–151, 181–189.

7 Sauer, *Spanish Main*, 151–156.

8 Las Casas attributed Enriquillo's revolt of 1519—which lasted until he came to terms with the Spaniards in the 1530s—to the rape of the cacique's wife by an *encomendero*, an extremely common theme in Las Casas, if not in reality. Bartolomé de las Casas, *Historia de las Indias*, Madrid, 1875–1876, II, 497; and Floyd, *Columbian Dynasty*, 192, 222.

9 Of the 23,000 Indians enumerated in the *repartimiento* lists of 1514, some 15,000 were described as *Indios de servicio*, or slaves, and only 8,000 as *naborias*, indigenous serfs. In none of the 14 *villas* was there an average of one child per family; even in the royal estate at Santo Domingo there were only 123 children to 270 men, 351 women, and 104 "aged." According to Sauer, the population of Española in 1492 was 1,100,000. Of the 392 Spanish *vecinos* in the 14 *villas*, no less than 54 were listed with native wives, against 92 with Castilian wives. Sauer, *Spanish Main*, 202–204, 65–69.

10 In March 1542, Alvaro de Castro reported from Española "that he believed that there were more than 25,000 or 30,000 Negroes there compared to no more than 1,200 settlers on the plantations or at the mines; and that he thought there were over 2,000 or 3,000 runaway slaves hidden in the Cape of San Nicolás, in the Ciguayos, or the Samana Peninsula, and on the Cape of Igüey. . . . There is much trade going on among them, based on articles stolen from farms

and ranches which they raid." Quoted in José L. Franco, "Maroons and Slave Rebellions in the Spanish Territories," in Richard Price (ed.), *Maroon Societies: Rebel Slave Communities in the Americas*, 2d ed., Baltimore, 1979, 38. One center of Arawak *cimarrones* in Española was Bahoruco, the hide-out of Enriquillo and the later site of LeManiel. Floyd, *Columbian Dynasty*, 222; and Price (ed.), *Maroon Societies*, 135–148. See also Francisco Perez de la Riva, "Cuban *Palenques*," in Price (ed.), *Maroon Societies*, 49–59.

11 Floyd, *Columbian Dynasty*, 97.

12 Proclamation of October 30, 1503, quoted in Williams (ed.), *Documents*, 62–63. *Cédula* of June 3, 1511, quoted in *Collección de documentos inéditos de Ultramar*, Madrid, 1886–1932, V, 258–262.

13 The islands declared to be *guatiao* (friendly) and not Carib were Trinidad, the Bahamas, Barbados, Margarita, and the "Gigantes," as was the mainland from the Guajira peninsula to the River Sinu. *Collección de documentos inéditos relativos al descubrimiento, conquista, y organización de las antiguas posesiones españolas de América y Oceanía*, Madrid, 1864–1884, I, 380–383, XXIII, 343–344; and Sauer, *Spanish Main*, 195.

14 Sauer, *Spanish Main*, 170–172, 191–192; Floyd, *Columbian Dynasty*, 135, 204–209; and Antonio de Herrera, *Historia general de los hechos de los Castellanos en las islas y tierra firme del Mar Océano*, Madrid, 1601–1615, I, chap. 8, 10.

15 Floyd, *Columbian Dynasty*, 95–105.

16 Francisco de Lando to Charles V, July 2, 1534, quoted in Williams (ed.), *Documents*, 40; and Antonio de Berrio to Philip II, November 14, 1593, in Williams (ed.), *Documents*, 243–244.

17 Irene A. Wright (ed.), *Documents concerning English Voyages to the Spanish Main, 1569–1580*, London, 1932; and Jose L. Franco, *La Presencia negra en el Nuevo Mundo*, Havana, 1968, 96. Drake also sought and obtained the aid of the island maroons in his unsuccessful attack on Santo Domingo in 1586. Arthur P. Newton, *The European Nations in the West Indies*, London, 1933, 101.

18 See Scott V. Parris, "Alliance and Competition: Four Case Studies of Maroon-European Relations," paper presented at the Waterloo Slavery Conference, University of Waterloo, 1979, 7–19.

19 For a contemporary narrative of the mainland ventures, see Scott's "Description of Guyana," British Library, Sloane MSS 3662; and Newton, *European Nations*, 131–142.

20 A vivid firsthand account was given by John Nicholl, *An Houre Glasse of Indian Newes*, London, 1607, quoted in James A. Williamson, *The Caribbee Islands under the Proprietary Patents*, Oxford, 1926, 13–14. Confusion over another stop made by the *Olive Branch* at Barbados led to errors about when that island was first claimed and settled. Williamson, *Caribbee Islands*, 15–18.

21 Scott's "Description of Grenada" (c. 1668), British Library, Sloane MSS 3662, 49–53, quoted in Williamson, *Caribbee Islands*, 18–20.

22 John Smith, *The True Travels, Adventures, and Observations of Captaine John Smith*, London, 1630, in Edward Arber (ed.), *The Scholar's Library*, No. 16, Birmingham, 1884, II, 881–916; Jean-Baptiste du Tertre, *Histoire générale des Antilles habités par les François*, Paris, 1667, I, 476–479; and British Library, Egerton MSS 2395, fol. 503–507, quoted in Vere Langford Oliver, *History of the Island of Antigua . . . from the First Settlement in 1635 to the Present Time*, London, 1894–1899, I, xiii–xvii.

23 Even acknowledged by Aucher Warner in his pious *Sir Thomas Warner, Pioneer of the West Indies: A Chronicle of His Family*, London, 1933, 79–80. Père Labat when visiting Dominica in 1700 met the aged Indian woman called Mme. Ouvenarde, said to have been the mistress of Sir Thomas Warner more than sixty years before, and to have had "many children" by him. John Eaden (ed.), *Memoirs of Père Labat, 1693–1705*, London, 1931, 92–93.

24 Smith, *True Travels*, 900.

25 In 1675 John Hilton related that Warner was alerted "by an old Indian woman yt did often freqt amongst ye english, who it seems they had used courteously, soe yt she had taken a great affeccon to ym," that the Carib feast was in fact a preparation for war. Two other anecdotes shed further light on the earliest colonial society of St. Kitts. By Hilton's account Tegreman was killed as he slept, the assailants "running him with their rapiers through ye ham'acco & into ye body." But sharing his hammock was an English boy whom Warner had brought from England and to whom the chief had "taken a great affeccon." Tegreman's bed mate escaped providentially, "for they had forgott ye boy." Tegreman's son and namesake also escaped and, according to John Smith, was carried to England and brought up by Ralph Merrifield, one of the colony's promoters, as one of his own children. Hilton's account in Oliver, *Antigua*, I, xiv; and Smith, *True Travels*, 903.

26 John Smith, not famous for understatement, put the Carib numbers at 400–500, but du Tertre, writing much later, gave 3,000–4,000, with 2,000 killed or wounded. *True Travels*, 901; and du Tertre, *Histoire générale*, I, 3–6.

27 Smith, *True Travels*, 901–903. Evidence given in 1676 mentioned that in the 1630s Sir Thomas Warner alone had twenty-four Indians in his household. *Calendar of State Papers, Colonial, America and West Indies*, 4:9 (1675–1676), 748, ii, iv.

28 Smith, *True Travels*, 908; and Richard S. Dunn, *Sugar and Slaves: The Rise of the Planter Class in the English West Indies, 1624–1713*, Chapel Hill, 1972, 55. Dunn reckons that the latter estimate is too high, arguing that there were only 8,707 taxpayers in 1639, but admitting that by then the population of Barbados was as great as that of either Massachusetts or Virginia.

29 Sir Robert Schomburgk, *The History of Barbados*, London, 1848.

30 Richard Ligon, *A True and Exact History of the Island of Barbados*, London, 1657, 54–55. The tale is almost symbolic of European rapine. Inkle was a young Englishman who, while among a party of stragglers on the Spanish Main, was saved from slaughter by the beautiful Indian maid Yarico. Falling instantly in love with the Englishman, Yarico went with him to Barbados. "But the youth, when he came ashoar in the *Barbadoes*, forgot the kindnesse of the poor maid, that she had ventured her life for his safety, and sold her for a slave, who was as free born as he. And so poor *Yarico* for her love, lost her liberty." While a domestic slave in Richard Ligon's household, Yarico conceived a child—whether or not by Inkle is not made clear—which out of modesty she delivered on her own near a pond still known as Yarico's in Schomburgk's day. Ligon in his appreciative way described Yarico as "of excellence shape and color, for it was a pure bright bay; small breasts, with the nipls of a porphyric color, this woman would not be woo'd by any meanes to wear Cloaths." *True and Exact*, 55.

31 Arthur Perceval Newton, *The Colonising Activities of the English Puritans: The Last Phase of the Elizabethan Struggle with Spain*, New Haven, 1914.

32 Ibid., 141–145.

33 Smith, *True Travels*, 902. The normal poison was the juice of the manchineel tree.

34 Eaden (ed.), *Memoirs of Père Labat*, 70–115. Labat quoted the frightful dictim "Frown on an Indian and you fight him. Fight an Indian and you must kill him or be killed."

35 Scott's "Description of Grenada," 49.

36 Williamson, *Caribbee Islands*, 152–153, citing British Library, Egerton MSS 2395, fol. 533–534; 2597, fol. 188.

37 Du Tertre, *Histoire générale*; and Jean-Baptiste Labat, *Nouveau voyage aux isles d'Amerique*, The Hague, 1724. These and other contemporary works were almost paraphrased in two narratives by Nellis M. Crouse, *French Pioneers in the West Indies, 1624–1664*, New York, 1940; and *The French Struggle for the West Indies, 1665–1713*, New York, 1943.

38 Crouse, *French Pioneers*, 205–229.

39 Du Tertre, *Histoire générale*, 572–580; and Oliver, *Antigua*, xxvii–xxviii, citing British Library, Egerton MSS 2395.

40 The diplomatic skill of the Caribs is attested by the treaty of 1659, which the English and French declared necessary, "not being able to suppress their Insolency, much less possible to Adventure to Declare unto them the Light of the Gospell the principal Motive of Establishing the Colonyes in America, because they allwayes had the Craft & Subbilty to make peace with one of the Two Nations before they would Enterprize anything against the other. By which means they politiquely did maintain friendshipp with one of the said two Nations." Oliver, *Antigua*, xxviii.

41 This act of generosity did not immunize Edward Warner from Carib attack. In 1640 his wife and children were carried off by a raiding party. Warner, *Sir Thomas Warner*, 57–58.

42 Ibid., 59–82; and Crouse, *French Struggle*, 8–10, 88.

43 Crouse, *French Struggle*, 8–10, 88; and Newton, *European Nations*, 243. Newton, however, mentioned incorrectly that Indian Warner was made governor of St. Vincent rather than Dominica.

44 Warner, *Sir Thomas Warner*, 63–71.

45 Signed by Captains Nicholas, Aloons, Bebura, Le Suroe, Nay, Wappya, the "Grand Brabba," and "14 more of the Chiefest Captains," on March 23, 1668. *C.S.P., C., A.W.I.*, 2:5 (1661–1668), 1717. The Carib signatories were enjoined to pass the news of the treaty among the other Caribs, and encourage them to make similar agreements with Governor Willoughby.

46 Colonel Philip Warner to Council of Trade and Plantations, April 3, 1676. *C.S.P., C., A.W.I.*, 4:9 (1675–1676), 861.

47 January 9, 1674, *C.S.P., C., A.W.I.*, 3:7 (1669–1674), 1, 201.

48 Annex to petition of Colonel Philip Warner to King in Council, *C.S.P., C., A.W.I.*, 4:9 (1675–1676), 750, i.

49 Stapleton to Council of Trade and Plantations, December 20, 1675, *C.S.P., C., A.W.I.*, 4:9 (1675–1676), 748.

50 *C.S.P., C., A.W.I.*, 4:9 (1675–1676), 750, i, 779.

51 *C.S.P., C., A.W.I.*, 4:9 (1675–1676), 750, ii, 1029.

52 Christopher Codrington to Council of Trade and Plantations, June 5, 1700, *C.S.P., C., A.W.I.*, 13:18 (1700), 499.

53 Clifford Evans, "The Lack of Archeology in Dominica," *Proceedings of the Second International Congress for the Study of Pre-Columbian Cultures in the Lesser Antilles*, Barbados, 1968, 93–102.

54 Eaden (ed.), *Memoirs of Père Labat*, 92–95.

55 Kenneth W. Porter, "Relations between Negroes and Indians within the Present Limits of the United States," *Journal of Negro History*, 17 (1932), 287–367; and *The Negro on the American Frontier*, New York, 1971; and Mary W. Helms, *Asang: Adaptation to Culture Contact in a Miskito Community*, Gainesville, 1971.

56 Sir William Young, *An Account of the Black Charaibs in the Island of St. Vincent*, London, 1795.

57 But ad interim, I. E. Kirby and C. I. Martin, *The Rise and Fall of the Black Caribs*, St. Vincent, 1972; Bernard Marshall, "Anglo-Black Carib Rivalry and the Subsequent War of 1772–1773 in St. Vincent: A Reassessment," paper delivered at the tenth meeting of the Association of Caribbean Historians, St. Thomas, April 1978; and Craton, *Testing the Chains*, 145–153, 201–207.

8

"The Family Tree Is Not Cut": Women and Cultural Resistance in Slave Family Life in the British Caribbean

BARBARA BUSH

The Asante proverb in the chapter title emphasizes the centrality of kinship bonds to traditional West African social and economic life.[1] Within this kinship structure, women played a central role. Until the recent upsurge of interest in the "black perspective" of the slave experience, it was assumed that transference to the New World destroyed or severely damaged these vital kinship bonds. Consequently a negative view of slave family life as highly disorganized has been presented in which women are portrayed as either scarlet wenches or domineering matriarchs.[2] Yet even contemporary accounts offer conflicting images of women and there is much evidence to contradict this view. If such evidence is reevaluated from a less-Eurocentric perspective, it may be argued that, in reality, slaves struggled to recreate their traditional kinship bonds, for it was within the family and community that they found the strength to survive servitude. Because of their central role as wives and mothers, slave women contributed significantly to this important area of cultural resistance.

Culture is not simply materialistic (artifacts) or idealistic (ideas) but encompasses all forms of social relationships and is interwoven with an individual's everyday existence from birth to death. Society and culture are inseparable concepts and must be studied historically, for they are not an integrated whole but an area of struggle and change. If the cultural base of any community is threatened, resistance becomes essential to survival. For New World slaves, their African cultural heritage became "a shield which frustrated the efforts of Europeans to dehumanise Africans through servitude."[3] It was the preservation of cultural identity that prevented "psychic annihilation." Slave women as the "principal exponents" and protectors of African-derived culture were arguably in the vanguard of a subtle but strong resistance against imposed European values.[4] To fully appreciate their contribution in the key area of family life, however, it is necessary to define and challenge the existing myths relating to the sexuality of black women (from which notions of slave family organizations *per se* stem), to reassess the theoretical context, particularly in relation to the concept of matrifocality and, finally, to reexamine the evidence in an Afro-Caribbean, as opposed to European, cultural context.

The Myths

According to contemporary observers, marriage and morality among slaves did not exist, or existed only in "uncivilized" inferior forms such as "polygamy" (a blanket term used to define *any* form of multiple or serial sexual relationships among slaves). While planters, with characteristic contrariness, utilized the alleged debased, "drudge" position of women in African polygynous marriages to justify their economic exploitation as field hands, they also conveniently blamed this institution for the "shocking licentiousness" of women slaves and hence the lack of Christian marriage.[5]

Conversely, abolitionist writers attacked the system and argued that the "misery and toils" of everyday labor on the plantation left women too exhausted "to promote the comfort of her household" and fully embrace the "pure and enlightened institution of Christian marriage."[6] Both sides agreed that the net result was immorality. Slave women were promiscuous from an early age and had "commerce with a multitude of men."[7] Together with the fact that slave marriages seldom held respectability or legitimacy in European eyes, this image of slave women provided white men with a suitable rationale for the sexual use and abuse of black women.

In the West Indies, black concubinage was regarded as an integral part of plantation life, inextricably woven into the social fabric. Though some writers piously blamed this miscegenous activity on lower-class white men—bookkeepers and overseers—planters preferred to portray black women as "easy," vying in competition for white men's favors, willing but also conniving.[8] This fitted in well with more general stereotyping of blacks as immoral, lying, and deceitful. In effect, white men of all classes, even those with legal European wives, continued to keep black or colored mistresses and to father mulatto children to the extent that severe intrasexual tensions and jealousies existed between black and white women.[9]

Disrespect for the marriage bond among slaves not only legitimized such sexual activities, but also rationalized and facilitated the economic exploitation of slave women. The "promiscuity" and other allied myths were well devised to meet the cynical needs of the plantocracy. It is no coincidence that faced with the threat of the abolition of the slave trade after 1790, slaveowners developed a new interest in women as "breeders."

Planters discussed "ameliorative" policies to promote slave family life and protect pregnant women. New laws were introduced to mitigate the worst aspects of sexual abuse of black women, particularly "criminal intercourse" of whites with married slaves.[10] Yet until this structural need arose to ensure the reproduction of the slave labor force, slave laws in the British Caribbean, passed by autonomous planter assemblies, failed to give any protection to the slave family, unlike the *Siete Partidas* and *Code Noir*, which governed the Spanish and French Caribbean colonies, respectively.[11]

In practice the effect of such legislation was negligible. The negative stereotype of black women and hence the black family remained entrenched and was utilized in defense of the slave system, to emphasize the inferiority of blacks. The image of the "hot-constitution'd" black woman had spawned other myths that compounded this view. Black women were poor mothers who neglected or were cruel to their "illegitimate" children. They shirked their maternal responsibilities for trivial pleasures such as dancing or "the gossip and fun of the field."[12] Like contemporary allegations that slaves did not feel or love in the same way as Europeans (having only "animal desires"),[13] this acted as a crude rationale for the enforced separation of mothers from children, husbands from wives.

Although the contradictory nature of plantocratic accounts indicates that slave masters were aware of the existence of viable family relationships among slaves that did not conform to the European model, the negative stereotypes have proved most durable. Until recently, secondary works on Caribbean societies perpetuated this bleak view of slave society that planters had utilized to justify their position as slave masters. With subtle differences in emphasis, many historians and sociologists have accepted the general idea that the cultural and physical dislocation of African slaves, together with the rigors of plantation life, precluded the establishment of any viable marriage forms.[14]

The "promiscuity" myth (where *promiscuity* is defined as any sexual behavior by women that deviates from the limitations of the Western, Christian model of monogamous marriage) has remained popular, with the proviso that, rather than constituting an inherent trait of the African, such behavior was the result of the peculiar conditions of slavery, actively encouraged by planters. This myth has contributed significantly to matrifocal theories of the slave family and the corollary—the weak or absent slave father.[15] In turn, such theories about slave marriage and family forms have strongly influenced sociological analyses of modern Afro-Caribbean society. The black Caribbean family has thus been described in terms of illegitimacy, common-law marriage, and "matrifocality," a pathological and inadequate deviation from the norm.[16]

In determining the domestic role of black women, there is no simple theoretical route. Though it is dangerous to read too much of the past into the present, it is equally unsound to engage in speculative or "inductivist" history, which relies on an analysis of modern Afro-Caribbean structures to hypothesize about the role of women in slave society.[17] Either approach ignores the profound socioeconomic changes that occurred since emancipation. Caribbean societies, past and present, may be closely linked but are not strictly comparable. For instance, matrifocality may be primarily a result of family disruption because of migrant labor patterns in the modern Caribbean rather than a direct result of the weakening of the father role in slave society.[18]

Another essential theoretical consideration, applicable to both primary and secondary works on the black woman in slavery and freedom, is the existence of a marked Eurocentric bias. Thus, any attempt to reassess the role of slave women must initially involve a reworking of definitions of family, marriage, and sexual morality within an African as opposed to a European matrix. Both past and present observers of Caribbean society have tended to adopt the essentially middle-class definitions associated with the rise of Western industrial society. Yet, as Sidney Mintz argues, such definitions are scarcely applicable to the study of a preindustrial slave society where African-derived mores were far more significant.[19] If such African-derived mores are taken into account, "matrifocality" and polygamy take on different meanings and thus the "promiscuity" myth is undermined. It is within this revised perspective that the concept of cultural resistance becomes significant.

The Western "convention of monogamy" defines *family* as an elementary coresidential nuclear unit, comprising two legally (in the eyes of the law or church) married partners with or without children. Contemporary observers judged the domestic role of slave women within this context. Although this form of family organization undoubtedly existed on a greater scale than has been assumed (modeled on African rather than European cultural precedents),[20] more flexible definitions of family and marriage are needed to account for the primary importance in slave society of consanguine (extended) as opposed to conjugal (nuclear) relationships.[21] Complex extended family links existed in the slave community. In the absence of blood kin, "fictive" kin, often newly arrived slaves, were "adopted" to reestablish traditional African-derived kinship patterns and ensure cultural continuity.[22] A strong sense of community existed among slaves, and interpersonal relations were marked by "warmth and dutiful sentiment." Children were cared for communally as were the elderly, who were afforded considerable respect in accordance with African practice.[23] Within this broader structure, the polygynous unit probably only accounted for a minority of slave marriages.[24] Marriage did not imply a lifelong relationship between two adults in a coresidential nuclear unit, and partners were often incorporated into wider extended family arrangements and may not have been continuously coresidential as in polygynous relationships.

From this fresh perspective, the role of slave women more closely parallels that of peasant women in preindustrial society in Europe than the idealized, leisured, bourgeois "ladies" they were unfavorably compared with. In such societies, women had a "separate but equal" status in marriage, making a vital contribution to the family economy and having considerable power in the domestic sphere. Individual privacy was neither expected nor attainable and this affected attitudes to modesty and codes of sexual behavior. "Mothering" in the modern sense of the word barely existed, for with vital work in the house or fields, women had little time to devote exclusively to children. The high infant mortality rate resulted in a certain degree of necessary "indifference" and surviving children were quickly incorporated into the economic life of the family and wider community. The nuclear family as such existed as a subunit within a more complex network of wider social relationships. Mutual affection existed between marriage partners but this was based on a pragmatic rather than "romantic" relationship.[25]

Traditional West African family patterns, which slaves strove to recreate, related far more closely to this preindustrial model than the bourgeois ideal adopted by middle-class commentators. Other factors specific to West African society may also help to better determine the cultural response of slave women, particularly the key role of the African mother and the relative ease of divorce as a right for both partners.[26] The bond between mother and child was regarded as the "keystone of all social relations"; it enabled women to play a strong and important role in the wider community. In polygynous unions, in contrast to the "drudge" status accorded to them by European observers, women had even greater authority and autonomy of action.[27]

Although it is not suggested here that Africans literally transferred identical patterns to the Caribbean, it may be argued that despite severe dislocation, they retained many elements of traditional culture. A greater cultural unity existed among slaves than was previously assumed by European observers and such unity strengthened the potential for cultural resistance.[28] If slave women readopted traditional roles outlined above, fundamental concepts such as matrifocality need to be radically revised. For instance, the traditional economic independence of women in both matrilineal and patrilineal societies in slaving areas (Asante and Ibo, for example), in addition to their authority over children, may have contributed to the "matriarch" myth. The glaring contrast between the roles and functions of black and white women in the contemporary cultural context (as perceived by white men), plus the custom of slave descent through the female line, may have led observers to equate the relative independence of black women with unnatural dominance.[29] Slave family organization could have retained certain features of matrilineal societies like the Asante (the "tribal" origin of a high percentage of Jamaican slaves), but it should be noted that even in such societies men are by no means devoid of power or authority.[30]

The oversimplified contrast between the dominant slave mother and the emasculated male slave is not borne out by contemporary evidence. Leaders of slave communities who adjudicated at slave disputes, for instance, were predominantly elderly male slaves or elite skilled craftsmen. According to Beckford and Long, primogeniture was the norm even though the only inheritance may have been rights to provision grounds. Slaves were interconnected by "the bond of family love on the one side and filial obedience on the other."[31] Arguably the only real "matriarchs," in the Western sense of the term, were the small minority of black or colored mistresses of white men whose roots in the black community had been weakened.

Sheer force of circumstance demanded that slave women adapt to their new environment. In the Caribbean, the cultures of Europe and Africa were continuously juxtaposed in situations of conflict and assimilation. Yet it may be argued that whenever possible black women strove to reestablish their traditional roles as wife and mother, even where this involved resistance to European cultural impositions. Slaves in general rejected European norms, and developed their own, no less viable, African-derived code of behavior. Through cultural conditioning, misinterpretation, or plain ignorance of "the manners and superstitions of Africans,"[32] or simply for propaganda purposes, contemporary observers gave a distorted account of the slave woman's domestic role and devalued African cultural practices as they elevated those of the European.

The Domestic Role of Women Slaves—A Reevaluation

In establishing the degrees of cultural resistance involved in adapting traditional roles, scholars must first challenge the myths and show that slave women did not conform to the European image of them. For instance, much evidence exists to belie contemporary accusations of promiscuity. Only a minority of women, often domestic servants or favored colored women (reputedly models of propriety), entered into unions with white men. Such unions were often longstanding and bonded by mutual affection.[33] Though the cruder variety of sexual abuse of black women undoubtedly existed, it was strongly resented and, according to John Stedman, drove slave women and their husbands to "distraction," causing "many murders" despite the threat of punishment. If women resisted white men's advances, they were "mercilessly flogged."[34] Undoubtedly some women entered into relations with European men and risked isolation from their community. Even they may have done so primarily out of ambition for themselves and their kin, not out of "lust." Such women who, according to Edward Long, "heartlessly exploited" their white paramours may have been engaged in a subtle form of resistance within apparent accommodation (as domestic slaves overtly adopted European manners while covertly retaining their African cultural roots).[35]

Similarly, little evidence exists to support the contention that women were promiscuous in relations with black men. Equiano commented on the "modesty" and "bashfulness" of African women; though men were allowed sexual license, women were rarely "incontinent." Richard Ligon noted of slaves of both sexes during the early days of slavery:

> Chaste they are as any people under the sun; for when men and women are together naked, they will cast their eyes towards the parts that ought to be covered and . . . I never saw so much as a kiss, or embrace, or wanton glance in their eyes between them.

Later observers made similar comments.[36]

Though, arguably, in slave society, the same high premium was not placed on premarital chastity as in middle-class European society, marital fidelity was highly valued and even "lapses of virtue" among unmarried women could bring the ridicule of fellow slaves. Though marriage was only a "voluntary connection," slave women exhibited a "sense of decency and decorum," in contrast to the freer behavior of male slaves.[37]

Despite allegations of sexual precocity, slave girls were arguably slower to arrive at sexual maturity than European women at that time.[38] Evidence suggests that parental and community controls restricted the sexual activities of young slaves. Some form of regulated trial marriage may have existed, based on traditional West African patterns where marriage is developmental and such is the premium placed on female fertility that the union may only be formalized *after* the birth of a child (Herbert Gutman noted a similar practice in nineteenth-century South Carolina).[39]

Divorce procedures amongst slaves, like premarital childbirth, could also have been construed as "loose" behavior without due reference to the slave cultural context. The relative ease of divorce in the slave community was remarked upon by planters. A common divorce rite in Jamaica was division of the *cotta*, a circular pad of dried, plaited plantain leaves on which slaves carried headloads.[40] In contemporary Europe, divorce was against all the teachings of the Christian church and extremely difficult to obtain, for women especially. From a Eurocentric view the relative equality in divorce of slave women would have appeared scandalous. In effect it protected black women from the worst abuse by men. After 1800, when planters tried to encourage Christian marriage among slaves, to improve sexual morality and hence the fertility rate of women slaves, women refused to leave their state of "lawless concubinage." Christian marriage held few attractions and threatened the relative independence women had under African-derived forms; they feared it would give their husbands license to "beat and ill-treat them."[41]

Despite the lack of Christian marriage most slaves lived in stable, long-lasting unions and were reputedly "fond of domestic lives." They frequently lived and grew old together and a "strong sense of family attachment" prevailed.[42] Women were essential to promoting this one area of stability that sustained the black community. In this private domestic sphere, as far as possible, they readopted the traditional role of African women. In an important sense they were performing the only labor in the slave community, with perhaps the exception of the cultivation of provision grounds, that could not be directly claimed by the master. As well as putting in a hard day's labor in the fields the woman slave was expected to cook, clean, and care for the family. The male slave had a less-onerous burden.[43] But though she gave her labor to the white man resentfully, under coercion, domestic labor in the house, community, and provision grounds was given freely and willingly.

But the precious family and kinship bonds of slaves were continuously disrupted by indiscriminate sales and enforced separation. Even in the "ameliorative" period after 1790 when laws were passed against such inhumane practices, many estates were sold off with "stock" to pay outstanding debts.[44] Severance from "old attachments" reputedly caused "a species of rebellion" in slaves and many a planter had cause to "regret his inhumanity" after purchasing separated slaves.[45] Husbands and wives who were separated endeavored to maintain their relationships despite the hardships involved. Advertisements for slave runaways from contemporary newspapers such as the *Jamaica Mercury* and *Royal Gazette* show that slave couples ran away together, and Long noted that the more generalized kinship ties of slaves survived and adapted to separation.[46]

Slave women reacted particularly strongly to separation from their children. Despite their burden of hard work, they were generally solicitous mothers who though necessarily strict were also tender and affectionate, particularly with infants.[47] They retained a degree of the traditional authority of African mothers and the respect they were accorded. Affections between mothers and offspring were "powerful and permanent." Enforced separation produced despair and re-bellious behavior, which caused grave troubles for planters. Some women disappeared or threatened suicide, and others became "desperate with grief" and were "most troublesome" until their children were restored to them.[48]

On a less-dramatic level, slave mothers resisted planters' attempts to change African-derived practices of child rearing. As in West Africa, slave women tended to suckle infants for two years, keeping them close to them at all times.[49] Owners, however, felt they could not extract the maximum amount of labor from nursing mothers. Jamaican planters, for instance, argued that long suckling was merely another form of malingering and thus sought to place infants in "weaning houses," out of the direct care of their mothers. Slave women were reported to have reacted with "high discontent."[50] Efforts to alter other traditional practices met with a similar lack of success. Monk Lewis, for instance, tried to introduce the practice of plunging Negro infants into a tub of cold water immediately after they had been born (a measure that was supposed to "infallibly" protect them from infant tetanus). Slave women, however, "took a prejudice against it" and were "so obstinate in their opposition" that Lewis was forced to abandon the idea.[51]

Pressures on women slaves that threatened to erode traditional mothering practices intensified in the late period of slavery when planters tried to boost the extremely low birthrate of women slaves. Planters began to redefine the woman's role in the plantation economy by placing far greater emphasis on childbearing. Measures were taken to promote a "healthy increase," including better treatment of pregnant women. Many of these measures were based on a false impression of the sexual life of slaves and thus involved more stringent impositions of European cultural codes to erode "bad African practices." The birthrate, however, remained low, despite improved physical conditions, and did not rise until after emancipation.[52] This demographic anomaly has been analyzed elsewhere,[53] but within a perspective of resistance an important angle on this debate is the degree to which slave women took control of their own childbearing patterns.

Pregnancy and childbirth on the slave plantation was frought with hardship. From the earliest days it was assumed that, unlike European women, black women gave birth with ease, like animals.[54] Planters were primarily concerned with women's productivity in the fields and made few concessions to pregnant women. Even after 1800, planters were still advised not to allow "too much indulgence."[55] Not surprisingly, slave women were reported to have a high rate of miscarriages, "abortions," and difficult pregnancies (often blamed on the lack of skill of Negro midwives).[56] Though prolific childbearing was honored in West African society, there was an unusually high sterility rate, particularly among newly arrived African women.[57]

Some planters were aware that certain deep and complex psychosomatic processes that inhibited childbirth may have been in operation. One planter described the woman's situation as "upheld by no consolation, animated by no hope, her nine-months torment issuing in production of a being doomed like herself to the rigors of eternal servitude." It was argued that in addition to the inconducive nature of the slave regime, the specter of sale of infants discouraged women from having children.[58] There is evidence that under conditions of extreme stress, the will to have children is diminished.[59] The disorientation of the middle passage and harsh seasoning period may also have suppressed women's desire to conceive. "Negresses," declared Monk Lewis, "can produce children at will . . . where they are barren it is just as hens will . . . not lay eggs on board ship because they do not like the situation."[60]

In addition to such deep-seated psychosomatic mechanisms, women may have consciously regulated their own childbearing through abortion or contraception. Richard Sheridan has speculated on this possibility and Edward Brathwaite regards it as a valid form of slave resistance.[61] Certainly slave women could have possessed the necessary cultural knowledge; abortifacient techniques were known and utilized in prescribed circumstances such as unsanctioned pregnancies in many of the parts of West Africa where slaves originated. Common abortifacients included herbs, leaves of special shrubs, and plant roots. They were administered by old women skilled in midwifery and the knowledge was transmitted from mother to daughter.[62]

Similar herbs and plants that "promoted terms in women" were known in the Caribbean, including wild tansy, a widely recognized abortifacient in the Old South.[63] Contemporary commentators accused women of inducing miscarriages by "violence" or through use of "simples of the country." Negro girls in Surinam reputedly used a vegetable flower called "seven-broom" in addition to green pineapples. In Jamaica, in the 1820s, "procuration of abortion" through "herbs and powders" administered by men and women was allegedly "very prevalent."[64] Europeans naturally linked self-induced abortion with the pleasure-seeking "promiscuous" activities of the women slaves, who were allegedly no more than "common prostitutes."[65] Yet evidence suggests that, as with other aspects of the slaves' private domestic lives, whites could merely surmise on such matters, for slaves jealously protected their knowledge of these secret practices.[66]

Throughout history, women, often in defiance of man-made religious and secular laws, have resorted to abortion and allied practices as a means of terminating unwanted pregnancies. Since such practices have by necessity been clandestine, little documentary evidence exists. Abortion belongs to a shadowy world outside the mainstream of history (as indeed has much of women's history until recently). Absence of documentation, therefore, cannot be used to refute the existence of such practices, for they are universal, transcending chronological and cultural barriers.

Women slaves had particularly strong motives for limiting the number of children they had. Too many children can be a burden when parents have a hard and bitter existence, but to this slave women must have added as a paramount reason to consciously control their childbearing the sheer lack of freedom. The fact that slaves were deprived "of free agency" meant their offspring too were doomed to enslavement. As Bryan Edwards frankly admitted, "slavery itself, in its mildest form, is unfriendly to population."[67] This may explain why the birthrate rose dramatically after emancipation though physical conditions had not noticeably improved.[68]

Women played a vital role in sustaining and uniting established family links and cared well for the children they had, within the constraints of the system. But there was little incentive for them to bear large numbers of children. Deliberate limitation of the number of children may have been an effective means by which they protested their enforced bondage. Against such methods planters were powerless and had little or no control (as failure of "ameliorative" policies illustrates). In refusing to breed at will, slave women frustrated planter ambitions and rejected attempts to interfere in the private sphere of their domestic lives. Thus women's attitudes to childbearing are integral, indeed fundamental, to a wider analysis of cultural resistance in slave family life.

Summary

Women took an active part in all forms of resistance against slavery in the British Caribbean. If slavery and the slave trade caused a "crude leveling" of sexual distinctions in the public or official domain of the slave women, in their private domain they tried against all odds to retrieve and maintain the essence of their black womanhood.[69] It was within the family and wider community that cultural resistance to imposed European values was strongest, and here women had a vital role to play in sustaining not only African-derived cultural practices but also a more general spirit of resistance that enabled slaves to survive slavery.

In order to justify slavery, however, planters had to denigrate this resilient and vital Afro-Caribbean culture. Their prime target was the moral code of the slaves, particularly the behavior of female slaves. Ignorance of the true nature of African marriages, polygyny in particular, spawned myths of black female promiscuity and heightened sexuality. This provided a convenient rationale for the miscegenous and adulterous activities of white men of all classes. Such adverse stereotyping of black women has proved highly durable and resulted in distorted theorizing about black family life in both slavery and freedom.

To reinstate the black woman in a more positive historical context and reformulate contemporary perceptions of the slave family, it is necessary to look beneath the superficial myths and reexamine the evidence from a less-Eurocentric but also less-middle-class perspective. Class as well as racial considerations must be taken into account. Whites, both proslavery and antislavery, interpreted the private lives of slaves according to the values of middle-class European society, which became the dominant or ruling ideas of nineteenth-century industrial society. Values of preindustrial peasant society and those of the new urban proletariat were denigrated by middle-class observers in much the same way as were the values of African slaves. The European proletariat, particularly the women, were frequently accused of "immorality" and "shameless freedom of the sexes."[70] Lower-class women were the targets of the sexual attentions of middle- and upper-class men. Lack of conformity to bourgeois morality constituted a potential threat to social order. Similar ideological considerations apply to slave and postslave societies with the added complications of racism. To justify slavery and maintain European dominance, Europeans had to devalue African codes of morality and perpetuate racist stereotypes. The slaves' essential humanity was thus denied, facilitating economic exploitation.

Thus to preserve all that was meaningful to them, slaves frequently came into conflict with the slave system and retained their own alternative, African-based belief system, which inspired resistance. The family was the crucible of this resistance. Family and kin supported the individual slave against the vagaries of plantation life. When Monk Lewis tried to demote a skilled slave to the rank of common field hand, he received supplications from the man's wife, then his mother, and finally his cousin's cousin.[71] Organized resistance was important but the strength of the slaves lay in the cultural support of the community. Kinship instilled a feeling of cooperation among slaves, and inspired and coordinated resistance.

Women slaves, strengthened by traditional African culture, were the backbone of the slave family and community. Though women had an influential position, male authority was not moribund, however, for the cooperation and efforts of both sexes were necessary to preserve the family in a system that militated against it in all ways. Women's role was unique in the sense that they were the childbearers and could effectively frustrate their owners by refusing to bear children at will. Women were also key figures in the transmission of cultural beliefs and were thus in the vanguard of cultural resistance.

It was in the interest of the planters to promote myths of the instability of the slave family, for this justified the exploitation and separation of slaves. With subtle variations, their image of slave immorality and disorganized family life has persisted until very recently. Contrary to these views slaves in fact developed viable family forms based on African rather than European values. Given the potential for sexual and social chaos, it is a tribute to women slaves in particular that they did not succumb to promiscuity and immorality in their relations with either white or black men. On the contrary, they made a valuable cultural contribution to the slave family and community in a situation where, in the words of Winthrop Jordan, anything but promiscuity represented a "tenacious cultural conservation," a form of resistance that ultimately represented a "triumph of cultural adaptivity."[72]

Notes

1 R. S. Rattray, *Ashanti Proverbs (The Primitive Ethics of a Savage People)*, Oxford, 1916, 124.

2 A more comprehensive analysis of stereotypes of slave women can be found in chapter 1, "'The Eye of the Beholder': The White Image of the Black Woman—Some Historical Reflections," in B. Bush, *'Lost Daughters of Afrik': Slave Women in the British Caribbean*, Ormskirk, 1983.

3 Walter Rodney, "Upper Guinea and the Significance of the Origins of Africans Enslaved in the New World," *Journal of Negro History*, 54:4 (October 1969), 327–345.

4 M. J. Herskovits and F. Herskovits, *Trinidad Village*, New York, 1936, 8–9.

5 See for instance Edward Long, *The History of Jamaica*, London, 1774, II, 303–304; and Bryan Edwards, *The History, Civil and Commercial, of the British Colonies in the West Indies*, London, 1801, II, 76, 148; and I, Appendix 2, 540–541.

6 John Riland, *Memoirs of a West Indian Planter*, London, 1837, 201–202.

7 Report of the Lords of Trade on the Slave Trade, *British Sessional Papers (BSP)*, (Commons), XXVI (1789), Part 3, Jamaica, Ans., No. 4, 646a; and Thomas Cooper, *Facts Illustrative of the Condition of Negro Slaves in Jamaica*, London, 1824, 3.

8 For "pious" views, see Riland, *Memoirs*, 191; Cooper, *Facts Illustrative*, 35–42; and Long, *History of Jamaica*, II, 289. The more stereotyped view is presented in Thomas Atwood, *The History of Domenica*, London, 1791, 273; Long, *History of Jamaica*, II, 331; and P. Wright (ed.), *Lady Nugent's Jamaica Journal*, Kingston, 1966, 29.

9 For a fuller examination of miscegenation in the Caribbean, see B. Bush, "White 'Ladies,' Coloured 'Favourites,' and Black 'Wenches': Some Considerations on Sex, Race, and Class Factors in Social Relations in White Creole Society in the British Caribbean," *Slavery and Abolition*, 2:3 (December 1981), 245–262. For contemporary observations, see Wright (ed.), *Lady Nugent*, 66, 86–87, 98; John Gabriel Stedman, *Narrative of a Five Years Expedition against the Revolted Negroes of Surinam, 1772 to 1777*, London, 1796, I, 112, 162; and Atwood, *History of Domenica*, 211–212.

10 Matthew Gregory Lewis, *Journal of a Residence among the Negroes in the West Indies*, London, 1845, 122; "Abstract from the Leeward Islands Act, 1798," Act No. 36, Clauses XXII and XXV; Edwards, *History, Civil and Commercial*, V, 183–185; "Abstract from the Slave Laws of Jamaica, 1826," Act Nos. 32 and 33; and Bernard M. Senior, *A Retired Military Officer*, London, 1831, 144.

11 Comparative evaluations of the three legal systems including "Ameliorative" legislation can be found in Elsa Goveia, *The West Indian Slave Laws of the Eighteenth Century*, Barbados, 1970, 13–48.

12 Edwards, *History, Civil and Commercial*, II, 148; Emma Carmichael, *Domestic Manners*, London, 1833, II, 201; and Lewis, *Journal*, 65.

13 Edwards, *History, Civil and Commercial*, II, 82; and William Beckford, *A Descriptive Account of the Islands of Jamaica*, London, 1790, II, 120.

14 See, for instance, Orlando Patterson, *The Sociology of Slavery*, London, 1967, 159–170; and Elsa Goveia, *Slave Society in the British Leeward Islands at the End of the Eighteenth Century*, Barbados, 1965, 234–237.

15 See, for instance, Michael Craton and James Walvin, *A Jamaican Plantation: The History of Worthy Park, 1670–1970*, Toronto, 1970, 127–133; and Richard S. Dunn, "A Tale of Two Plantations: Slave Life at Mesopotamia in Jamaica and Mount Airy in Virginia, 1799–1828," *William and Mary Quarterly*, 34:1 (January 1977), 63.

16 See, for example, William J. Goode, "Illegitimacy in the Caribbean Social Structure," *American Sociological Review*, 25:1 (February 1960), 21.

17 This whole dichotomy of theoretical approach is summed up in R. T. Smith's "Culture and Social Structure in the Caribbean: Some Recent Work on Family and Kinship Studies," *Comparative Studies in Society and History*, 6:1 (January 1964), 24.

18 See, for instance, Edith Clarke, *My Mother Who Fathered Me*, London, 1957, 68–84.

19 Sidney Mintz, "History and Anthropology: A Brief Reprise," in E. Genovese and S. Engerman (eds.), *Race and Slavery in the Western Hemisphere: Quantitative Studies*, New York, 1975, 490–493.

20 See Barry Higman, "The Slave Family and Household in the British West Indies, 1800–1834," *Journal of Interdisciplinary History*, 6:2 (Autumn 1975), 275–277; and Michael Craton, "Hobbesian or Panglossian? The Two Extremes of Slave Conditions in the British Caribbean, 1783 to 1834," *William and Mary Quarterly*, 35:2 (April 1978), 339.

21 For a useful theoretical discussion on family and kinship organization, see Nancie L. Solien, "Household and Family in the Caribbean: Some Definitions and Concepts," in M. M. Horowitz (ed.), *Peoples and Cultures of the Caribbean*, New York, 1971, 404–406.

22 Edwards, *History, Civil and Commercial*, II, 131; and Stedman, *Narrative*, I, 114. A similar practice was noted in the Old South. See Herbert G. Gutman, *The Black Family in Slavery and Freedom, 1750–1925*, New York, 1976, 154–155.

23 Beckford, *Descriptive Account*, II, 326; John Stewart, *A View of Jamaica*, New York, 1969, 249–250; Robert C. Dallas, *The History of the Maroons*, London, 1803, I, cxi; and Daryll Forde, "Kinship and Marriage among the Matrilineal Ashanti," in A. R. Radcliffe-Brown and Daryll Forde (eds.), *African Systems of Kinship and Marriage*, London, 1956, 276.

24 Higman, "Slave Family," 277.

25 Philippe Ariés, *Centuries of Childhood: A Social History of Family Life*, New York, 1962, 71, 368–369, 39; Edward Shorter, *The Making of the Modern Family*, New York, 1975, 16–18, 67–68, 168–170; and Peter Laslett, *The World We Have Lost*, London, 1971, 4, 45.

26 Useful data on the "separate but equal" status of African women in marriage and divorce may be found in Denise Paulme (ed.), *Women in Tropical Africa*, Berkeley, 1963, 6; Radcliffe-Brown and Forde (eds.), *African Systems*, 46, 50; and Forde, "Kinship and Marriage," 280–283.

27 Forde, "Kinship and Marriage," 262; Paulme (ed.), *Women*, 8–9, 12; and Radcliffe-Brown and Forde (eds.), *African Systems*, 49–52, 77. Asante proverbs also reflect this importance of the mother. Rattray, *Ashanti*, 125, 128–129.

28 Rodney, "Upper Guinea," 345; and Sidney Mintz, cited in Gutman, *Black Family*, 345.

29 Bush, "White 'Ladies,'" 249–252.

30 Forde, "Kinship and Marriage," 262, 256. Remnants of matrilineal organization still exist

among the present-day Djuka of Surinam and Guyana. See, for instance, A. J. F. Köbben, "Unity and Disunity: Cottica Djuka Society as a Kinship System," in Richard Price (ed.), *Maroon Societies: Rebel Slave Communities in the Americas*, Garden City, N.Y., 1973, 323; and M. J. Herskovits and F. Herskovits, *Rebel Destiny among the Bush Negroes of Dutch Guiana*, New York, 1934, 132.

31 Stewart, *View*, 262; Beckford, *Descriptive Account*, II, 324; and Long, *History of Jamaica*, II, 410–411.

32 Edwards, *History, Civil and Commercial*, II, 147. A similar observation is made by Stewart, *View*, 252, who noted that slaves were "jealous" of their culture, and slave villages were concealed by trees "beyond the ken" of slave masters.

33 Lewis, *Journal*, 87; and Wright (ed.), *Lady Nugent*, 66–68. See also Bush, "White 'Ladies.'"

34 Stedman, *Narrative*, I, 370, 106; and John Jeremie, *Four Essays on Colonial Slavery*, London, 1831, 26.

35 Long, *History of Jamaica*, II, 331. This form of resistance is discussed by Eugene Genovese, *Roll, Jordan, Roll: The World the Slaves Made*, New York, 1974, 111, and a similar duality of behavior of blacks in the Caribbean has been noted by Peter J. Wilson, *Oscar: An Enquiry into the Nature of Sanity*, New York, 1975, 16, 114–116.

36 Paul Edwards (ed.), *Equiano's Travels*, London, 1967, 8; Richard Ligon, *A True and Exact History of the Island of Barbados*, London, 1657, 47; Stedman, *Narrative*, I, 368; and Carmichael, *Domestic Manners*, II, 24.

37 Ligon, *True and Exact*, 47; Sir Hans Sloane, *A Voyage to the Islands of Barbados, Nieves, St Christopher, and Jamaica*, London, 1707, I, xlviii; and *BSP*, 1789, Part 3, Barbados, Ans., No. 15.

38 Michael Craton, *Searching for the Invisible Man: Slaves and Plantation Life in Jamaica*, Cambridge, 1978, 103–104; and Dunn, "Tale of Two," 59.

39 Stedman, *Narrative*, II, 253; Beckford, *Descriptive Account*, I, 231; and Dallas, *History of the Maroons*, I, 115. Trial marriages exist among the Asante, the ethnic origin of many Jamaican slaves. Forde, "Kinship and Marriage," 280. For examples in the New World, see Gutman, *Black Family*, 42, 60–65.

40 Long, *History of Jamaica*, I, 415, 313.

41 John Quier, "A Slave Doctor's Views on Childbirth," *Report of the Assembly on Slave Issues*, Jamaica House of Assembly, enclosed in Lt. Gov. Clarke's report No. 92 of November 20, 1788, CO 137/38, Appendix C, 492; Riland, *Memoirs*, 187–189; Cooper, *Facts Illustrative*, 42–47; and Senior, *Retired*, 42–43.

42 Sloane, *Voyage*, I, xlvii; Long, *History of Jamaica*, II, 414; and *BSP*, 1789, Bermuda, Ans., No. 17, and Jamaica, Ans., No. 14.

43 Carmichael, *Domestic Manners*, I, 80, 179; and Cooper, *Facts Illustrative*, 33–34.

44 Edwards, *History, Civil and Commercial*, II, 153–154.

45 William Beckford, *Remarks upon the Situation of Negroes in Jamaica*, London, 1788, 8; Cooper, *Facts Illustrative*, 26; and Stewart, *View*, 179.

46 *BSP*, 1789, Barbados, Ans., No. 15; and Long, *History of Jamaica*, II, 414.

47 Long, *History of Jamaica*, II, 414; Ligon, *True and Exact*, 51; Lewis, *Journal*, 90; Beckford, *Remarks*, 24; Stedman, *Narrative*, II, 368; and Stewart, *View*, 249–250.

48 Bickell, cited in Edward Brathwaite, *The Development of Creole Society in Jamaica*, Oxford, 1971, 215; Lewis, *Journal*, 179; and Riland, *Memoirs*, 87–89.

49 Stedman, *Narrative*, II, 368; and Carmichael, *Domestic Manners*, II, 191.

50 Lewis, *Journal*, 145–146.

51 Lewis, *Journal*, 141.

52 Barry W. Higman, *Slave Population and Economy in Jamaica, 1807–1834*, London, 1976, 153–155; and Richard Sheridan, "Mortality and Medical Treatment of Slaves in the British West Indies," in Genovese and Engerman (eds.), *Race and Slavery*, 289–300.

53 See, for instance, recent work carried out by Craton, Dunn, and Higman. The debate is summarized in chapter 7, "Childbirth in the Slave Community," in Bush, '*Lost Daughters.*'

54 See, for example, Long, *History of Jamaica*, II, 385; Stedman, *Narrative*, II, 359; Sloane, *Voyage*, I, cxlvii; and Wright (ed.), *Lady Nugent*, 69.

55 Beckford, *Remarks*, 24–25; and Wright (ed.), *Lady Nugent*, 77–79.

56 *BSP*, 1789, Barbados, Ans., No. 17; Craton, *Searching*, 103–111; and Long, *History of Jamaica*, II, 436.

57 Paulme (ed.), *Women*, 14; and Forde, "Kinship and Marriage," 262–263. The high sterility rate is commented on by Craton, *Searching*, 107, and Higman, *Slave Population*, 49.

58 Dr. Collins, cited in Patterson, *Sociology of Slavery*, 206; and *BSP*, 1789, Barbados, Ans., No. 15.

59 See contemporary sources cited in George Devereux, *A Study of Abortion in Primitive Society*, London, 1960, 240–275. Other African examples are given in Herbert Aptekar, *Anjea: Infanticide, Abortion, and Contraception in Savage Society*, New York, 1931, 62–63. See also Terrence Des Pres, *The Survivor: An Anatomy of Life in the Death Camps*, New York, 1976, 189–191.

60 Lewis, *Journal*, 41.

61 Sheridan, "Mortality and Medical Treatment," 300; and Brathwaite, *Development of Creole Society*, 206–207.

62 Rattray, *Ashanti*, 55; Devereux, *Study of Abortion*, 131, 218, 289, 258, 204; and Aptekar, *Anjea*, 35. See also G. W. Harley, *Native African Medicine*, London, 1941, 73; and M. J. Herskovits, *Dahomey: An Ancient West African Kingdom*, New York, 1938, I, 268.

63 Dr. Thomas Dancer, *The Medical Assistant; or, Jamaica Practice of Physic*, Kingston, 1809, 263–264, 386; and Gutman, *Black Family*, 81–82.

64 Dr. Collins, cited in Patterson, *Sociology of Slavery*, 134; and Stedman, *Narrative*, I, 334. Rev. Henry Beame, cited in Michael Craton, James Walvin, and David Wright (eds.), *Slavery, Abolition, and Emancipation: Black Slaves and the British Empire*, London, 1976, 141. Similar practices have been reported from other New World slave societies—the French Caribbean, Brazil, and the Old South—and also the modern Caribbean. See, for example, Herskovits and Herskovits, *Trinidad Village*, 128.

65 Quier, "Slave Doctor," 491; Long, *History of Jamaica*, II, 436; and Edwards, *History, Civil and Commercial*, II, 148.

66 Rev. Henry Beame, cited in Craton, Walvin, and Wright (eds.), *Slavery, Abolition*, 141.

67 Edwards, *History, Civil and Commercial*, II, 148.

68 Sheridan, "Mortality and Medical Treatment," 289.

69 Lucille Mathurin, "The Arrivals of Black Women," *Jamaica Journal*, 9:2 and 3 (February 1975), 2; and Edward Brathwaite, "Submerged Mothers," *Jamaica Journal*, 9:2 and 3 (February 1975), 48.

70 Hans Medick, "The Proto-Industrial Family Economy: The Structural Function of Household and Family during the Transition from Peasant Society to Industrial Capitalism," *Social History*, 3:3 (October 1976), 313–314.

71 Lewis, *Journal*, 109.

72 Winthrop D. Jordan, *American Attitudes toward the Negro, 1550 to 1812*, New York, 1968, 114.

9

Historiography and Slave Revolt and Rebelliousness in the United States: A Class Approach

HERBERT SHAPIRO

Donald Robinson has written that it is extremely difficult to assess resistance by slaves to bondage and that the obstacles to obtaining a reliable portrait of this aspect of slavery are nearly insurmountable.[1] The obstacles may exist but despite Robinson's caution it is now well established in the historiography of Afro-American slavery that black resistance to enslavement was widespread, persistent, heroic, and politically consequential in hastening the demise of the "peculiar institution." We can confirm that the image of the Sambo stereotype does not illuminate the reality of slave psychology but rather the masters' self-deception and Stanley Elkins's misapprehension of slavery. A number of scholars have contributed to a history of slave resistance. The way was opened by the efforts of such pioneers as Carter G. Woodson, Benjamin Quarles, Harvey Wish, W. E. B. Du Bois, Raymond Bauer and Alice Bauer, Joseph Carroll, John Hope Franklin, Philip Foner, and Kenneth Stampp. In more recent years the works of such scholars as George Rawick, Paul Escott, Vincent Harding, Peter Wood, James Oakes, John Blassingame, Gerald Mullin, and Leslie Owens have enriched our understanding of resistance, and so also has much of the work of Herbert Gutman and particularly the more recent work of Eugene Genovese.

Above all there has been the continuing trailblazing scholarship of Herbert Aptheker, whose passionate commitment to the cause of the oppressed and responsible, meticulous concern for evidence have enabled him to systematically

outline the evidence pointing to the conclusion that "discontent and rebelliousness were not only exceedingly common, but, indeed, characteristic of
American Negro slaves."[2] Aptheker has proceeded from the humanism of
Angelina Grimké's comment that slavery "always has, and always will produce
insurrections wherever it exists, because it is a violation of the natural order of
things, and no human power can much longer perpetuate it," and related that
viewpoint to a class analysis of slavery and slave resistance.[3] The result has been
a body of work that has played a major role in bringing from shadows the history of a people's fight for freedom that is at the same time a central feature of
the history of American class struggle.

Certainly for Aptheker, a class, Marxian approach to slavery has not been a
mere adornment to otherwise valuable scholarship but instead has represented
an integral part of his work. Eugene Genovese has written that all Marxian
history "may from one point of view, be judged good or poor by the extent to
which it contributes to our understanding of class."[4] If that is the case, and because there is continuing discussion on what constitutes a class view, it is particularly appropriate to further consider the elements of a class understanding of
slavery and of resistance by slaves and what this view has added to what we
know of Afro-American slavery. The conceptual frameworks offered by Marx
and Engels may perhaps have meaning for the specialist in Afro-American history beyond that of the casual reading one might take along on a summer
vacation.

To approach the study of slave resistance from the standpoint of a class analysis involves viewing slavery within the context of the world in which it existed,
examining the actual class relationship that produced and maintained slavery.
Those interested in class are naturally concerned with the interaction of masters
and slaves, the class alignments of Southern white society, the relationship of
slavery to national mechanism of class rule, the genesis of slavery in the rise of
a class of merchant capitalists, and the dooming of slavery that was foreshadowed by the emergence of industrial capitalism. The slaves are seen not
merely as individual dependents of masters but as members of a class, brought
to life despite the relative isolation of plantation society by shared experience
and need. This class developed an ethos of its own, a culture and a network of
institutions and values. The scholar who relates to the Marxian conception of
class will take into account the exploitative nature of slavery, will consider
slaveholder ideology in the light of that nature, and, attuned to the theme of
contradiction, will recognize the inherent antagonism between master and
slave. That antagonism, unless American slavery was absolutely unrelated to
any other human experience, of course generated conflict. Eugene Genovese
has agreed with Herbert Aptheker that in the last analysis the cause of slave

revolts was slavery and the point is a fundamental one.[5] The slaves knew their human identity, matched slaveholder rhetoric against perceived reality, and could not be relied upon to join the masters in defining themselves as pieces of property. Slavery was a stimulus to the will for freedom and that will, joined to the historic rupture between the American ruling classes and the democratic strivings of many white people, led to the ending of bondage.

A class approach to slave resistance leads us away from preconceived standards for what constitutes meaningful struggle and calls for studying the activity of slaves within the existing circumstances determined by American reality. Those circumstances caution the historian against making mechanistic comparisons with patterns of resistance in other parts of the Americas. North American slaves had to contend with the formidable armed power of a slaveowning class that set in place an extensive apparatus of control and was able, for reasons we need to study further, to secure or dragoon the support of most nonslaveholding whites. Given the prevailing extent of racism, the population statistics were an obstacle to successful revolt. In 1860 in the South as a whole, slaves constituted only 34 percent of the population and in that same year only in two states did slaves form a majority. Precisely because of the bourgeois-democratic origins of the United States, slaveowners had some success in presenting themselves to poorer whites, not as class enemies, but as fellow strivers for affluence. The slaveholders had available not only their own immediate reserves but also the power of the federal government, which gave its support repeatedly in suppressing slave uprisings. In these circumstances, the resistance that was manifested by slaves was indeed remarkable. The Nat Turner revolt, I hope we will now all agree, does not recede in magnitude but rather stands as an event, according to Kenneth Stampp, that no antebellum Southerner could forget.[6] The Southampton insurrection, setting off an insurrection panic in much of the South, traumatized the plantation owners and was a factor impelling them to an increasingly self-isolating course. The revolt entered the cultural heritage of black people and for many whites it served as a powerful challenge to the myth of the contented slave. The essential point is that the Turner revolt and other manifestations of rebelliousness fulfilled a vital role: They served as a destabilizing influence upon the slaveholders, fueling their fears of catastrophe and driving them to seek ever-stronger assurances against challenge from within and without. The Southern fear of insurrections had a core of reality, for slaves had rebelled and might rebel again. Horace Greeley knew what he was doing in 1856 when he mocked the slaveowner South, referring to its "nonsense about the contented condition of the slave" matched by alarms of impending uprisings.[7]

Eugene Genovese has noted that all of the slave revolts in American history "made vital contributions to the democratization of the modern world . . . [and] helped to establish the claims of the people against their oppressors."[8] These are profoundly political matters, as were the other varied forms of resistance employed by slaves. Slaves, of course, had no access to the electoral machinery or to the forums of debate, and were excluded from all constitutional guarantees, as indeed blacks in general were denied such guarantees. For a myriad of reasons the course of general insurrection was closed but the actions of slaves were influential in determining the agenda of political issues, in determining who would win political power in the United States and who would lose it. And these actions had political meaning, for they spurred the abolition of chattel status and provided an opening wedge toward gaining the democratic rights to which other Americans were entitled.

A class view of the resistance of slaves is likely to avoid such mechanistic errors as that made by Richard Wade in determining that the Denmark Vesey plot probably did not exist because the urban context worked against the likelihood of uprisings.[9] A class approach does not dictate predetermined answers, but it does call upon us to keep in mind that the city environment affected the unfolding of relations between masters and slaves yet it did not bridge the gap between the owners and the owned. We know that in other cities slave revolts did occur and for all the attractions of Charleston, there is no reason to believe that this city could not also be the setting for insurrection.

The warping of historical reality that can result from ignoring class considerations in the study of slavery is perhaps nowhere more clearly seen than in the work of Stanley Elkins and in the crude caricature of Elkins given us by William Styron. Anyone who understood that slaves constituted a class of human beings and that the members of this class labored, produced most of the wealth of the South, raised families, and developed varied forms of cultural expression would not likely have accepted the Sambo stereotype as a valid description of slave personality structure. The slaves did not confront the masters merely as atomized, infantilized ciphers and any attention to the collective experience generated by slavery would have shown this to be the case.

The work of a number of scholars, work relative to the theme of resistance, has been influenced, directly or indirectly, by an emphasis upon class. Herbert Gutman has written of the achievements of black slaves in maintaining a viable family structure, moving the ground out from under Daniel Moynihan's fanciful view of slavery.[10] Gutman relates the black family structure to the strength of extended kinship networks, but I would suggest this continuing strength is comprehensible only on the basis of the struggles of slaves as a class to resist the will of the masters and to establish a measure of control over their own lives. The will of slaves for meaningful, caring family life was more than a desire manifest by particular extended families; it represented the aspirations of the slave community, the members of whom were bound to each other by shared experience and social status that transcended blood relationship. If Gutman's conclusions, however, presuppose the activity of slaves as a class, he limits the understanding of that activity in abstracting black family experience from the exploitative slave-master relationship that denied slave family life legal status and continually threatened its security. One of the great sagas of American history is that the slave family structure was not crushed despite all of the monstrous burdens placed upon it by enslavement.

Eugene Genovese's work, both that written individually and that written jointly with Elizabeth Fox-Genovese, has reflected efforts to apply class analysis to the study of slavery. In some of the recent work, what stands out is an emphasis upon understanding slavery as shaped by the growth of the capitalist world market and the role of slave revolts in precipitating the national crisis that led to the Civil War and the abolition of slavery. Earlier, particularly in *The Political Economy of Slavery*, there is the perception that the activity of a class is shaped by the tendencies inherent in its position; the logic of slavery prevails over anyone's subjective will. Genovese had called attention to Du Bois's emphasis upon the role of revolts in abolishing the slave trade and concurred with C. L. R. James's view that Nat Turner made Garrison a household word.[11] In their most recent work, Fox-Genovese and Genovese arraign capitalism for its crimes of "having carried slavery, serfdom, peonage, genocide, and, in general mass murder and cruelty" beyond what sadistic minds might conceive. They point to the anomaly that capitalism, which rests upon free labor, created new unfree forms of labor, "including systems of chattel slavery" on an unprecedented scale. They refer to the grounding of slavery in "economic exploitation and class relations." Fox-Genovese and Genovese have identified slavery as a prebourgeois property relationship functioning within American capitalism. They have drawn attention to the important work of Maurice Dobb in showing us how capitalism emerged upon the world scene. They refer to the retrograde historical role of the slaveholders and note it was Northern freedom, not Southern slavery, that provided the means "for the nation's survival, development, and rise to world power."[12] Taking into account the formidable obstacles to the initiation of slave revolts in the United States, Eugene Genovese writes that the fact of such revolts, to whatever extent they occurred, "demonstrated to the world the impossibility of crushing completely the slaves' rebellious spirit."[13] Fox-Genovese and Genovese have outlined a thesis on the class nature of slavery that addresses, as they observe, "the central issues" concerning the system. This thesis begins with the existence of a ruling class "spawned by the expansion of European capitalism but increasingly shaped by the precapitalist nature of its relation to the labor force," and brings us to a struggle of the contending classes, "which for some meant their very freedom." [14]

Some of the earlier problems found in Genovese's view of the relations between master and slave arose because he tended to write of the economic structure of slavery with little reference to the slave, and his treatment of slave culture was inadequately grounded on the system's material context. The result was that a particular form of slaveholder rule was elevated over the substance of the exploitative relationship between the owners and the enslaved.

The discussion by Fox-Genovese and Genovese of slave resistance is weakened by a tendency to underestimate the dimension of the resistance that transcended the limits of the system. The setting forth of accommodation as the concept that mediates the whole range of behavior from docility to rebelliousness is a problem, for though accommodation is not presented as an acquiescent response, it is limited to "a struggle to avoid the worst." [15] But is there not abundant evidence that an essential feature of slavery was the slaves' will to be free? If this was the case, then we may properly conclude that what mediated the black response to bondage was the natural human desire to become more than the master's chattel property, that this desire was the source of the varied forms of resistance manifested by slaves. The concept of "accommodation" continues to add confusion rather than clarity to the discussion of slave resistance.

All of us who seek to better understand the history of Afro-American slavery owe a great debt to the work of Herbert Aptheker. Although at some places there may still be graduate students who are encouraged to infer that his work is not quite scholarly or to forget that his work is part of a living trend in the profession, Aptheker's studies of slavery have, since the late 1930s, materially influenced American historical scholarship. If today the historian who would write of contented, carefree slaves is not likely to achieve credible standing, that change from the past is related to what Aptheker has done to depict the many-sided struggle of blacks for freedom. As scholar and activist he has manifested the radical's commitment to humanizing the world, his sympathies and engagement are there for all to discern, but he has joined to commitment a concern for precise rendering of evidence and a respect for the honest scholarship of others. In a variety of settings, formal and informal, he has served as a teacher of numerous historians who established significant careers as productive scholars. He has consistently stressed the role of black scholars in challenging racist domination of the social sciences, recognizing, for example, the vitally important work, what Du Bois termed "the long hammering," of Carter G. Woodson at a time when most white scholars ignored Woodson's scholarship, even if they knew the name, and at least one distinguished historian of the South at the University of Chicago, Avery Craven, reportedly told black graduate students they could not write objectively of their people's history. Aptheker's *Documentary History of the Negro People* furnished overwhelming evidence that black people had fought by every available means against oppression and in his work blacks appeared not only as the acted upon but also as the makers of history. Du Bois hailed the work as capturing "the very words and thoughts" of scores of American blacks, and noted that the world preserved the records of kings and gentlemen "in stupid detail" but saved all too little of the record left by "the half or wholly submerged working group."[16] The apologists for slavery sought to establish a myth of race inferiority, which would preclude blacks from making any human response to bondage.

In Aptheker's work there is evident deep feeling and a profound moral sense of the monstrous nature of slavery. His perspective has always been one that views the world not only as it is but as it is becoming. Regarding the struggle of American black people he has observed that for "sheer courage and ingenuity" this conflict has been unsurpassed in all the history of human struggle.[17]

In numerous articles and especially in *American Negro Slave Revolts*, Aptheker has presented a powerful rejoinder to U. B. Phillips's view of slavery as an arrangement for the control and instruction of naturally inferior, submissive blacks. Committed to the democratic transformation of the contemporary world, Aptheker had no need for the rationale for subjection that Phillips claimed to have found in the record of slavery. Aptheker cited evidence pointing to the conclusion that the history of Afro-American slavery includes more than two hundred and fifty reported revolts and conspiracies. He carefully set out his standards for determining the existence of such events. Leslie Owens has written that further attention to plantation records would probably uncover many more such incidents.[18] But in any event, it needs to be said here that despite what occasionally has been said by some, no historian, neither J. G. de Roulhac Hamilton nor anyone else, has effectively challenged Aptheker's findings.[19]

Aptheker's work reflects his humanism but also his class view of slavery and slave resistance. In one of his early essays he pointed to American slavery as a system of exploitation that produced staples for a world market.[20] It was because Afro-American slavery was set in the context of expanding world capitalism that the system was as exploitative as it was. Throughout his work on slave revolts he relates such events to the impact of economic cycles and to the existing relation of classes. He examines the question of slaveholder cruelty from the standpoint of the tendencies inherent in slavery. Slaves were instruments of production but as reasoning human beings they could not be equated with inanimate pieces of equipment. They dreamed of a better future but they knew that slavery would normally consign themselves and their children to lifelong bondage. Given that profit was to be made from the labor of slaves, they had to be maltreated in order to extract from them the labor that could be turned into more land and more slaves.[21] Aptheker would not exclude a range of behavior on the part of individual masters; some masters emancipated slaves and a few became determined opponents of slavery, but what most drew his attention were the dynamics of slavery that affected slaveholders as a class. It was also this question of the inherent features of the slave-master relationship that Frederick Douglass addressed when he observed that the slave who had the best master dreams of having no master at all.[22]

Aptheker's essay "Class Conflicts in the South: 1850–1860," published in 1939, draws our attention to a theme that has not received adequate study, the theme of the complex interaction of slave resistance and discontent with the planter regime manifested by nonslaveholding whites.[23] The sharpening tensions of the national antislavery struggle set the context for these conflicts. The point is not to imagine conscious white-black alliance where it did not exist, but to recognize that the slaveholder regime was becoming increasingly unstable and the planters consequently became more inclined to adopt strategies of desperation.

Aptheker notes that the abolitionist movement succeeded only with the maturing of the rising class of industrial capitalists. But in his work social change is not automatic. The success of destroying slavery, he writes, was produced "by men and women, Negro and white, who had for decades been sowing the seed, talking, writing, petitioning, voting, and who finally piloted an aroused America through the maelstrom of a four-year Civil War."[24] A consistent theme in his view of slave resistance is an emphasis upon its impact on the political arena, the understanding that class conflict ultimately is expressed in political struggle. If, as he writes, rebelliousness and discontent were characteristics of American black slaves, then it was inconceivable that in a society in which the existence of slavery was a central issue, such rebelliousness did not contribute to shaping the American political scene.

Permeating Aptheker's work on slavery is the perception that class analysis cannot be isolated from the antagonism of exploiter and exploited classes and the expression of such antagonism in struggle. Others have contributed much to what we know of slave culture and of plantation routine, but Aptheker has been preeminent among scholars in establishing a central feature of slavery that all serious students must take into account.

The process of developing a class analysis of slave resistance continues and will be part of the discussion seeking a fuller understanding of the Afro-American heritage. I would want here to comment on three aspects of that process. The first is that slave resistance had not adequately been seen as part of American labor history. The struggles mounted by slaves are included in the inheritance passed on to the American working class of the modern era. Black people had to fight against incredible obstacles to attain the status of wage workers, a struggle that stretched long beyond the legal abolition of slavery, but in waging that fight they secured experience of organization and established a militant fighting spirit that has added much to the American labor movement. Those who would deny the existence of a meaningful pattern of slave resistance would ignore what has been a source of inspiration and strength to all who assert the claims of democracy against privileged authority. They would have us believe that the planters created a wonder of wonders, a system in which a class of laboring people could be exploited and yet not resist. In short they would take a record of unusual heroism and turn it into its opposite.

Second, we need to look more carefully at the class implications found in the historical work that denies rebelliousness and resistance. Elkins's Sambo view is not unrelated to the circumstance that it appeared as the civil rights movement was gathering new strength, challenging the ideology of gradualism. It appeared as the issue of black leadership in setting an agenda for social change was coming to the fore. Whatever motivated the historian, the conclusions drawn in the work served those interests in American society that feared black initiative and assertiveness and believed all radical change to be dangerous. The Fogel-Engerman work, *Time on the Cross* (1974), also did more than express a philosophy of liberal integrationism. The authors saw slavery as a fundamental constituent of American capitalism and in the last analysis what emerged was a capitalism that treated its most unfree workers relatively well for its time. The book is less an examination of plantation slavery than it is a tribute to the American social system.

A third theme calling for attention is that of the relation of slave resistance to the situation of free blacks. The oppression of slaves was linked to the general conditions of racial oppression confronting all blacks. How did slave resistance affect the lives of free blacks? To what extent did the possibility of attaining free status, however remote, impinge upon the forms of resistance manifested by slaves? These questions deserve further investigation and analysis.

This book provides confirming evidence that the issue of resistance continues to be of major significance in the study of Afro-American slavery. Scholars interested in formulating a class analysis of this theme have made important contributions and in the future such scholars will surely continue to use class as an insightful approach to the complex issues of race, caste, class, and gender presented by Afro-American history.

Notes

1 Donald Robinson, *Slavery in the Structure of American Politics*, New York, 1979, 451–452.
2 Herbert Aptheker, *American Negro Slave Revolts*, New York, 1974, 374.

3 Angelina Grimké, quoted in Bettina Aptheker, *Woman's Legacy: Essays on Race, Sex, and Class in American History*, Amherst, 1982, 23.

4 Eugene D. Genovese, *In Red and Black: Marxian Explorations in Southern and Afro-American History*, New York, 1971, 20.

5 Eugene D. Genovese, *From Rebellion to Revolution: Afro-American Slave Revolts in the Making of the Modern World*, Baton Rouge, 1979, preface.

6 Kenneth Stampp, *The Peculiar Institution*, New York, 1956, 132.

7 Herbert Aptheker, *Essays in the History of the American Negro*, New York, 1945, 118.

8 *From Rebellion to Revolution*, 83.

9 Richard C. Wade, "The Vesey Plot: A Reconsideration," *Journal of Southern History*, 30:2 (May 1964), 143–161.

10 Herbert G. Gutman, *The Black Family in Slavery and Freedom, 1750–1925*, New York, 1976.

11 *From Rebellion to Revolution*, 112–113.

12 Elizabeth Fox-Genovese and Eugene D. Genovese, *Fruits of Merchant Capital*, New York, 1983, vii, 60, 125.

13 *From Rebellion to Revolution*, 50.

14 Fox-Genovese and Genovese, *Fruits of Merchant Capital*, 167.

15 Ibid., 123.

16 Herbert Aptheker, *A Documentary History of the Negro People in the United States from Colonial Times to the Founding of the NAACP in 1910*, New York, 1951, preface by W. E. B. Du Bois.

17 Herbert Aptheker, *The Negro in the Civil War*, New York, 1938, 4.

18 Leslie Howard Owens, *This Species of Property: Slave Life and Culture in the Old South*, New York, 1976, 262.

19 J. G. de Roulhac Hamilton, in his review of *Negro Slave Revolts*, wrote that the book was "the result of tireless industry and tremendous research" but also declared that Aptheker "does not know the South of the period of slavery, nor yet does he know slavery as it was." *American Historical Review*, 49:3 (April 1944), 504–506. Also see Kenneth W. Porter's response to Hamilton's review, *American Historical Review*, 50:1 (October 1944), 210–212. More recently Orlando Patterson, while noting that "the total rejection of Aptheker has gone too far," also states that *Negro Slave Revolts* "was largely wrong in its conclusions and biased in its interpretations." Patterson does not specify what was wrong with Aptheker's conclusions and in what respect the interpretations biased. Patterson acknowledges that Aptheker's work "did break new ground" but contends that Aptheker "sees revolution and rebellion where they can be hardly said to exist and . . . draws conclusions about the revolutionary potential of the American slave that in no way relate to the facts of the case." Patterson appears to base his criticisms, not upon the actual thesis and evidence contained in *Negro Slave Revolts*, but rather upon a caricature of the book. See Orlando Patterson, "Slavery," *Annual Review of Sociology*, 3 (1977), 425–426.

20 *Essays*, 4.

21 Aptheker, *Negro Slave Revolts*, 131–133.

22 Frederick Douglass, *My Bondage and My Freedom*, New York, 1855, 263.

23 Herbert Aptheker (Herbert Biel), "Class Conflicts in the South: 1850–1860," *Communist*, 18 (February-March 1939), 170–181, 274–279.

24 Aptheker, *Essays*, 136.

10

Strategies and Forms of Resistance: Focus on Slave Women in the United States

ELIZABETH FOX-GENOVESE

Harriet Tubman, Sojourner Truth, Linda Brent, Ellen Craft: History has preserved the names of women who resisted slavery in a variety of ways. Jane, "a mulatto woman, slave," who was indicted for the murder of her infant child, also may be taken to have resisted, albeit presumably at a high cost to herself. And her name is on record for those who are willing to seek it in the appropriate court records. Those records, like the diaries of such white women as Mary Boykin Chesnut, the narratives of slave men, and the various ex-slave narratives, also provide those who seek a poignant record of the varieties of female slave resistance.[1] Perhaps more telling yet, they bear witness to the resistance of women, whom the record keepers did not even deem worthy of being named at all: "the Rolling-house was maliciously burnt by a Negro woman of the Defts. [defendants] whereof she was Convicted . . . and Executed for it." The court was unwilling to convict the woman's master, deciding that he "is not Chargeable for the wilful wrong of his servant."[2]

Such testimonies to women's opposition to enslavement, or to those who enslaved them, shed an invaluable light on the resistance of Afro-Americans as a people, as well as on slave women themselves. Not least, they help us to fill out the record of multiple forms of resistance—a subject to which I shall return. Perhaps more important yet, they demonstrate that the slaveholders, including, and indeed especially, those most deeply committed to a paternalistic ideology, recognized on some level the intentional resistance of their bondwomen: The nameless female arsonist was "malicious" and "wilful." Perhaps the slaveholders knew in their hearts that she differed only in degree from the house servant, whom they dubbed "impudent" and "uppity." But the records provide, at best, an imperfect guide to the nature, extent, and meaning of slave women's resistance to their enslavement.

The fortieth anniversary of the publication of Herbert Aptheker's pioneering study *American Negro Slave Revolts* provides an especially appropriate context in which to consider the role of slave women in the resistance of Afro-Americans to their enslavement.[3] For Aptheker, long before the emergence of women's history in its contemporary guise, insisted upon recording the presence of women among slave rebels wherever he found it. He may rank among the few historians of his generation to have understood that any people includes both men and women, and to have written history as if it resulted from the combined efforts of men and women. I can find no place in *American Negro Slave Revolts* in which women should have been included and were not.[4] If anything, Aptheker errs in the opposite direction. One suspects that at least occasionally he added "and women" following "men" because his human instinct, knowledge of the world, and commitment to women's social significance told him that women must have participated in forms of resistance, even if the records did not mention them. His willingness to credit women's contribution to the resistance of the enslaved cannot, in short, be questioned. But even his determined quest for evidence of women's participation did not unearth a plethora of forgotten female leaders of revolts; in fact, he found few specific female names. Women figure primarily as members of groups of resisters, or embodiments of specific forms of resistance. Historians of Afro-American women have recently called attention to what we might call gender-specific forms of female resistance that Aptheker did not directly address.[5] But resistance, although an essential dimension of his work, was not his main story.

That main story concerned revolts. And in telling it, Aptheker demonstrated, beyond contention, that Afro-American slaves not merely resisted degradation and dehumanization but revolted against their enslavement. Aptheker's critics have suggested that he may have exaggerated the number and significance of slave revolts, but their very differences with him have implicitly underscored his central point, namely, that some slaves, under the most adverse circumstances, engaged in armed political struggle—armed class struggle, if you prefer. The point at issue between Aptheker and these critics concerns how best to distinguish full-scale revolts from ubiquitous acts of violent resistance. The very existence of this debate confronts historians of slave women with the problem of how to interpret the role of slave women in the collective struggle of their people. For North American slave women appear not to have participated significantly in the direct planning and execution of the most explicitly political revolts of the nineteenth century, notably those of Gabriel Prosser, Denmark Vesey, and Nat Turner.[6] And women probably also did not participate in large numbers, if at all, in the smaller but explicitly millitary insurrections, or attempted insurrections, that punctuated the eighteenth and early nineteenth centuries.[7] Yet however we ultimately draw the line between revolt and non-insurrectionary resistance, the explicitly political and military revolts cannot be understood in isolation from the backdrop of steady resistance that could, at any moment, be both collective and violent, and in which women indisputably did not participate. Recognition of these two aspects of the struggle against slavery helps to establish a viable context for a preliminary assessment of the role of slave women in the resistance of Afro-American people.

It is impossible to discuss the specific roles of women in the general struggle of Afro-American slaves without taking account of male and female roles— gender roles—among the slaves. Gender roles, like gender relations, among the slaves remain a topic of considerable debate, and insufficient study. Scholars are slowly beginning to acknowledge that notions of what it means to be a man and what it means to be a woman, as well as the notion of appropriate relations between the two, are among the most sensitive and deeply rooted aspects of any individual's or any people's sense of identity. But to date, most of the attention to gender relations among Afro-Americans, under slavery and thereafter, has focused on discussions of family life. This ideologically charged literature has taken as its standard middle-class, Euro-American ideas of normal, in contrast to pathological, male and female roles and relations. Even at its best, and at its most appreciative of Afro-American cultural vigor, it has assumed that commitment to nuclear families and to companionate marriages under firm male leadership offers the most convincing evidence of health and stability. The Afro-Americans' struggle to defend these values under adverse conditions is presented as evidence of the slaves' successful resistance to the most brutal and dehumanizing aspects of enslavement.[8] But the discussion has not adequately assessed the perturbing problem of the extent to which these norms derived from African traditions, or the extent to which they reflected white values. Nor has it fully penetrated the yet more perturbing problem of the sources of and the links between behavior and belief: Masters could impose some forms of behavior on their slaves and encourage others, but the slaves retained considerable latitude to endow those forms that they adopted or observed with their own meanings. It remains extremely difficult to ascribe precise measures to the respective parts of African traditions and American conditions in Afro-American practice and belief, all the more since the slaves' experience of American conditions led them to reinterpret African traditions.[9] It remains more difficult yet to determine the extent to which slaves appropriated any of the values of American culture, and, to the extent that they did, the degree to which they modified them to conform to either their experience of enslavement or their transformed African values. If the discussion, at this level, appears abstract, it nonetheless casts a long shadow over the possible history of slave women in resistance and revolt. Let us consider a concrete example: If slave women can be shown to have been decisively more active in resistance and revolt than their white counterparts in time and place, should their activity be attributed to the survival of African patterns of female strength—and, if so, which ones—or to the demoralizing impact of enslavement on male leadership and authority? For the moment, the point is less to solve the problem than to recognize that it is highly charged.

The truth is that we have no comparative study of the role of slave women in resistance, and no consensus about what would constitute an appropriate comparative framework. Comparison of women's roles in the slave revolts throughout the New World would elucidate an additional dimension of those revolts, and of the various slave systems.[10] Comparison of the roles of slave women in revolts with the roles of women in the revolts of other oppressed peoples and popular classes would presumably add an important element to our understanding of the dynamics of popular rebellion in different societies, and assuredly contribute to our understanding of women's participation in different peoples' resistance to oppression. But this work has not yet received sustained attention. Some recent scholarship is beginning to compare the experience of Afro-American women to that of North American white women, but has not yet addressed specific outbreaks of violent class struggle.[11] Nonetheless, recent work on the multiple contributions of women to war, resistance, and revolution among various peoples at various times leaves no doubt that women have everywhere and at all times participated in the struggles of peoples for national liberation and self-determination. Analogous work on class struggles also reveals the ubiquity and importance of women's contributions. In any particular struggle, women can be found in almost any role, from leadership to armed combat to spying to providing a variety of support services. In struggles for national or class liberation, it is not uncommon for at least some women to depart radically from what are taken to be normal female activities among their people. It is uncommon, historically, for women to assume primary leadership of armed combat, or even to engage directly in combat on a regular basis—but women have done both. It is, in short, probably safe to say that there is no form of insurrectionary struggle in which some women have not, at some time, engaged. But that being said, it is also true that historically, as in the contemporary world, women are less likely than men to assume the political and military leadership of the struggles for liberation of their people and class.[12]

Whatever women's roles in the struggles of the oppressed against their oppression have been, they have been singularly difficult to document, especially among nonliterate peoples. Sources on the role of slave women in resistance and revolt have proved especially sparse, and those that exist must be recognized as themselves the product of a continuing historical struggle. Most of the early sources are white. In assessing them, we must take account of the blinders that white assumptions imposed on white perceptions. White commentators may well have missed many female contributions to resistance because they did not expect them. Enslaved and oppressed peoples, as Frantz Fanon so movingly demonstrates in "Algeria Unveiled," are quite prepared to capitalize on the "invisibility" of their women in the interests of a victorious struggle. Many of the other sources on Afro-American slave revolts derive from black men who were actively engaged in a total struggle.[13] For such men, their testimonies concerning events constituted part of that struggle. It is not impossible that they borrowed more than the ideology of revolution and democratic rights from the emerging Euro-American ideology of their period. It is also not impossible that they have drawn especially on those African traditions that emphasized the leadership of men in political and military affairs. Whether drawing upon one or the other of these currents, or combining the two, black men may—consciously or unconsciously, and for a variety of reasons—have made a political choice to prefer the leadership of men in the struggles of the enslaved.

If the nature of the sources shapes our perceptions of slave women's contributions to resistance and revolt, the conditions of enslavement, which were also those of struggle, shaped the historical possibilities for slave men's and women's actual contributions to resistance and revolt. And however much we have learned to recognize the role of slaves in setting limits to their oppression and in shaping their own lives, the master class did establish the conditions. Those conditions varied according to time, place, and size of plantation, but, overall, scholars concur that they never invited the kind of massive rebellions or establishment of maroon societies that occurred elsewhere in the Western Hemisphere.[14] I cannot in this essay begin to do justice to the impact of variations in size and location of plantations on women's roles in resistance and revolt, although it must have been considerable. But however much the conditions imposed by individual masters varied, they also fell within the general structures of prevailing legal and political relations, and of a society that can, in important respects, be viewed as a network of households that included the decisive productive as well as reproductive relations.[15] These general structural conditions changed significantly over time. From the perspective of slave revolts and resistance, the most important changes probably occurred toward the first third of the eighteenth century, as the fluidity and experimentation of early settlement gave way to more rigid structures that reflected the greater stability and will to ordered domination of white society, and following the wave of revolution that characterized the late eighteenth century. Both of these shifts confronted slaves with an increase in the resolution and sophistication of white society, but both—especially the second—also offered slaves new sources of collective identity and purpose as Afro-Americans. The net result can perhaps best be grasped in the tendency of nineteenth-century slave revolts to claim the explicit political purpose of realizing for Afro-Americans the promises of the new democratic ideology of individual freedom. And by the time that the slaves were claiming this message for themselves they indeed constituted a distinct Afro-American people—creoles who had become the only self-reproducing slave population in the New World.

The following preliminary discussion of the role of slave women in resistance rests on a series of working assumptions—all of which must be advanced tentatively. (1) However hard it may be to draw the lines, violent resistance and revolt should be distinguished. Revolt, to paraphrase Clausewitz, is the continuation of violent resistance by other means. (2) The relation between violent resistance and revolt changed over time, with the decisive shift occurring in the late eighteenth and early nineteenth centuries when the slaves appropriated for themselves the ideology of democratic revolution. (3) The African legacy, if difficult to identify precisely, made a central contribution to slave women's self-perceptions, and hence to their patterns of resistance. (4) White culture and institutions constituted the conditions of oppression and hence shaped the patterns of resistance. (5) Although it is not uncommon that a cataclysmic struggle against oppression encourages the temporary disregard of prevailing gender roles, it is more than likely that a protracted struggle of resistance will build upon and shape the continuing life of a people, including its gender roles. In short, the resistance activities of women are likely to reflect their roles as women, as much as their commitment to resistance. Or, to put it differently, though women may fight as soldiers, they will normally resist as women. (6) Any attempt to understand the resistance of slave women as women must acknowledge the dreadful paucity of sources that testify directly to those women's self-perceptions. If we can make a preliminary attempt to identify women's patterns of behavior, we must simultaneously recognize that we have very limited evidence of the meaning that the women themselves attributed to their behavior. (7) Any assessment of slave women's resistance must make a preliminary and cautious attempt to understand the complex relation between the resistance of the individual and collective resistance and to attempt to identify the institutions and movements through which women might have contributed directly, as opposed to indirectly, to collective resistance.

THE FRAGMENTARY SOURCES and partial, if growing, scholarship on the middle passage, the early period, and other New World slave societies strongly

suggest that in the early periods of enslavement women were likely to participate in nearly direct proportion to their numbers—which were fewer than
those of men—in revolt and violent resistance. Certainly on the slave ships,
women, whom white slavers chose to see as more docile than men, enjoyed
greater freedom of movement than men and were, consequently, well positioned to play important roles. Then, as later, their occasional betrayal of revolts
can at least be taken as an indication of their participation in, or proximity to,
the planning of them.[16] The fragmentary evidence from the early period of
settlement further suggests that arrival in the New World did not dissipate the
rebelliousness many women had evinced on the middle passage. In fact, at least
some women appear to have rebelled or resisted in whatever way available,
whenever the opportunity offered itself or could be seized. But precise patterns
remain difficult to establish. High demographic casualties among both black
and white populations, as well as increasing importations of fresh Africans,
themselves from different peoples and states, delayed the establishment of distinct social patterns. There is no reason to doubt that during this early period,
which was characterized by a constant influx of Africans and the complex class
and race relations of a slave society in the making, women rejected their enslavement as wholeheartedly as men. Nor is there any special reason to believe,
given the patterns of African slave trading, that women necessarily made the
crossing or began life in the Americas in the company of the men of their families and communities. It is more than likely that the violent removal first from
their native societies and then from Africa not merely separated women from
the men of their kinship but also at least temporarily disrupted accepted patterns of relations between men and women. Many women must have confronted their enslavement as uprooted individuals. And the white society into
which they were introduced may not yet have developed, or been able to implement, a fixed notion of the gender relations and roles appropriate to their new
servants. With a firm eye on rapid profits, many planters proved entirely willing to exploit female slaves to the limits of their physical endurance—if not
beyond—with little regard to the niceties of male and female tasks. The forms
of female resistance in this early period may safely be taken to have been as
varied and as violent as the complexity of the class, race, and gender relations of
an emerging, frontier slave society.[17]

The increasingly cohesive slave society that emerged during the eighteenth
century, especially in Virginia and South Carolina, generated considerably
more information on the resistance and rebellion of slaves, just as the slaveholders manoeuvred more systematically to set about mastering and to prevent
revolts by their slaves. With slaves distributed, however unevenly, throughout
the colonies, slave revolts occurred throughout them as well. The records of
these revolts testify to women's participation in them, and frequently to their

leadership as well. There was, for example, the revolt in Louisiana in the early 1770s, after which Mariana received one hundred lashes and lost her ears for her part. Although with respect to white perceptions, it is worth noting that she received a substantially lighter punishment than did the men, Temba and Pedro, despite her apparent status as leader.[18] But women could be punished as severely as men for their roles in conspiracies, or for suspicion of having committed arson. Frequently they were burned alive.[19]

The eighteenth century witnessed the emergence of forms of violent resistance, notably arson and poison, that would characterize the entire antebellum period. Women regularly played their part, or were accused of so doing, in these activities. Peter Wood has argued that in the wake of the Stono Rebellion in South Carolina the white ruling class systematically curtailed the de facto liberties that the slaves had theretofore enjoyed. The comprehensive Negro Act of 1740 deprived slaves of those personal opportunities to which they had never been entitled, but had nonetheless seized under the frontier conditions of the early years of the colony: "freedom of movement, freedom of assembly, freedom to raise food, to earn money, to learn to read English."[20] This legislation, and above all the determination of the masters that it represented, established the ownership and discipline of slaves as a matter of class, not merely individual, responsibility. It may also have sharpened the distinction between male and female forms of resistance and revolt if only by systematizing the constraints of enslavement and thus making some forms of women's activities more visible. Or, to put it differently, it may have begun to subject female slaves to the same structural constraints that relegated white women to households and male supervision.

The case of runaways suggests that slave society hedged in women even more stringently than men. At least the scholars who have analyzed the advertisements for runaways during the eighteenth century have found far fewer women than men: Wood estimated one woman to three men during the middle decades of the century; Gerald Mullin found that 11 percent of the advertisements for runaways that specified gender were for women in Virginia between 1736 and 1801.[21] It would be rash to conclude, on the basis of this evidence, that women were intrinsically more reconciled to slavery than men. More likely, for reasons discussed below, they had more trouble in passing unobserved outside the plantation. But it is also possible that the fewer ads for female runaways also reflected masters' assumptions that a temporarily missing female had not really run away, but might only have gone to visit kin in the neighborhood. An advertisement from the *Carolina Centinel* of Newberry, North Carolina, in 1818, requested help in securing the return of a female runaway who had already been known to be absent for a considerable period of time during which she had been "harboured" by slaves on various plantations in the neighborhood.[22] Another advertisement from the *Virginia Gazette* of Williamsburg, in 1767, sought assistance in securing the return of a female slave who clearly had been anything but docile: "Hannah, about 35 years of age, had on when she went away a green plains petticoat, and sundry other clothes, but what sort I do not know, as she stole many from the other Negroes." Hannah was further described as having remarkable "long hair, or wool," and being "much scarified under the throat from one ear to the other," and having "many scars on her back, occasioned by whipping." The master clearly regarded Hannah as a serious runaway. "She pretends much to the religion the Negroes of late have practised, and may probably endeavor to pass for a free woman, as I understand she intended when she went away, by the Negroes in the neighbourhood." He believed that under the pretense of being a "free woman" she was heading for Carolina.[23] The two ads reflect the combination of actual conditions and masters' perceptions: A slave woman might "visit" neighboring plantations, where she would disappear among the other slaves without causing comment or provoking a search, at least initially. If she undertook serious flight, she would probably have to attempt to pass for a "free woman" in order to have a plausible reason to be abroad. To be sure, some women did run away to join groups of maroons, but probably in far fewer numbers than men, and probably with diminishing frequency as the possibilities for establishing maroon societies were eroded. Women also, like men, ran away to the British during the Revolution.[24]

The evidence from the eighteenth century remains difficult to interpret. There has been little work on slave women during the eighteenth century, and none on their roles in resistance and revolt specifically. Given the continued influx of new Africans, we can be sure that African influences played a more direct role than they would after the closing of the trade. But we lack adequate studies of the nature of those influences on gender roles and relations. Recently Afro-American and Pan-African feminists have begun to call attention to the importance of women's roles and the degree of women's authority and autonomy in African societies. They have correctly reminded us of the prevalence of matrilineality and matrifocality among West African peoples, and of the presence of queens and female leaders among them. The example of Nanny the Maroon in Jamaica has also been advanced as evidence of women's leadership in New World revolts.[25] As I have tried to suggest, the evidence from the middle passage, the early period, and the eighteenth century testifies to women's active participation in resistance and revolt. But other evidence suggests that from very early, and certainly by the time of Stono, some forms of revolt were considered primarily male affairs. No record survives, for example, of a female leader during the Stono Rebellion itself. Furthermore, scattered evidence indicates that at least some organized insurrections assumed a distinct military and masculine cast. The Stono Rebellion began with twenty black men who marched southwest toward St. Augustine with "colors flying and two drums beating." Vincent Harding emphasizes the importance that those rebellious slave men attached to their having become soldiers: "Sounding the forbidden drums, they were warriors again." [26] African history offers reason to believe that African women might fight as soldiers, but it also suggests that Africans normally viewed warfare as primarily an affair of men. It is, in short, probable that even during the early period African arrivals and Afro-Americans themselves assumed that armed insurrection constituted an essentially male activity. [27] The conditions imposed by white society, not to mention the whites' own visible commitment to male soldiers, can only have reinforced the Afro-American's indigenous tendencies to ascribe warfare to men.

AS THE EIGHTEENTH century gave way to the nineteenth, a series of interrelated events set the distinctive contours of antebellum slave society in the Southern states. In their various ways, the American Revolution, the French Revolution, the revolution in St. Domingue, the invention of the cotton gin, the closing of the African slave trade, and more set Southern society on the course that would lead through the development of a mature slave society to the conflagration of war with a rapidly developing industrial capitalist society. These developments established not merely the social relations within which slave resistance became endemic but also the terrain on which the great slave revolts of the period 1800–1831 would be launched, and they drew the lines within which slavery and its abolition would become national issues. Not incidentally, the same period also witnessed the consolidation of the bourgeois ideology of gender roles in general, and the distinctive Southern ideology of the lady—to be distinguished from the Northern ideology of true womanhood—in particular. Although there is scant reason to believe that Afro-American slaves grasped that ideology to their breasts, there is some reason to believe that its development had indirect consequences for the role of slave women in resistance. Assuredly, the implementation of the Southern ideal of the lady included a tendency to confine women to households and to discourage their freedom from a male "protection" that imposed special burdens and limitations on slave women.

The consolidation of North American slave society, for well-examined reasons, hedged in Afro-American slaves. The role of maroons and other groups of outlyers (runaway slaves) declined. Spontaneous violent revolts of large numbers of slaves probably also declined—although Aptheker might disagree. But the political character and self-consciousness of those revolts that did materialize were heightened. Revolt seems to have become even more a specialized political and insurrectionary male responsibility. And resistance, which became the very essence of the system, fell into some recognizable patterns. As the slaveholding class attempted to impose its own paternalistic ideology upon the enslaved, and to encourage the reproduction and expansion of the slaves, it also seems to have made a minimal effort to apply general notions of gender roles in its treatment of slaves and allocation of tasks. The gender ideology of the master class bore no organic relation to the values of the slaves themselves, although they too had their own ideas of manhood and womanhood. Moreover, with respect to their slaves, the masters clearly observed the ideology of gender difference erratically and according to their own convenience. Nonetheless, the existence of notions of gender difference and gender roles among the masters and the slaves clearly shaped the distinctive patterns of female resistance.

If we are to believe our sources, black women's resistance to slavery was much more likely to be individual than collective. The cumulative effect of individual acts of resistance did contribute decisively, as both Aptheker and Genovese, who follows him on this matter, argue, to the undermining of the system from within and to the confrontationist attitudes of the slaveholders without, but I do believe that the implications of the individual acts of resistance varied and that all must be distinguished from explicitly collective resistance. Furthermore, the characteristic forms of individual female resistance differed somewhat from those of men, perhaps because of Afro-American attitudes toward womanhood, certainly because of opportunities offered and denied by white-dominated slave society. Male and female forms of resistance differed most in those instances in which the physiological differences between the genders were most significant and in those instances in which the attitudes of the slaveholders toward gender roles most directly affected the opportunities available to the enslaved. The most difficult problem consists in identifying Afro-American attitudes toward the respective gender roles of men and women, and identifying the specific African components in those attitudes.

By the time that antebellum slave society assumed its mature form, African gender attitudes are not likely to have appeared in their original form. Like all other aspects of Afro-American culture, African attitudes toward gender had been transformed and reinterpreted in the light of American experience—the discrete experience of the slaves as well as the possible influence of white practices and values. Obviously, male and female physiology constituted the bedrock of gender differences, and physiology did distinguish between some forms of resistance that were specific to slave men and slave women. Women's reproductive capacities offered both special opportunities for resistance and some possible deterrents against particular forms of resistance. If Afro-American attitudes toward gender began with the slaves' own interpretation of physiological differences, they also must have been shaped by the gender distinctions imposed by the conditions of life in a slave society. Whether or not the slaveholding class could influence Afro-American belief, it could assuredly influence Afro-American practice. To the extent that masters distinguished between male and female slaves—and they did in innumerable ways—male and female slaves enjoyed gender-specific opportunities for specific kinds of resistance and revolt. It seems likely that those conditions also encouraged slaves to reinterpret their African values, and perhaps slowly to include some elements of white attitudes toward gender in their own distinct emerging world view.

But let me begin with those forms of resistance that were least differentiated by gender. To the extent that slaveholders pressed women into the same kinds of heavy labor in the fields and in clearing ground as they did men, women seem to have resisted in the same ways as did men. The breaking of tools and the challenging—even the murdering—of overseers was not the monopoly of male slaves. Such sources as we have clearly demonstrated—and I shall return to the point—that female slaves took enslavement and wanton oppression personally. In 1857, a slave, David, appealed his conviction for the murder of the overseer whom he had assisted another slave, Fanny, in killing. Prior to the act, Fanny had been heard to say that she was not about to allow that overseer to mess in her affairs—and the affairs in question had nothing to do with sexual exploitation.[28] Men's and women's conspiring together to kill overseers, and indeed masters, was nothing new. In December 1774, the *Georgia Gazette* of Savannah reported the "following melancholy account, viz."

> That on Tuesday morning the 29th ult. six new Negro fellows and four wenches, belonging to Capt. Morris, killed the Overseer in the field, after which they went to the house, murdered his wife, and dangerously wounded a carpenter named Wright, also a boy who died the next day; they then proceeded to the house of Angus McIntosh, whom they likewise dangerously wounded; and being there joined by a sensible fellow, the property of said McIntosh, they went to the house of Roderick M'Leod, wounded him very much, and killed his son, who had fired upon them on their coming up and broke the arm of the fellow who had joined them. Their leader and McIntosh's negro have been taken and burnt, and two of the wenches have returned to the plantation.[29]

The incident provides much to reflect upon. To begin with, why did the white authorities not see fit to punish the "wenches" as severely as the men? There is nothing surprising in recently arrived Africans' banding together at the point of visible oppression—labor—to strike out at their oppressors. There is also nothing surprising in the persistence of such resentment and violence against overseers, as immediate oppressors, throughout the antebellum period. But such concerted actions, which began in the fields, seem to have been less common during the nineteenth century. Furthermore, at least on large plantations, during the nineteenth century masters seem to have frequently organized men and women into different work gangs, even if the women undertook work as heavy as that of the men.[30] At this point, it is difficult to determine the precise reasons for the masters' gender-specific organization of labor gangs. It may only have reflected a desire to cut down on distractions among the slaves during work hours. It may possibly have reflected an attempt to apply the masters' own notions of male and female spheres—however imperfectly—to their slaves. But it assuredly diminished the opportunities for collective male and female resistance at the point of production. When Fanny and David acted together, they did so, as it were, after hours. But even if male and female slaves did not often engage in collective violent resistance in the fields, there is ample evidence that among field hands, especially on large plantations on which life in the quarters remained sharply separated from life in the big house, female slaves frequently resisted their enslavement in much the same ways as did male slaves.

In a crude way, we could say that female slaves resisted as laborers harsh conditions of labor and unusual abuse of the power to supervise labor. Yet even as laborers, female slaves had recourse to forms of resistance normally denied male slaves. The extent to which the slaveholders attributed social significance to the womanhood of their female slaves—the extent to which they attempted to implement gender distinctions—limited the ways in which those slave women might resist, but also offered them special opportunities for resistance. The gender relations and norms of white society made it unlikely that female slaves would be trained for most of the specialized crafts or hired out for jobs that would provide them with an excuse for mobility. Female slaves were unlikely to become carpenters, blacksmiths, masons, or coopers, or to acquire skills in comparable specialized crafts that would lead them to be hired around. And the pool of skilled craftsmen provided not merely the leadership for the most important slave revolts but also the largest number of fugitives. Even those female slaves who did receive specialized training, as cooks or seamstresses, for example, would be expected to remain not merely within plantation households but largely within houses. Since female slaves, like white women, were not expected to be abroad unaccompanied, they enjoyed far fewer opportunities for successful flight, unless they dressed as men.

Yet specialization of skills according to gender offered female slaves other opportunities for resistance. As cooks and house servants, they were in a privileged position for poisoning. And there can be no doubt that the ubiquitous fear of poison decisively contributed to exacerbating the disquiet of the slaveholding class. Plantation letters and diaries abound with references to poisonings, and testify to the uneasiness of the whites. Poison could not always be detected as the cause of death, but was frequently suspected. One slave woman poisoner, "an old sullen house negress," was identified when she complained to a fellow slave, who reported, of having misjudged the necessary amount of arsenic: "I thought my master and mistress would get enough, but it was not sufficient."[31] Another slave woman profited from her specialized position as a nurse to poison an infant and to attempt to do the same to her master. She was burned alive in Charleston, together with the man who supplied the poison.[32] These acts of resistance occurred after the South Carolinians had made a concerted attempt to curtail slaves' knowledge of and access to drugs by an addition to the Negro Act in 1751. The legislation prescribed punishment for any black who should instruct another "in the knowledge of any poisonous root, plant, herb, or other poison whatever, he or she, so offending shall upon conviction thereof suffer death as a felon." It also prohibited physicians, apothecaries, or druggists from admitting slaves to places in which drugs were kept, or allowing them to administer drugs to other slaves.[33] This kind of legislation, and the cautious spirit it reflected, may have decreased whites' mindlessly introducing slaves to the nature and use of medicinal drugs, but probably did not abolish the practice entirely. Slave women did serve as nurses on large plantations, and as midwives. It is also clear that slave women must have transmitted knowledge of poisonous herbs down through the generations. But white precautions, together with the gender conventions that assigned slave women to kitchens and to nursing, may have resulted in poisoning's becoming an increasingly female activity.

The position of slave women within the big house gave them uncommon access to the goods of the slaveholders. It is widely recognized that cooks and other house servants supplemented the diets of their near and dear from the storerooms of the masters. An occasional house servant, such as Clara, could scour the big house for bullets for a son who intended to murder his master. Clara's son succeeded. And she was convicted with him.[34]

The position of slave women within the big house further permitted them special kinds of psychological resistance, the consequences of which are almost impossible to assess. Impudence and uppitiness did constitute forms of resistance that provoked responses disproportionate to the acts. House servants proverbially tried the patience and the nerves of mistresses to whom it fell to oversee their work. Since the mistress lacked the full authority that adhered to the master of the plantation, her relations with her servants could easily lapse into a kind of personal struggle. When servants compounded sauciness and subtle disrespect with a studied cheerful resistance to accomplishing the task at hand, the mistress could rapidly find herself losing control—of herself as well as her servant. "Puttin' on ole massa" must have been, if anything, more trying in its female embodiment. In 1808, a group of South Carolinians acknowledged the undermining potential of mockery in their request to the legislature that slave apparel receive the serious attention it deserved: The citizens of Charleston argued that the dress of persons of color had become so expensive "as to tempt the slaves to dishonesty; to give them ideas not consistent with their conditions; to render them insolent to the whites, and so fond of parade and show as to cause it extremely difficult to keep them at home." They should only be allowed to wear coarse materials. Liveries were another matter, for they, no matter how elaborate, constituted a badge of servitude. But it was necessary "to prevent the slaves from wearing silks, satins, crapes, lace muslins, and such costly stuffs, as are looked upon and considered the luxury of dress." For an orderly slave society required that "every distinction should be created between the whites and the negroes, calculated to make the latter feel the superiority of the former."[35] But slave women who worked in the big house were uniquely positioned to resist that message, to undermine the distinctions, and to make the lives of privileged mistresses an unending war of nerves.

Slave women could also take advantage of their special role as reproducers to resist various forms of labor through shamming. Although male slaves too could fake illness, female slaves could and did claim pregnancy when they were not pregnant, and claim unusual discomfort or weakness when they were pregnant. The tactic did not always work, but frequently it did, and if it undoubtedly reflected a simple desire to be relieved of labor—not to work—it also reflected a marvelous challenge to the master: You want me to reproduce as a woman, treat me as a woman. John Campbell's recent study of the treatment of pregnant slaves on George J. Kollock's Georgia plantations demonstrates that, at least in this case, the records suggest that the master did give the benefit of the doubt to pregnant slave women, especially in their third trimester, and that this latitude helps to account for the successful self-reproduction of Afro-American slaves in the antebellum South.[36] So this particular form of female resistance did more than alleviate the workload of the individual slave woman: It contributed to strengthening her people.

The relation between slave women's roles as mothers and their resistance to enslavement has generated considerable interest, albeit with contradictory conclusions. If none doubt that slave women frequently took advantage of real or claimed pregnancy to avoid labor, some have argued that they also practiced abortion and infanticide as systematic resistance to the perpetuation of the system. Court records do reveal prosecution of slave women for infanticide. And surely some cases of infanticide and numerous abortions escaped the attention of the masters and authorities. But Michael P. Johnson has recently, and convincingly, questioned whether all cases of infant death that were attributed to infanticide should have been. His discussion of the Sudden Infant Death Syndrome (SIDS) suggests that the death of slave infants by apparent smothering should be linked to their mother's labor in the fields rather than to any attempt to deprive the system of slave infants.[37] In any event, it would be difficult to argue that infanticide and abortion dealt a decisive blow to a slave society that boasted a self-reproducing and expanding slave population. And those who argue for resistance against reproduction—if it occurred with any frequency— must take into account the well-documented attachment of slave mothers to their children. It may be that some slave women practiced abortion and infanticide and that other slave women did or did not run away because of attachment to their children. But it is difficult to fit these contradictory patterns into a single explanation for female slave resistance, much less a general explanation of the significance of that resistance. We have no way of knowing whether slave women practiced abortion—and perhaps infanticide—selectively: Could they, for example, have been more likely to terminate pregnancies, if not lives, that resulted from the sexual exploitation of white men? That, indeed, would have been resistance—perhaps the primary resistance with which to counter the predatory sexuality of white men. At the present state of research, we can, at best, say only that the sexual vulnerability and reproductive capacities of slave women influenced the ways in which they resisted. We can say little about the social significance that they attached to that womanhood.[38]

THE LIST OF slave women's acts of resistance to their enslavement in particular and to the slave system in general could be extended indefinitely. Some scholars, notably Deborah Grey White and Darlene Clark Hine and Kate Wittenstein, are beginning to address that history.[39] As women, female slaves engaged in various forms of resistance associated with their sexuality and reproductive capacities. As female slaves, they especially engaged in poisoning and theft, and were much less likely than male slaves to be fugitives or even truants. Although when they did become truants, they could melt into the slave community of another plantation, which may hint at special links among women that bound slave kin and fictive kin networks. As slaves, they engaged in murder, arson, and grand larceny. However deeply their acts of individual resistance undermined the slave system, their direct contribution to political revolt appears to have been considerably less than that of men. In short, the current state of scholarship—that is, the current reading of available evidence—suggests that female slaves, for reasons closely associated with their gender, were more likely to engage in individual than collective resistance in the period following the consolidation of North American slave society and the beginnings of an Afro-American revolutionary tradition.

But this bald assessment will not do, even for a preliminary reading. The very use of the categories of "individual" and "collective" forces us to ask other questions—with full recognition that the answers will depend upon a fresh look at the sources. For a broad gap separates the random acts of individual resistance from the political and military resistance of revolt. And if we accept Aptheker's general assessment of the systematic and cumulative resistance of Afro-American people to their enslavement, we must force ourselves to identify and understand the networks and institutions through which that people forged itself as a people and supported the efforts of its most self-conscious rebels against slavery as a social system.

As Vincent Harding has especially insisted, the various records of revolts invariably make some mention of churches or funerals or religious gatherings as a backdrop for revolt itself. As we all know, there is wide acknowledgment of secret black churches and religious meetings and networks. The significance of religion in the forging of Afro-American culture can hardly be disputed.[40] But my point here is somewhat different. In my judgment, the churches and secret religious networks undoubtedly provided the institutional links between acts of individual resistance and revolts in the name of collectivity. And women were integral members of those churches and religious associations. If our sources seem not to have revealed the roles of women in continuing, collective resistance, it may be that we have not read them with the most interesting questions in mind. It seems obvious enough that those who were caught and tried for their leadership in the great revolts would not mention the networks and institutions on which their plans depended. Why sacrifice brothers and sisters needlessly? Even more, why jeopardize the future revolts of the enslaved by betraying their collective underground organizations? Long-term resistance had to have some collective focus, and its institutions and networks had to remain invisible to the oppressor. But recognizing the likelihood that such institutions and networks bound the daily lives of individuals to the most spectacular attacks against the system that oppressed them, we must also recognize the certainty of women's integral participation in them.

This recognition itself commands a further effort of research and imagination. Albert Raboteau explicitly and other scholars of Afro-American religion implicitly have minimized the importance of women's roles in the leadership of slave religion. Female religious leaders surfaced occasionally, especially in New Orleans and in conjunction with the persistence of voodoo. But slave women appear not to have become preachers and leaders of Afro-American Christian-ity—certainly not in large numbers. It is nonetheless difficult to believe that informal—and perhaps formal—associations of women, or sisterhoods, did not take shape in association with slave religious communities. Especially after the prohibition of separate black churches, such associations would likely have been as secret as the congregations to which they were linked. But Betty M. Kuyk's recent work on black fraternal orders in the United States opens new possibili-ties. For she finds that the black men's associations that took shape so rapidly during Reconstruction had roots in slavery, and beyond slavery in African cul-ture.[41] If men's organizations, why not women's? Such gender groupings are rea-sonably common in societies in which gender constitutes one of the principal forms of social organization, as it did among many West African peoples. But for all the reasons advanced throughout this essay to explain the greater con-straints on slave women than slave men, notably, the conditions of gender divi-sions within the dominant white society, should such women's organizations have existed in whatever form, they would surely have been even less visible than those of men. Deborah Grey White has been insisting on the importance of the female community of slaves in work and as the locus of female traditions of rites of passage, motherhood, and female identity.[42] It appears at least plausible that the community of female slaves generated some kind of religious sister-hood, however fragile and informal. At the least, it remains indisputable that slave women saw themselves as sisters in religion, as essential members of the religious community of slaves. To the extent that the religious community pro-vided the context or underpinnings for the revolts, the women of that commu-nity constituted its backbone—not least because not being active members of the revolt they did not risk being cut down with their brothers, but would per-sist and keep the tradition alive.

The preoccupations of historians have, perhaps, mirrored the biases of ante-bellum white Southerners and of subsequent bourgeois ideology in missing the contributions of slave women to collective violent resistance and even insurrec-tionary revolts. By the same token, they may also have failed to take adequate account of the full individual opposition of slave women to their enslavement. There is a danger to which we all, including women's historians, are vulnerable in insisting upon the specific experience of women as women: We can miss the recalcitrant and determined struggle of the individual soul or consciousness against reduction to the status of thing. It has become a commonplace that slave women suffered under a double burden of enslavement as workers and as women. I should be the last to dispute that harsh truth and, indeed, shall argue shortly that its implications for the growing commitment to antislavery were decisive. But first, let me point out that however deeply slave women themselves felt their exploitation and vulnerability as women, they also seem to have insisted, in the end, on their oppression as slaves. Despite the extensive commentary that has arisen from Judge Thomas Ruffin's celebrated decision in *State vs. Mann*, there has been almost no comment on the gender of the slave who provoked the action that led to the case. Lydia "had committed some small offence, for which the Defendant undertook to chastise her—that while in the act of so doing, the slave ran off, whereupon the Defendant called upon her to stop, which being refused, he shot at and wounded her." The Supreme Court of North Carolina acquitted the white man. In Ruffin's words: "The Power of the master must be absolute to render the submission of the slave perfect."[43] Power and submission: The conflict here is one of wills. Happily, we possess direct confirmation of a slave woman's perception of that conflict as one between the will of her master and her own.

Harriet Jacobs, who published her narrative under the name of Linda Brent, structured her entire account of her escape from slavery as a remorseless and unmediated struggle against the imposition of her master's will. Although the narrative includes much on her sexuality and her children, and her master's sexual designs upon her—so much as to have earned it a description as a modern *Pamela*—in the end everything falls by the wayside except her own refusal to accept the imposition of his will. Her womanhood accounts for many of the specific forms of her oppression, but not for her rejection of oppression. And that refusal of his will was the refusal of his power, the refusal to submit perfectly, or indeed at all. Psychologically, her struggle with her master is one with the most celebrated revolts. The object is not to ease oppression, to lighten a burden, even to protect loved ones: The object is to reject slavery.[44]

The Brent narrative is all the more remarkable for being cast in the language of Northern, sentimental domestic fiction. Brent, ably seconded by the editorial efforts of Lydia Maria Child, apparently intended to ensure the recognition of her tale by Northern, middle-class women, who were steeped in their own culture's pieties of vulnerable womanhood. But her tactical adoption of the literary conventions does not obscure the inner logic of her account, which remains not the violation of womanhood but the conflict of wills. Withal, the rhetoric of the Brent narrative has its own significance and adds a final dimension to the resistance of slave women. Northern abolitionists insisted on assessing slavery from the perspective of their own concerns. And the growing success of their opposition to the slave system depended in no small measure on their casting it as the antithesis of their own bourgeois values—presented as absolute moral standards. To their credit, they did flatly oppose enslavement. But as abolition swelled to join a more general antislavery movement, the emphasis fell increasingly upon the inherent opposition between slavery and the work ethic, slavery

Elizabeth Fox-Genovese

and initiative, slavery and democracy. In this context, the growing perception of the exploitation of slave women as a violation of the norms of true womanhood gained in importance. However deeply Northern women may have misperceived and misinterpreted the experience of slave women by imposing on them white, middle-class norms, their very misrepresentations added indispensable fuel to Northern opposition to slavery and thus, albeit ironically, added a discrete female component to that national resistance which would result in the abolition of slavery.

Notes

1 C. Vann Woodward, *Mary Chesnut's Civil War*, New Haven, 1980; Arna Bontemps (ed.), *Great Slave Narratives*, Boston, 1969; George P. Rawick (ed.), *The American Slave*, vols. 2–19, Westport, CT, 1972; and Solomon Northup, *Twelve Years a Slave*, ed. by Philip S. Foner, New York, 1970, among many.

2 Helen T. Catterall (ed.), *Judicial Cases concerning American Slavery and the Negro*, Washington, DC, 1936, I:1, 84.

3 Herbert Aptheker, *American Negro Slave Revolts*, New York, 1943.

4 Aptheker, *Negro Slave Revolts*, e.g., 84, 89, 92, 127, 138, 148, 181, 201, 259. Aptheker does not pay special attention to women's gender-specific forms of resistance, but systematically includes them as challenges to the system.

5 Darlene Clark Hine and Kate Wittenstein, "Female Slave Resistance: The Economics of Sex," in Filomina Chioma Steady (ed.), *The Black Woman Cross-Culturally*, Cambridge, 1981, 289–300; and Gerda Lerner, "The Struggle for Survival—Day to Day Resistance," in Lerner (ed.), *Black Women in White America: A Documentary History*, New York, 1973, 27–45. Other scholars have discussed the gender-specific form of slave women's oppression, but not paid much attention to related forms of resistance; for example, Angela Y. Davis, "Reflections on the Black Woman's Role in the Community of Slaves," *Black Scholar*, 3 (December 1971), 3–15; and *Women, Race, and Class*, New York, 1981; Bell Hooks, *Ain't I a Woman: Black Women and Feminism*, Boston, 1981; and Jacqueline Jones, "'My Mother Was Much of a Woman': Black Women, Work, and the Family under Slavery," *Feminist Studies*, 8:2 (Summer 1982), 235–270. For women's roles in day-to-day resistance, see Raymond A. Bauer and Alice H. Bauer, "Day to Day Resistance to Slavery," *Journal of Negro History*, 27 (October 1942), 388–419.

6 Aptheker, *Negro Slave Revolts*; and Vincent Harding, *There Is a River: The Black Struggle for Freedom in America*, New York, 1981. These general studies, like specific studies of individual revolts, simply do not mention female participants, although both Aptheker and Harding are exemplary in mentioning women in those cases in which the records even hint at their presence. See also, among many, Richard C. Wade, "The Vesey Plot: A Reconsideration," *Journal of Southern History*, 30:2 (May 1964), 143–161; Robert S. Starobin, "Denmark Vesey's Slave Conspiracy of 1822: A Study in Rebellion and Repression," in John Bracey et al. (eds.), *American Slavery: The Question of Resistance*, Belmont, CA, 1971, 142–158; William Freehling, *Prelude to Civil War: The Nullification Controversy in South Carolina, 1816–1836*, New York, 1966, 53–60; *An Account of the Late Intended Insurrection among a Portion of the Blacks of This City*, Charleston, 1822, repr. 1970; Joseph Cephas Carroll, *Slave Insurrections in the United States 1800–1865*, New York, 1938, repr. 1968; John Lofton, *Insurrection in*

South Carolina: The Turbulent World of Denmark Vesey, Yellow Springs, OH, 1964; John B. Duff and Peter M. Mitchell (eds.), *The Nat Turner Rebellion: The Historical Event and the Modern Controversy*, New York, 1971; Stephen B. Oates, *The Fires of Jubilee: Nat Turner's Fierce Rebellion*, New York, 1975; and Thomas Wentworth Higginson, *Black Rebellion*, ed. by James M. McPherson, New York, 1969. For contemporaneous testimony, see John Oliver Killens (ed.), *The Trial Record of Denmark Vesey*, Boston, 1970; and Henry Irving Tragle (ed.), *The Southampton Slave Revolt of 1831*, New York, 1973.

7 Aptheker, *Negro Slave Revolts*, and Harding, *There Is a River*, like Peter Wood, *Black Majority: Negroes in Colonial South Carolina from 1670 through the Stono Rebellion*, New York, 1974, do not make a point of women's absence from these military bands, but their evidence clearly indicates that women did not belong to such bands. But women, as Aptheker and Harding show, clearly did participate in other kinds of collective risings. See Daniel Horsmanden, *The New York Conspiracy*, ed. by Thomas J. Davis, Boston, 1971.

8 Among many, see, Eugene D. Genovese, *Roll, Jordan, Roll: The World the Slaves Made*, New York, 1974; Herbert G. Gutman, *The Black Family in Slavery and Freedom, 1750–1925*, New York, 1976; John Blassingame, *The Slave Community: Plantation Life in the Antebellum South*, rev. ed., New York, 1979; Leslie Howard Owens, *This Species of Property: Slave Life and Culture in the Old South*, New York, 1976; George P. Rawick, *The American Slave: A Composite Autobiography*, I, *From Sundown to Sunup: The Making of the Black Community*, Westport, CT, 1972; and Robert W. Fogel and Stanley L. Engerman, *Time on the Cross*, 2 vols., Boston, 1974.

9 For an excellent analysis of this process, see Sydney W. Mintz, *Caribbean Transformations*, Chicago, 1974, esp., "Afro-Caribbeana: An Introduction." See also Lawrence Levine, *Black Culture and Black Consciousness: Afro-American Folk Thought from Slavery to Freedom*, New York, 1977.

10 Steady (ed.), *Black Woman*, provides a comparative perspective on the experience of African and Afro-American women, but not on the role of women in revolts in the different new world societies. Richard Price (ed.), *Maroon Societies: Rebel Slave Communities in the Americas*, Garden City, NY, 1973, provides some information on women in different maroon societies.

11 For example, Deborah Grey White, "Ain't I a Woman? Female Slaves in the Antebellum South," Ph.D. dissertation, University of Illinois at Chicago Circle, 1979; and Suzanne Lebsock, "Free Black Women and the Question of Matriarchy: Petersburg, Virginia, 1784–1820," *Feminist Studies*, 8:2 (Summer 1982), 271–292. Much of the comparison between the experience of black and white women concerns the postbellum period; see, for example, Cynthia Neverdon-Morton, "The Black Woman's Struggle for Equality in the South, 1895–1925," in Sharon Harley and Rosalyn Terborg-Penn (eds.), *The Afro-American Woman: Struggles and Images*, Port Washington, NY, 1978, 43–57; and Terborg-Penn's "Discrimination against Afro-American Women in the Woman's Movement, 1830–1920," in Harley and Terborg-Penn (eds.), *Afro-American Woman*, 17–27.

12 Carol Berkin and Clara Lovett (eds.), *Women, War, and Revolution*, New York, 1980; Stephanie Urdang, *Fighting Two Colonialisms: Women in Guinea-Bissau*, New York, 1979; Juliette Minces, "Women in Algeria," in Lois Beck and Nikki Keddie (eds.), *Women in the Muslim World*, Cambridge, 1978, 159–171; and Mangol Bayat Philipp, "Women and Revolution in Iran, 1905–1911," in Beck and Keddie (eds.), *Women in the Muslim World*, 295–308.

13 Frantz Fanon, "Algeria Unveiled," in *A Dying Colonialism*, New York, 1965.

14 Price (ed.), *Maroon Societies*; Eugene D. Genovese, *From Rebellion to Revolution: Afro-American Slave Revolts in the Making of the Modern World*, Baton Rouge, 1979; Aptheker, *Negro Slave Revolts*; and Aptheker, "Additional Data on American Maroons," *Journal of Negro*

History, 32 (October 1947), 452–460. Cf. Barbara Kopytoff, "Jamaican Maroon Political Organization: The Effects of the Treaties," *Social and Economic Studies*, 25 (June 1976), 87–105; and her "The Early Political Development of Jamaican Maroon Societies," *William and Mary Quarterly*, 35 (April 1978), 287–307; and Orlando Patterson, "Slavery and Slave Revolts: A Socio-Historical Analysis of the First Maroon War, 1655–1740," *Social and Economic Studies*, 19 (September 1970), 289–325, among many.

15 Elizabeth Fox-Genovese, "Antebellum Southern Households; A New Perspective on a Familiar Question," *Review*, 7:2 (Fall 1983), 215–253.

16 Harding, *There Is a River*, 3–23, passim; Daniel P. Mannix and Malcolm Cowley, *Black Cargoes: A History of the Atlantic Slave Trade*, New York, 1962; Basil Davidson, *The African Slave Trade*, Boston, 1961; Lorenzo Greene, "Mutiny on Slave Ships," *Phylon*, 5 (January 1944), 346–354; and Darold D. Wax, "Negro Resistance to the Early American Slave Trade," *Journal of Negro History*, 51 (January 1966), 1–15. Elizabeth Donnan, *Documents Illustrative of the Slave Trade to America*, 4 vols., New York, 1935, repr. 1965, contains many references to women's activities on the middle passage.

17 Wood, *Black Majority*; Gerald W. Mullin, *Flight and Rebellion: Slave Resistance in Eighteenth-Century Virginia*, New York, 1972; Edmund S. Morgan, *American Slavery, American Freedom: The Ordeal of Colonial Virginia*, New York, 1975, esp. 295–337; Philip Alexander Bruce, *Economic History of Virginia in the Seventeenth Century*, New York, 1895, repr. 1935, II, 57–130; James Thomas McGowan, "Creation of a Slave Society: Louisiana Plantations in the Eighteenth Century," Ph.D. dissertation, University of Rochester, 1976; Jack D. L. Holmes, "The Abortive Slave Revolt at Pointe Coupee, Louisiana, 1795," *Louisiana History*, 11 (Fall 1970), 341–362; James H. Dorman, "The Persistent Spectre: Slave Rebellion in Territorial Louisiana," *Louisiana History*, 18 (Fall 1977), 389–404; and Allan Kulikoff, *Tobacco and Slaves: The Making of Southern Cultures* (forthcoming).

18 Harding, *There Is a River*, 39; and Catterall (ed.), *Judicial Cases*, III, 424.

19 For example, Wood, *Black Majority*, 292; Aptheker, *Negro Slave Revolts*, 90–91, 189–190, 242, 281; and Harding, *There Is a River*, 61.

20 Wood, *Black Majority*, 324–325.

21 Ibid., 241; and Mullin, *Flight and Rebellion*, 40.

22 Ulrich B. Phillips (ed.), *Plantation and Frontier Documents, 1649–1863*, Cleveland, 1909, repr. 1965, II, 90.

23 Ibid., 93.

24 Chester W. Gregory, "Black Women in Pre-Federal America," in Mabel E. Deutrich and Virginia C. Purdy (eds.), *Cleo Was a Woman*, Washington, D.C., 1980, 53–72. Benjamin Quarles, *The Negro in the American Revolution*, Chapel Hill, 1961, contains passing references to women (e.g., 27, 120–121), but pays special attention to black men's participation in the war.

25 Lucille Mathurin, *The Rebel Woman in the British West Indies during Slavery*, Kingston, 1975; Alan Tuelon, "Nanny—Maroon Chieftainess," *Caribbean Quarterly*, 19 (December 1973), 20–27; Joseph J. Williams, S.J., *The Maroons of Jamaica*, in Anthropological Series of the Boston College Graduate School, III:4, Chestnut Hill, MA, 1938, 379–480; and Rosalyn Terborg-Penn in this volume.

26 Harding, *There Is a River*, 35.

27 Basil Davidson, *Black Mother: The Years of the African Slave Trade*, Boston, 1961, e.g., 151–152; and his *A History of West Africa to the Nineteenth Century*, with F. K. Buah and the advice of J. F. Ade Ajayi, Garden City, NY, 1966; and Paul Lovejoy, *Transformations in Slavery: A History of Slavery in Africa*, Cambridge, 1983, esp. 66–87, 108–128.

28 Catterall (ed.), *Judicial Cases*, II:1, 206–207.

29 Phillips (ed.), *Plantation and Frontier*, II, 118–119.

30 Edwin Adam Davis (ed.), *Plantation Life in the Florida Parishes of Louisiana, 1836–1846, as Reflected in the Diary of Bennet H. Barrow*, New York, 1943, throughout refers to "women" doing thus and so, frequently spinning; and Phillips (ed.), *Plantation and Frontier*, I, "Extracts from journal of the manager of Belmead Plantation, Powhaton County, Virginia, 1854," e.g., 213–214, "Women cleaning water furrows . . .", "Women open water furrows . . .", and "Men and Women grubbing the Land too hard frozen to plough."

31 Wood, *Black Majority*, 292.

32 Ibid.

33 Ibid., 290. See Thomas Cooper and David J. McCord (eds.), *The Statutes at Large of South Carolina*, 10 vols., Columbia, 1836–1841, VII, 422–423.

34 Catterall (ed.), *Judicial Cases*, 2:1, 241–242.

35 Phillips (ed.), *Plantation and Frontier*, II, 113. The citation is from the "Memorial of the Citizens of Charleston to the Senate and House of Representatives of the State of South Carolina [Charleston 1822]."

36 John Campbell, "Work, Pregnancy, and Infant Mortality among Southern Slaves," *Journal of Interdisciplinary History*, 14:4 (Spring 1984), 793–812.

37 Hine and Wittenstein, "Female Slave Resistance"; and Michael P. Johnson, "Smothered Slave Infants: Were Slave Mothers at Fault?" *Journal of Southern History*, 47 (1981), 510–515.

38 Bauer and Bauer, "Day to Day Resistance," 50–57. Angela Davis and Bell Hooks (see references in note 5, above) emphasize the sexual exploitation of slave women, but do not discuss this in relation to slave women's resistance.

39 Hine and Wittenstein, "Female Slave Resistance"; and Deborah Grey White, "Ain't I a Woman?"; and her "Female Slaves, Sex Roles, and Status in the Antebellum Plantation South," *Journal of Family History*, 8:3 (Fall 1983), 248–261.

40 Harding, *There Is a River*, 55, but throughout; Genovese, *Roll*; and Mechal Sobel, *Trabelin' On: The Slave Journey to an Afro-Baptist Faith*, Westport, CT, 1979.

41 Albert J. Raboteau, *Slave Religion: The "Invisible Institution" in the Antebellum South*, New York, 1978, minimizes the role of women throughout, but see references on 79 and 238. Betty M. Kuyk, "The African Derivation of Black Fraternal Orders in the United States," *Comparative Studies in Society and History*, 25:4 (October 1983), 559–592. See also Bennetta Jules-Rosette, "Women in Indigenous African Cults and Churches," in Steady (ed.), *Black Woman*, 185–207, which focuses on the recent past and the contemporary period.

42 White, "Female Slaves."

43 Catterall (ed.), *Judicial Cases*, II:1, 57.

44 Linda Brent [Harriet Jacobs], *Incidents in the Life of a Slave Girl*, ed. by Lydia Maria Child, new ed. by Walter Teller, New York, 1973, orig. 1861. For the identification of Brent as Harriet Jacobs, and as her own author, see Jean Fagan Yellin, "Written by Herself: *Harriet Jacobs' Slave Narrative*," *American Literature*, 53:3 (November 1981), 479–486. The Brent narrative should be compared with that of Ellen Craft, who was no less determined, but who ran dressed as a man and in the company of her husband. See her "Running a Thousand Miles for Freedom; or, The Escape of William and Ellen Craft from Slavery," in Bontemps (ed.), *Great Slave Narratives*.

11

"The Dream Deferred": Black Freedom
Struggles on the Eve of White Independence

PETER H. WOOD

One night in August of 1967 I sat before a small Sony television watching the "Evening News."* It had been a summer of urban violence, and now the CBS camera hovered over Detroit. It peered down from a helicopter toward rising smoke and distant nonwhite people, just as it regularly hovered over villages in Vietnam. The commentator struggled to explain what was happening, but he clearly had no real idea who these Americans were, where they had come from, or what they wanted. And if the explainer was ignorant, much of his audience was more so. Suddenly, through that televised column of smoke, I glimpsed my calling as a colonial historian more clearly than before. For myself, if not for others, the present and the future would make more sense if I could help illuminate some corner of the black past.

I began by reading everything that had been written on early American slavery—still a plausible ambition in those days. I even purchased the new edition of Herbert Aptheker's *American Negro Slave Revolts* when it appeared in 1969, though I sensed it would be of little value. No one had told me specifically not

* This paper was delivered to the Organization of American Historians' Annual Meeting in Cincinnati on April 8, 1983, at a session entitled "Herbert Aptheker's *American Negro Slave Revolts*: A Forty-Year Retrospective." An earlier draft was presented at a conference of the U.S. Capitol Historical Society entitled "Slavery in the Age of the American Revolution" in Washington, DC, March 25, 1980, and a shorter version appeared in the November-December 1984 issue of *Southern Exposure* under the title "Impatient of Oppression: Black Freedom Struggles on the Eve of White Independence."

to look at the volume, but no one had ever mentioned it positively to me either. Growing up among Cold War liberals I had learned somehow through osmosis that Herbert Aptheker was beyond the pale; I had been led to believe by veiled inferences that his work would be shallow, dated, and dogmatic. So, with the smugness of the world that trained me, I took up this book more to prove that I was thorough and open-minded than to gain substantive insight.

Imagine my surprise. For here was a book that did *for all* the colonies and states what no other writer had yet done *for any one* of them. And here was an author willing to acknowledge the continuities between past and present that other mentors shunned and downplayed. Listen to the first eye-opening sentences.

> Writing on slave unrest in the United States—and doing this in 1969— one feels more like a news reporter than a historian. While recently the California statesman, Ronald Reagan, found the ghetto rebels of today to be "mad dogs," a South Carolina statesman of 1823 found plantation rebels of his day to be "monsters in human shape."
>
> Which humans are dogs and monsters depends, I suggest, upon class and, often, upon color and nationality, too.[1]

I was struck not simply by the book's broad overview and democratic principles—I did not yet realize how rare those commodities would be in my chosen line of work—but by its evidence. For myself, and I suspect for others in my generation, *American Negro Slave Revolts* provided the first clear confirmation that we could locate the kinds of documentary sources on slave activity we were setting out to find. I remember going to a labor hall one Sunday afternoon to hear Herbert Aptheker speak; I wanted to see this man for myself. After the talk I waited behind, but there were too many questioners, and I never met him.

So it is a special pleasure to join with others in honoring this powerful book and this pioneering historian; we thank him on behalf of our colleagues and students, and especially on behalf of all the people from times past whose stories he first salvaged from oblivion. I am a firm believer that in the related struggles for historical truth and social justice, the best way to honor a fellow seeker is to carry on the search, and in that spirit I offer an essay concerning slave resistance on the eve of white independence.

As my starting point I take this observation from the preface to the 1969 edition of *American Negro Slave Revolts*: "The plots came in waves, as though anger accumulated and vented itself and then a period of rest and recuperation was needed before the next upsurge. Certainly, waves were the rule," Aptheker continues, "with clearly defined periods, as: 1710–1722, 1730–1740, 1790–

1802, 1819–1823, 1828–1832, 1850–1860." I believe at least one other notable wave occurred—during the 1770s—and I shall argue that it was cresting in the eventful year before the Declaration of Independence with more force than scholars of black history have acknowledged or than most historians of the American Revolution have imagined.[2]

In brief, the argument is this. Between 1765 and 1776, a wave of hope and discontent welled among American blacks. While the manifestations of this spirit have been best documented in the North among urban slaves and free Negroes, they were even more important in the South, where blacks made up a major proportion of the total population, especially in the vital coastal regions. Though not universal, this wave of struggle was also not isolated, sporadic, and uninformed. It touched every major slave colony, and it was closely related to—even influential upon—the political unrest gripping many white subjects in these years. The wave can be divided, at least for purposes of analysis and discussion, into three separate phases before it crests at the time of white independence, blurs into the chaos of a bitter anticolonial war, and then dissipates in the early 1780s for a brief lull "before the next upsurge."

PHASE ONE: The long groundswell of increased frustration and heightened expectation that builds during the decade between the Stamp Act controversy in 1765 and the emergence of armed violence between whites at Concord Bridge in April 1775.

PHASE TWO: The crucial seven-month period from the early spring to the late fall of 1775, in which the prospect of imminent freedom and impending war prompts coordinated resistance efforts and harsh reprisals.

PHASE THREE: The hectic months after Lord Dunmore's proclamation (November 15, 1775) when several thousand slaves seek to seize their freedom and work to free others, only to be rewarded with death, disappointment, and what Langston Hughes has called "the dream deferred."

From trough to crest, this wave builds, not through a simple two-way tug of war between slaves and masters, but through a three-way battle. We must envision the merchant-planter revolutionaries, the English officer-bureaucrats, and the black worker—liberators at opposing corners of a triangle, or, if you prefer, at the separate points of a standard tricornered hat of the day. Everyone in the colonial society fell somewhere within this triangle of competing beliefs and aspirations, and each person or group, depending upon their background and situation, was drawn with varying degrees of intensity toward one or another corner. Despite most existing historiography of the prerevolutionary era, "choosing sides" was more than a two-sided proposition. The existence of a significant third dimension to traditional arguments and events gives the study of this era an added complexity, logic, and meaning that it has lacked in the past.

IN FEBRUARY 1774 twenty-year-old Phillis Wheatley, the African-born poetess living in Boston, wrote to another non-European, the Indian minister Samson Occom, that "in every human Breast, God had implanted a Principle, which we call love of freedom; it is impatient of Oppression, and pants for Deliverance; and by the leave of our modern Egyptians I will assert, that the same Principle lives in us."[3] Among more than half a million Afro-Americans living in the thirteen colonies, few were in a position to record their feelings so clearly for posterity. But for nearly a decade thousands of persons, particularly in the South, where nine out of ten blacks resided, had been expressing a similar impatience with oppression by the "modern Egyptians" in a variety of overt ways.

Among an increasingly Christian slave population, itinerant preaching developed rapidly during these years until outlawed by whites as a political liability.[4] In music black songs often became political and threatening to authorities, much as reggae can be today. By the mid-1770s we find reports of slaves playing the African gourd-guitar and singing about "the usage they have received from their Masters or Mistresses in a very satirical stile and manner."[5] Stories of secret night meetings involving "deep and solemn consultation upon life or death" and apparent "deliberations" by "private committees" raised anxiety among whites.[6] So did the frequency of slave runaways and their suspected motives. For example, word of Lord Mansfield's decision in the *Somerset* case reached Virginia in 1772, and the next year a planter stated he had lost a slave couple who were heading to England "where they imagine they will be free (a Notion now too prevalent among the Negroes, greatly to the Vexation and Prejudice of their Masters)." By the following summer the news had reached the frontier, where Bacchus absconded from Augusta County and set out "to board a vessel for Great Britain . . . from the knowledge he had of the late determination of Somerset's Case."[7]

Occasionally, especially in the coastal towns where the divisions among whites were most apparent, groups of blacks moved openly to exploit these rifts to their own advantage, often using tactics drawn from the white independence struggle. In the fall of 1765 Christopher Gadsden's Sons of Liberty took to the streets of Charleston to protest the Stamp Act, chanting "Liberty, Liberty" and carrying a British flag with the word spelled across it. During the New Year holiday, according to Henry Laurens, Charleston blacks began "crying out 'Liberty'" on their own, and the whites "all were Soldiers in Arms for more than a Week," while "patrols were riding day and night" throughout the province.[8] In Boston in 1774, where political petitioning had become a high art, blacks incorporated the process into their freedom struggle. In September Abigail Adams wrote to her husband in Philadelphia.

> There has been in town a conspiracy of the negroes. At present it is kept pretty private, and was discovered by one who attempted to dissuade them from it. . . . They . . . got an Irishman to draw up a petition to the Governor, telling him they would fight for him provided he would arm them and engage to liberate them if he conquered.[9]

Since Governor Thomas Gage was also the general in command of an expanding military force, the plan was a logical and plausible one. According to Herbert Aptheker, "It has been said that the governor thought enough of the proposal to call it to the attention of a Colonel Percy of the Fifth Regiment and to detail a Lieutenant Small to look carefully into the matter."[10]

The British, from their corner of the triangle, had been looking into such matters for several years as part of their contingency planning. They knew that the mass of discontented workers made slave colonies highly vulnerable: "The great Disproportion, there is between White men and Negroes in South Carolina," an agent reminded the Lords of Trade in 1770, renders the colony "less formidable to a foreign or an Indian Enemy, in Case of Hostilities."[11] Moreover, they were equally aware that armed and loyal blacks could be a considerable asset. In 1771 the English governor of West Florida prepared an assessment of Spanish strength at New Orleans, noting that their forces included "upwards of four thousand Negroes upon whom they have great dependence being all used to Muskets and the Woods."[12]

In 1772 Virginia's Governor Dunmore summarized these perceptions when he described conditions in the southern tidewater region for Lord Hillsborough. "At present," he said, "the Negroes are double the number of white people in this colony, which by natural increase, and the great addition of new imported ones every year is sufficient to alarm not only this colony but all the Colonies of America." Dunmore, who would give further attention to this subject in the years ahead, observed to the secretary of state that

> in case of a war . . . the people, with great reason, trembled at the facility that an enemy would find in procuring Such a body of men, attached by no tye to their Masters or to the Country, on the Contrary it is natural to Suppose that their Condition must inspire them with an aversion to both, and therefore are ready to join the first that would encourage them to revenge themselves by which means a conquest of this Country\would inevitably be effected in a very Short time.[13]

From the third corner of the triangle, the patriot colonists sought to assess the relative strength and restiveness of the slave population and speculated about Britain's willingness to exploit it. When the young Bostonian Josiah Quincy, Jr., visited Charleston in 1773, he found white South Carolinians at a loss to gauge the size of the black majority. "A few years ago it was allowed that the blacks exceeded the whites as seventeen to one," he wrote. "There are those who now tell you that the slaves are not more than three to one; but they who talk thus are afraid that the slaves should by some means discover their superiority. Many people express great fears of an insurrection, others treat the idea as chimerical." [14]

Tensions were similar in Virginia as the slave impatience with oppression grew. Late in 1774, young James Madison, beginning his political career as a member of the Committee on Public Safety for Orange County, wrote to printer William Bradford in Philadelphia.

> If America & Britain should come to a hostile rupture I am afraid an Insurrection among the slaves may and will be promoted. In one of our Counties lately a few of those unhappy wretches met together and chose a leader who was to conduct them when the English troops should arrive— which they foolishly thought would be very soon and that by revolting to them they should be rewarded with their freedom. Their intentions were soon discovered and the proper precautions taken to prevent the Infection. It is prudent such attempts should be concealed as well as suppressed. [15]

Six weeks later Bradford replied, "Your fear with regard to an insurrection being excited among the slaves seems too well founded." The Philadelphian informed Madison that "a letter from a Gentleman in England was read yesterday in the Coffee-house, which mentioned the design of [the] administration to pass an act (in case of rupture) declaring [']all Slaves & Servants free that would take arms against the Americans.' By this," Bradford concluded, "you see such a scheme is thought on and talked of; but I cannot believe the Spirit of the English would ever allow them publicly to adopt so slavish a way of Conquering." [16]

As the prospects for insurrectionary acts improved and the anxiety of white patriots grew, the frequency and harshness of punishments increased, though one must make allowance for the standards of the time. (There were roughly two hundred capital offenses on the books in England, and brutal sentences were accepted throughout the empire: In London in 1773, a woman accused of murder was burned at the stake before a large crowd.) [17] Nevertheless, whether through mounting insurgency or broader reprisals, the rate of slave executions (always with due remuneration for the master) seems to have risen during these years. "The most significant exceptions to the rule of moderacy," writes Pauline Maier, "lay with those accused of inciting slave insurrections in the South." [18] In October 1773, a North Carolina slave charged with murder was burned at the stake by the sheriff of Granville County.[19] The next fall, two Georgia blacks accused of arson and poisoning were burned alive on the Savannah Common, and in December several more slaves were "taken and burnt" for leading an uprising in nearby St. Andrew's Parish that killed four whites and wounded others.[20]

Significantly, some white colonists, because of religious scruples, ideological consistency, and strategic necessity, reacted to these mounting tensions with thoughts other than harsh reprisal. Weeks after the murders and executions in St. Andrew's Parish, Georgia, for example, a group of local Scottish parishioners met at Darien. On January 12, 1775, they adopted a resolution that slavery was an "unnatural practice . . . founded in injustice and cruelty, and highly dangerous to our liberties, (as well as lives), debasing part of our fellow-creatures below men, and corrupting the virtues and morals of the rest." Slavery's existence, they asserted, "is laying the basis of that liberty we contend for . . . upon a very wrong foundation," and they pledged to work for the manumission of Georgia slaves.[21]

Another immigrant had similar sentiments. On March 8, 1775, Thomas Paine (who had been in Philadelphia only three months—and was still spelling his name without a final e) published his first article in the *Pennsylvania Journal and Weekly Advertiser*, using the pen name "Humanus." The piece, entitled "African Slavery in America," points out that blacks had been "industrious farmers" who "lived quietly" in Africa before "Europeans debauched them with liquors" and brought them to the New World. Paine reminds white Americans that because they have "enslaved multitudes, and shed much innocent blood in doing it," the Lord might balance the scales by allowing England to enslave them. To avoid such retribution and give greater consistency to the patriot cause, "Humanus" urges the abolition of slavery and suggests (in terms that will resurface later in the year) that freed Negroes be given land in the West to support themselves, where they might "form useful settlements on the frontiers. Thus they may become interested in the public welfare, and assist in promoting it; instead of being dangerous as now they are, should any enemy promise them a better condition."[22] The newcomer Paine may actually have been picking up on an idea raised in Philadelphia two years earlier by the Quaker abolitionist Anthony Benezet, who had suggested in a letter to Dr. John Fothergill that freed slaves might be settled with whites in new communities beyond the Alleghenies.[23]

DURING THE SPRING of 1775, even as Paine wrote, the interlocking struggles of tories, patriots, and blacks intensified. In this new phase, as talk of rebellion grew, the issue of who controlled supplies of powder and shot took on central importance, and Loyalists charged white radicals with spreading rumors of slave unrest. "In the beginning of 1775," Thomas Knox Gordon of South Carolina recalled, "the Malecontents being very anxious to have some plausible pretence for arming with great industry propagated a Report that the Negroes were meditating an Insurrection." [24] Patriots, in turn, claimed authorities were prepared to enlist black strength if necessary to quell white dissent. The Committee of Safety in New Bern, North Carolina, announced in a circular letter that "there is much reason to fear, in these Times of General Tumult and Confusion, that the Slaves may be instigated and encouraged by our inveterate Enemies to an Insurrection, which in our present defenseless State might have the most dreadful Consequences." [25]

The evidence bears out both these opposing charges but it also supports a third assertion. Whatever the schemes of patriot and tory leaders during 1775, local slave leaders from their corner of the triangle were attentive and active participants rather than ignorant and passive objects. Black activists sought to capitalize on the white struggle in their plans for freedom fully as much as white factions tried to implicate half a million blacks in their political designs. Consider a report from back country New York that was being publicized and discussed as far away as Virginia by mid-March. In Ulster County one Johannes Schoonmaker caught part of a conversation between two of his slaves, discussing the powder needed and the support available to carry out a plot that included burning houses and executing the slaveowning families as they tried to escape. This organized liberation plan involved blacks from the villages of Kingston, Hurly, Keysereck, and Marbletown, and the twenty persons who were taken into custody had considerable powder and shot in their possession. In addition, rumor had it that these Negroes were to be joined in their freedom struggle by five or six hundred Indians. [26]

Because we have studied both slavery and the Revolution on a colony-by-colony basis, we have failed to appreciate fully the extent of the black freedom struggle in the summer of 1775. In every Southern colony, from Maryland to Georgia, slaves threatened armed revolt. Their local leaders engaged in desperate high-stakes calculations about when to assert themselves and gain liberation with the help of outside forces. In this they were perhaps not unlike the Jews and other resistance fighters who awaited Allied aid during World War II; premature action in each instance was suicidal. Enough weapons were confiscated during the year so that even if one allows for frame-ups, the extent of the wave is still considerable when we look at each colony in turn.

In Virginia in mid-April, Governor Dunmore ordered the barrels of gunpowder in the Williamsburg magazine removed to a ship under cover of night. [27] The local mayor immediately submitted a petition claiming that widespread rumors of a slave revolt made internal security a crucial matter, and news reached the capital of irate citizens coming from the west to reclaim the powder by force. Word spread that Dunmore was fortifying the governor's palace and had issued arms to his servants; a physician testified that the governor swore to him "by the living God that he would declare Freedom to the slaves and reduce the City of *Williamsburg* to Ashes" if disorder continued.[28] Hearing this, several blacks presented themselves at the palace to offer their services but were turned away.[29] On April 29, a special supplement of the *Virginia Gazette* reported that two Negroes had been sentenced to death in nearby Norfolk "for being concerned in a conspiracy to raise an insurrection in that town."[30]

Word of Lord Dunmore's threat quickly reached Gage in Boston. "We hear," he wrote in mid-May, "that a Declaration his Lordship has made, of proclaiming all the Negroes free, who should join him, has Startled the Insurgents."[31] And on June 12, a week before the disastrous engagement at Bunker Hill, which was to cost him his command, Gage wrote to his friend Lord Barrington, the British secretary of war.

> You will have heard of the boldness of the rebels, in surprising Ticon-deroga; and making excurtions to the frontiers of Montreal; but I hope such hostilities, will justify General Carleton in raising all the Canadians and Indians in his power to attack them in his turn. . . . You may be tender of using Indians, but the rebels have shown us the example, and brought all they could down upon us here. Things are come to that crisis, that we must avail ourselves of every resource, even to raise the Negros, in our cause.[32]

Two weeks later Dunmore himself observed, regarding Virginia's planter elite: "My declaration that I would arm and set free such Slaves as should assist me if I was attacked has stirred up fears in them which cannot easily subside."[33] Within a month he was at work on a secret plan with John Connelly of Fort Pitt to add the threat of an Indian attack on the back country to the prospect of slave insurrections.[34]

In Maryland in late April planters pressured Governor Robert Eden into issuing arms and ammunition to guard against rumored insurrections, though the governor feared their acts "were only going to accelerate the evil they dreaded from their servants and slaves."[35] In May John Simmons of Dorchester County refused to attend militia muster, saying "he understood that the gentlemen were intending to make us all fight for their land and negroes, and then said damn them (meaning the gentlemen) if I had a few more white people to join me I could get all the Negroes in the county to back us, and they would do more good in the night than the white people could do in the day."[36] In August a

Maryland minister—a strict believer in the "outside agitator" creed—protested that "the governor of Virginia, the captains of the men of war, and mariners, have been tampering with our Negroes; and have held nightly meetings with them; and all for the glorious purpose of enticing them to cut their masters' throats while they are asleep. Gracious God!" he exclaimed, "that men noble by birth and fortune should descend to such ignoble base servility."[37] By fall the Dorchester County Committee of Inspection reported, "The insolence of the Negroes in this county is come to such a height, that we are under a necessity of disarming them which we affected on Saturday last. We took about eighty guns, some bayonets, swords, etc."[38]

In North Carolina, as Aptheker and other writers have shown, the black freedom struggle during the summer of 1775 was even more intense. "Every man is in arms and the patroles going thro' all the town, and searching every Negro's house, to see they are all at home by nine at night," wrote Janet Schaw, an English visitor to Wilmington. "My hypothesis is," she said, "that the Negroes will revolt."[39] Her view was confirmed when a massive uprising in the Tar River area of northeastern North Carolina was revealed just before it was to begin, on the night of July 8. Scores of blacks were rounded up and brought before the Pitt County Committee of Safety, which "Ordered several to be severely whipt and sentenced several to receive 80 lashes each [and] to have both Ears crap^d which was executed in the presence of the Committee and a great number of spectators." Colonel John Simpson reported that "in disarming the negroes we found considerable ammunition," and he stated:

> We keep taking up, examining and scourging more or less every day; from whichever part of the County they come they all confess nearly the same thing, vizt that they were one and all on the night of the 8th inst to fall on and destroy the family where they lived, then to proceed from House to House (Burning as they went) until they arrived in the Back Country where they were to be received with open arms by a number of Persons there appointed and armed by [the] Government for their Protection, and as a further reward they were to be settled in a free government of their own.[40]

In South Carolina, meanwhile, the impending arrival of a new royal governor fueled mounting speculation among both blacks and whites. A Charleston merchant wrote:

> Our Province at present is in a ticklish Situation, on account of our numerous Domesticks, who have been unhappily deluded by some villanous Persons in the notion of being all set free on the Arrival of . . . new Gov[erno]r Lord W[illia]m Campbell[;] it is their common Talk throughout the Prov-

ince, and has occasioned impertinent behaviour in many of them, inso-
much that our Provincial Congress now sitting hath voted the immediate
raising of Two Thousand Men Horse and food, to keep those mistaken
creatures in awe, as well as to oppose any Troops that may be sent among
us with coercive Orders.[41]

When Campbell arrived he found the story circulating that the "Ministry
had in agitation not only to bring down the Indians on the Inhabitants of this
province, but also to instigate, and encourage an insurrection amongst the
Slaves. It was also reported, and universally believed," Campbell stated, "that to
effect this plan 14,000 Stand of Arms were actually on board the Scorpion, the
Sloop of War I came out in. Words, I am told, cannot express the flame that this
occasion'd amongst all ranks and degrees, the cruelty and savage barbarity of
the scheme was the conversation of all Companies."[42] A free black pilot named
Thomas Jeremiah was jailed on charges of being in contact with the British
navy and seeking to distribute arms. Black witnesses for the prosecution testified Jeremiah had alerted them to the impending war and informed them that it
could well mean freedom for blacks. As I have described elsewhere, Jeremiah
was publicly hanged and burned in Charleston on the afternoon of August 18.[43]

The situation in Georgia was scarcely different, as John Adams learned
through a discussion with several other delegates to the Continental Congress
in Philadelphia. "In the evening . . . two gentlemen from Georgia, came into
my room," Adams recorded in his diary for September 24.

> These gentlemen gave a melancholy account of the State of Georgia and
> South Carolina. They say that if one thousand regular troops should land
> in Georgia, and their commander be provided with arms and clothes
> enough, and proclaim freedom to all the negroes who would join his camp,
> twenty thousand negroes would join it from the two Provinces in a fort-
> night. The negroes have a wonderful art of communicating intelligence
> among themselves; it will run several hundreds of miles in a week or
> fortnight.[44]

Such an acknowledgment of the effective oral network that kept blacks informed is rare indeed among the print-oriented leaders of the independence
movement. But such a grapevine clearly existed, and it would be stretched and
strengthened in the months ahead as the triangular freedom struggle entered a
third and climactic phase.

IN VIRGINIA Governor Dunmore, who had retreated to the safety of a British
ship, was preparing to use the desperate card he had threatened to play, and

perhaps should have played, six months earlier. When his marines raided a printing office in Norfolk in September, they were joined by cheering blacks.[45] During October he continued to conduct raids and to remove slaves via small sloops and cutters, as he had been doing for several months. "Lord Dunmore," charged the Committee of Safety in Williamsburg on October 21, "not contented with . . . inciting an insurrection of our slaves, hath lately, in conjunction with the officers of the navy, proceeded to commence hostilities against his Majesty's peaceable subjects in the town and neighborhood of Norfolk; captivated many, and seized the property of others, particularly slaves, who are detained from the owners."[46] A week later a Norfolk resident wrote to London that "Lord Dunmore sails up and down the river, and where he finds a defenceless place he lands, plunders the plantation and carries off the negroes."[47]

Edmund Pendleton estimated in early November that perhaps fewer than one hundred slaves had taken refuge with Dunmore, but the situation changed drastically on November 14, when the governor's forces won a skirmish at Kemp's Landing. Dunmore capitalized on this small victory in two ways. First, he sent off John Connelly toward Detroit with secret orders approved by Gage to return to Virginia with Indian troops, seize Alexandria, and await forces from the coast.[48] Second, Dunmore used the occasion to publish the less-than-sweeping proclamation he had drawn up the week before, emancipating any servants or slaves of the opposition faction who would serve in his army. It read in part, "I do hereby further declare all indented servants, negroes, or others (appertaining to Rebels) free, that are able and willing to bear arms, they joining his Majesty's Troops, as soon as may be, for the more speedily reducing this Colony to a proper sense of their duty, to his Majesty's crown and dignity."[49] Connelly was soon captured, but the proclamation had its intended effect.[50] "Letters mention that slaves flock to him in abundance," Pendleton wrote to Richard Henry Lee at the end of the month, "but I hope it magnified."[51] "Whoever considers well the meaning of the word Rebel," stated a white resident of Williamsburg, "will discover that the author of the Proclamation is now himself in actual rebellion, having armed our slaves against us and having excited them to an insurrection . . . there is a treason against the State, for which such men as Lord *Dunmore*, and even Kings, have lost their heads."[52]

Since it ultimately failed from both the British and the black vantage points, there is a tendency to minimize the combined initiative of the months following November 15.[53] But at the time, events in Virginia had enormous potential significance for blacks and whites alike. On December 14, a Philadelphia newspaper related that a gentlewoman walking near Christ Church had been "insulted" by a Negro, who remained near the wall on the narrow sidewalk, refusing to step off into the muddy street as expected. When she reprimanded him he replied, according to the report, "Stay, you d--d white bitch, till Lord Dunmore and his black regiment come, and then we will see who is to take the wall."[54] That same day George Washington urged Congress "to Dispossess Lord Dunmore of his hold in Virginia" as soon as possible. In repeated letters the planter-general stressed that "the fate of America a good deal depends on his being obliged to evacuate Norfolk this winter." Washington spelled out his fears to Richard Henry Lee on December 26: "If, my dear Sir, that man is not crushed before spring, he will become the most formidable enemy America has; his strength will increase as a snow ball by rolling; and faster, if some expedient cannot be hit upon to convince the slaves and servants of the impotency of his designs."[55]

Reports from the Chesapeake southward after Dunmore's proclamation are suggestive of the events that followed Lincoln's emancipation order.[56] With the prospect of freedom at hand, flight became the logical form of rebellion, and along the coast hundreds took direct action despite terrible odds. The newspapers told of "boatloads of slaves" seeking out British ships, not always successfully.[57] Seven men and two women from Maryland "who had been endeavouring to get to Norfolk in an open boat" were apprehended near Point Comfort.[58] Three blacks who boarded a Virginia boat that they mistakenly took to be a British vessel were only "undeceived" after they had openly "declared their resolution to spend the last drop of *their blood* in Lord *Dunmore's* service."[59] Though perhaps more than a thousand reached Dunmore's ships safely, an outbreak of smallpox among the refugees the next spring reduced their numbers and discouraged others from following. If it had "not been for this horrid disorder," he wrote, "I should have had two thousand blacks; with whom I should have had no doubt of penetrating into the heart of this Colony."[60]

News that black freedom had been sanctioned in Virginia must have reached South Carolina by early December. On Sullivan's Island at the mouth of Charleston harbor, fugitive slaves hopeful of freedom were gathering near the pesthouse, the small structure beside the water supervised by a black named Robinson and used to quarantine the sick from incoming ships from Africa and the Caribbean. From here, some runaways had already joined the British fleet and begun to participate in raiding parties to liberate their comrades. On December 5, Captain Jacob Milligan of the sloop *Hetty* reached Charleston with a cargo of rum and sugar, but not before he had been seized and searched by Captain Tollemache of the *H.M.S. Scorpion*. The next day Milligan informed the Council of Safety "that there were considerable number of slaves upon Sullivan's Island, and that he learnt huts were building for them in the woods."[61]

The Council of Safety took swift action. The next day it issued the following instructions to Colonel William Moultrie.

Sir—you are hereby ordered to detach two hundred men of the regiments under your command, with proper officers, this ensuing night, to . . . Sullivan's Island, there to seize and apprehend a number of negroes, who are said to have deserted to the enemy, together with every person who may be found on that island. . . .

P.S. The pest house to be burned, and every kind of live stock to be driven off or destroyed.[62]

According to a Charleston merchant, Josiah Smith, Jr., Moultrie moved against the encampment at night with a force of fifty or sixty men and "early in the Morning sett Fire to the Pest house, took some Negroes and Sailors Prisoners, killed 50 of the former that would not be taken, and unfortunately lost near 20 that were unseen by them till taken off the Beach by the Men [of] Warrs Boats."[63] When a local citizen spoke with officers of the *Scorpion* several days later, he reported that "Capt. Tollemach did not deny having some of our negroes on board, but said they came as freemen, and demanding protection; that he could have had near five hundred, who had offered."[64]

Within weeks similar conditions prevailed in Georgia. On March 13, Stephen Bull wrote to Henry Laurens from Savannah to report that two hundred enslaved workers had deserted (nearly fifty from Arthur Middleton's plantation alone) and were on Tybee Island, apparently in contact with the British ships frequenting the coast.[65] The next day Bull added an extraordinary handwritten note at the end of a dictated letter to Colonel Laurens:

This in my own hand. If the Congress is still setting, no doubt my letters will be read in Congress, if so, I hope the Council will think as I do; that is, *not* to have this last paragraph read to so large a number of people, but to be known only to the Council, for no one does, at least ought not to know, anything of the following matter, but the members of the Council of Safety of this Province and myself. The matter is this: It is far better for the public and the owners, if the deserted negroes on Tybee Island, who are on Tybee Island, be shot, if they cannot be taken, [even] if the public is obliged to pay for them; for if they are carried away, and converted into money, which is the sinew of war, it will only enable an enemy to fight us with our own money or property.

Therefore, all who cannot be taken, had better be shot by the Creek Indians, as it, perhaps, may deter other negroes from deserting, and will establish a hatred or aversion between the Indians and negroes.[66]

Henry Laurens had already faced such a situation and dealt with it through the search-and-destroy mission to Sullivan's Island. As the president of South

Carolina's Council of Safety, he had authority over Bull's mission into Georgia, and he was subtle but clear in responding to the request for permission to act. "Now for the grand we may say awful business contained in your Letter," he responded on March 16; "it is an awful business notwithstanding it has the sanction of the Law, to put even fugitives and Rebellious Slaves to death—the prospect is horrible—." But then, without hesitation, he continued, "We think the Council of Safety in Georgia ought to give that encouragement which is necessary to induce proper persons to seize and if nothing else will do to destroy all those Rebellious Negroes upon Tybee Island or wherever they may be found." [67] Apparently Bull left Savannah hours before this authorization arrived and received word of it while on his way back to Charleston. "Could I have heard from you but twelve hours sooner," he wrote Laurens, "I should not have left Savannah as soon as I have done, as there is one piece of service which I wanted to have put into execution, which I did not think myself properly authorised to do." [68] The fate of the two hundred "fugitives and Rebellious Slaves" on Tybee Island remains unknown.

A GREAT DEAL had changed in the year since Tom Paine had advocated emancipation and western resettlement. The British had co-opted these ideas and used them to their own advantage, capitalizing on slave aspirations for freedom and tipping black hopes decidedly toward the Loyalist position with the carrot of emancipation. When Dunmore's proclamation gave public substance to this stance, the planter elite viewed the threat to their property as a compelling argument for independence, just as their grandchildren would more than four score years later. Patriot opinion had solidified around the notion that the freedom struggles of enslaved Africans were a liability rather than an asset. When Paine's *Common Sense* first appeared on January 9, 1776, it spoke of the British as barbarous and hellish agitators and of Indians and blacks as brutal and destructive enemies.

Paine's widely publicized views both reflected and influenced the thoughts of delegates to the Continental Congress gathering in Philadelphia several months later. In Jefferson's original draft for the Declaration of Independence, submitted June 28, 1776, the Virginia planter (supported by Adams and Franklin) listed as a final grievance against George III that the king had encouraged the "execrable commerce" in African slaves and was now adding insult to injury by "exciting those very people to rise in arms among us, and to purchase that liberty of which *he* had deprived them, by murdering the people upon whom *he* also obtruded them." [69] A majority of the Congress found this objection to the slave trade and its consequences divisive, untimely, or far-fetched, and they removed the clause during debate. But as Sidney Kaplan has shown, they then instructed

Jefferson to introduce a new final item, playing upon fears of slave revolts and Indian attacks while avoiding any direct reference to slavery. Kaplan rightly concludes that "in its final charge against George III—'He has excited domestic insurrections amongst us, and has endeavoured to bring on the inhabitants of our frontiers the merciless Indian Savages' . . .—an indictment of the monarch for stirring up an enslaved and an oppressed people to seek their freedom from freedom-seeking revolutionaries,—the Declaration is perhaps doubly flawed." [70]

Preoccupied with imperial misrule and prejudiced from the start against members of another class and a different race, colonial leaders could not acknowledge accurately (or perhaps even perceive) the nature of the struggle for liberation that was being waged passionately around them. When this struggle was diverted, postponed, crushed in its early stages—as is the way with most difficult liberation movements—they could hardly sense the full weight of the despair or measure the full extent of the contradictions. Rather than elaborate upon the difficult triangular struggle, acknowledging the shifts and compromises of their own course and the strength of the opposition from below as well as from abroad, they instead adopted the hypocritical view that outside agitators had been at work, unsuccessfully, among passive and anonymous victims of enslavement. By relying upon their persuasive and partisan words, we ourselves have been largely blinded for two centuries to a major factor in the turmoil leading up to the Revolution. Hemmed in by our categories of color, we have failed to recognize a significant chapter in the story of worker and artisan political unrest. We have underestimated the complexity and coherence of this brief but important wave on the unending river of struggle.

Notes

1 Herbert Aptheker, *American Negro Slave Revolts*, New York, 1969, preface, 1.
2 Ibid., 3. I have drawn upon Aptheker's own work and the valuable monographs of other scholars in shaping my argument. For a discussion of much of the literature, see Peter H. Wood, " 'I Did the Best I Could for My Day': The Study of Early Black History during the Second Reconstruction, 1960–1976," *William and Mary Quarterly*, 35:2 (April 1978), 218–219. Other recent articles include two pieces in *William and Mary Quarterly*, 37:1 (January 1980): F. Nwabueze Okoye, "Chattel Slavery as the Nightmare of the American Revolutionaries," 3–28; and Jeffrey J. Crow's prize-winning essay "Slave Rebelliousness and Social Conflict in North Carolina, 1775 to 1802," 79–102; see also two pieces by Sylvia R. Frey, "The British and the Black: A New Perspective," *Historian*, 38 (February 1976), 225–238; and "Between Slavery and Freedom: Virginia Blacks in the American Revolution," *Journal of Southern History*, 49 (August 1983), 375–398. Dr. Frey is currently preparing an analysis of blacks during the Revolution that will augment the meticulous study of Benjamin Quarles, *The Negro in the American Revolution*, Chapel Hill, 1961.

Four suggestive, recent books that provide a broader context for this essay are Ira Berlin and Ronald Hoffman (eds.), *Slavery and Freedom in the Age of the American Revolution*,

Charlottesville, 1983; Michael Craton, *Testing the Chains: Resistance to Slavery in the British West Indies*, Ithaca, 1982; Eugene D. Genovese, *From Rebellion to Revolution: Afro-American Slave Revolts in the Making of the Modern World*, Baton Rouge, 1979; and Orlando Patterson, *Slavery and Social Death: A Comparative Study*, Cambridge, 1982.

3 Charles W. Akers, "'Our Modern Egyptians': Phillis Wheatley and the Whig Campaign against Slavery in Revolutionary Boston," *Journal of Negro History*, 60 (July 1975), 405–406.

4 Ellen Gibson Wilson, *The Loyal Blacks*, New York, 1976, chapter 1. In 1772 the Virginia House of Burgesses Committee for Religion, chaired by slaveowner Robert Carter Nicholas, drafted a Toleration Bill intended to define the limits of dissenting worship among Baptists, who frequently included blacks in their meetings. The law prohibited slaves from attending church without their master's permission, and it forbade any night services. Rhys Isaac, *The Transformation of Virginia, 1740–1790*, Chapel Hill, 1982, 201, 220.

5 Quoted in John Lovell, Jr., *Black Song: The Forge and the Flame*, New York, 1972, 401.

6 Report by "Stranger," *South Carolina Gazette*, September 17, 1772, reprinted as appendix in Peter H. Wood, *Black Majority: Negroes in Colonial South Carolina from 1670 through the Stono Rebellion*, New York, 1974, 342–343.

7 *Virginia Gazette* (Purdie and Dixon), September 30, 1773, and June 30, 1774, cited in Gerald W. Mullin, *Flight and Rebellion: Slave Resistance in Eighteenth-Century Virginia*, New York, 1972, 131. On the *Somerset* case in England, see A. Leon Higginbotham, Jr., *In the Matter of Color: Race and the American Legal Process: The Colonial Period*, New York, 1978, 333–363.

8 Laurens to John Lewis Gervais, January 29, 1766, cited in Harvey H. Jackson, "'American Slavery, American Freedom' and the Revolution in the Lower South: The Case of Lachlan McIntosh," *Southern Studies*, 19 (Spring 1980), 87n. Though Laurens suggested "there was little or no cause for all that bustle," see Peter H. Wood, "'Taking Care of Business' in Revolutionary South Carolina: Republicanism and the Slave Society," in Jeffrey J. Crow and Larry E. Tise (eds.), *The Southern Experience in the American Revolution*, Chapel Hill, 1978, 277–278; and Aptheker, *Negro Slave Revolts*, 198, notes 101, 102.

9 Charles Francis Adams (ed.), *Familiar Letters of John Adams and His Wife Abigail Adams*, New York, 1876, 41–42. "I wish most sincerely there was not a slave in the province," she added. "It always appeared a most iniquitous scheme to me—to fight ourselves for what we are daily robbing and plundering from those who have as good a right to freedom as we have."

10 Aptheker, *Negro Slave Revolts*, 87, 201.

11 Memorial to the Lords of Trade and Plantations, February 5, 1770, *South Carolina Historical and Genealogical Magazine*, 31 (April 1930), 151–152. South Carolina agent Charles Garth argued the necessity "of Peopling this Colony with White Men for their better Defence and Protection against the Danger of Insurrections of the Negroes: whose numbers must continually encrease with an encrease of their important commercial Staple Commodities, to the great Advantage and Emolument of Great Britain, as well as of the Colony."

12 Eron Dunbar Rowland (ed.), "Peter Chester: Third Governor of the Province of West Florida under British Dominion, 1770–1781," *Publications of the Mississippi Historical Society: Centenary Series*, 5 (1925), 34–35.

13 Letter of May 1, 1772, PRO, CO 5/1372; see *William and Mary Quarterly*, 16 (1907–1908), 44.

14 March 25, 1773, "Journal of a Voyage to South Carolina, &c.," in Josiah Quincy, *Memoir of the Life of Josiah Quincy, Junior, of Massachusetts: 1774–1775*, Boston, 1874, 88–89.

15 Letter of November 26, 1774, William T. Hutchinson and William M. E. Rachal (eds.), *The Papers of James Madison*, Chicago, 1962, I, 129–130.

16 William Bradford to James Madison, Philadelphia, January 4, 1775, Hutchinson and Rachal (eds.), *Papers*, I, 132.

17 Ivor Noël Hume, *1775: Another Part of the Field*, New York, 1966, 62.

18 Pauline Maier, *From Resistance to Revolution: Colonial Radicals and the Development of American Opposition to Britain, 1765–1776*, New York, 1972, 283. Cf. Harold Davis, *The Fledgling Province: Social and Cultural Life in Colonial Georgia, 1773–1776*, Chapel Hill, 1976, 129–130.

19 *North Carolina Historical Review*, 9 (1932), 82.

20 *Georgia Gazette*, September 14 and 21, December 7, 1774; Herbert Aptheker, *The American Revolution, 1763–1783*, New York, 1960, 220; and Aptheker, *Negro Slave Revolts*, 201.

21 Jackson, "'American Slavery, American Freedom,'" 81; and Kenneth Coleman, *The American Revolution in Georgia, 1763–1789*, Athens, GA, 1958, 45–46.

22 Quoted in David Freeman Hawke, *Paine*, New York, 1974, 36. Hawke dismisses Paine's work with the dubious observation that "the essay rings false from start to finish." For the text, see Philip S. Foner (ed.), *The Complete Writings of Thomas Paine*, New York, 1945, II, 19.

23 Wilson, *Loyal Blacks*, 15–16.

24 This Loyalist claims memorial, filed in London, n.d., is in Audit Office 12, Volume 51, f. 289. Gordon goes on, ff. 290–291, to explain how he tried to quiet these fears. The claims memorial of Thomas Irving, another South Carolina official (Volume 51, ff. 306–307), also addresses this matter. I am indebted to Prof. Mary Beth Norton for these references.

25 May 31, 1775, Adelaide L. Fries (ed.), *Records of the Moravians of North Carolina*, Raleigh, 1968, II, 847, 928–930. The committee advised inhabitants to form companies and to
    send out Detachments to patrol and search the Negro Houses, and all other suspected
    Places within their several Districts . . . to seize all Arms and Ammunition found in
    their Possession, and to apprehend and carry before the next Magistrate all such Negroes
    as they shall find under Circumstances of Suspicion, to be dealt with according to
    the Law.

26 *Virginia Gazette* (Dixon and Hunter), March 18, 1775.

27 For a discussion of events during this month, see Noël Hume, *1775*, chapter 4.

28 "Deposition of Dr. William Pasteur," *Virginia Magazine of History and Biography*, 13 (July 1905), 48–49. Cf. "Deposition of John Randolph" in the same journal, 15 (October 1907), 150.

29 *Virginia Gazette* (Pickney), May 4, 1775.

30 *Virginia Gazette* (Dixon and Hunter), *Supplement*, April 29, 1775. On continuing unrest in Norfolk and Williamsburg during the summer of 1775, see Frey, "Between Slavery and Freedom," 377–378.

31 Gage to Dartmouth, Boston, May 15, 1775, quoted in Quarles, *Negro in the American Revolution*, 21–22.

32 Gage to Barrington, Boston, June 12, 1775, in Howard H. Peckman (ed.), *Sources of American Independence: Selected Manuscripts from the Collections of the William L. Clements Library*, Chicago, 1978, I, 133.

33 Dunmore to Secretary of State, June 25, 1775, CO 5/1353, quoted in Wilson, *Loyal Blacks*, 25. The governor, quipped the *Virginia Gazette* bitterly on June 1, "who for some time past has been suspected of acting the part of an incendiary in this colony, is to take the field as generalissimo at the head of the Africans." As a parting shot, the editor added: "N.B. The BLACK LADIES, is it supposed, will be jollily entertained in the p——e." The same month James Madison noted, "If we should be subdued, we shall fall like Achilles by the hand of one that knows that secret." Quoted in Sydney Kaplan, "The 'Domestic Insurrections' of the Declaration of Independence," *Journal of Negro History*, 61 (July 1976), 243.

34 Noël Hume, *1775*, 328ff.

35 Robert Eden to William Eden, April 28, 1775, quoted in Ronald Hoffman, *A Spirit of Dissension: Economics, Politics, and the Revolution in Maryland*, Baltimore, 1973, 147–148, as are other items in this paragraph, notes 36–38.

36 Simmons, a wheelwright, reportedly told James Mullineux "that if all the gentlemen were killed we should have the best of the land to tend and besides could get money enough while they were about it as they have got all the money in their hands." Mullineux told a grand jury "that the said Simmons appeared to be in earnest and desirous that the negroes should get the better of the white people." He was later tarred, feathered, and banished for fomenting a slave insurrection. See Maier, *Resistance to Rebellion*, 284, where he is listed as James Simmons.

37 "Extracts of a Letter from a Clergyman in Maryland to His Friend in England," August 2, 1775.

38 Report of Dorchester County Committee of Inspection, Fall 1775. The report regarding slaves continued: "The malicious and imprudent speeches of some of the lower classes of whites have induced them to believe, that their freedom depended on the success of the King's troops. We cannot therefore be too vigilant nor too rigorous with those who promote and encourage this disposition in our slaves."

39 Evangeline Walker Andrews and Charles M. Andrews (eds.), *Janet Schaw: Journal of a Lady of Quality*, New Haven, 1921, 200–201.

40 William L. Saunders et al. (eds.), *The Colonial Records of North Carolina*, Raleigh, 1890, X, 94–95. Besides Aptheker, *Negro Slave Revolts*, 202–203, see also Crow, "Slave Rebelliousness," and Alan D. Watson, "Impulse toward Independence: Resistance and Rebellion among North Carolina Slaves, 1750–1775," *Journal of Negro History*, 63 (1978), 317–328.

41 Josiah Smith, Jr., to James Poyas, May 18, 1775, and to George Appleby, June 16, 1775, as cited in Crow, "Slave Rebelliousness," 84–85n. Early in 1775 General Gage had written to John Stuart, the superintendent of Indian affairs in South Carolina, that the radicals in that colony could hardly afford to promote too much "Serious Opposition" and local unrest, or they might find that "Rice and Indigo will be brought to market by negroes instead of white people." Stuart's recollection of this letter, quoted here, is given in John R. Alden, "John Stuart Accuses William Bull," *William and Mary Quarterly*, 2 (July 1945), 318.

42 British Public Record Office Transcripts, xxxv, 192–193, South Carolina Archives, Columbia, SC.

43 "'Taking Care of Business,'" cited in note 8, above. Also see Robert M. Weir, *Colonial South Carolina—A History*, Millwood, NY, 1983, 200–203.

44 Charles Francis Adams (ed.), *The Works of John Adams*, Boston, 1850, II, 428. Adams continues, "They say their only security is this; that all the king's friends, and tools of government, have large plantations and property in negroes; so that the slaves of the Tories would be lost, as well as those of the Whigs."

45 *Virginia Gazette*, October 7, 1775; and *Constitutional Gazette*, October 21, 1775.

46 *Maryland Gazette*, November 9, 1775.

47 *Morning Chronicle and London Advertiser*, December 22, 1775, quoted in Quarles, *Negro in the American Revolution*, 22.

48 Noël Hume, *1775*, 389.

49 Quoted in James W. St. G. Walker, *The Black Loyalists: The Search for a Promised Land in Nova Scotia and Sierra Leone, 1783–1870*, New York, 1976, 1. Cf. Francis L. Berkeley, *Dunmore's Proclamation of Emancipation*, Charlottesville, 1941.

50 For an illustration of both the prejudices of our historical heritage and the linking of these two

events, see the stilted turn-of-the-century account of Cuyler Smith, "The American Negro," *Frank Leslie's Popular Monthly* (September 1902).

51 Edmund Pendleton, letter of November 27, 1775, quoted in Quarles, *Negro in the American Revolution*, 23. Frey, "Between Slavery and Freedom," 387, reminds us: "Despite his ambitious plans to organize a black army and to use it to discipline the rebellious Virginians, Dunmore was no champion of emancipation. A slaveowner himself, he persistently invited slave defections without, however, freeing his own stricken slaves or unleashing the black violence feared by the horror-stricken proprietor class—a fact that escaped neither the Patriot press nor Virginia slaves."

52 November 30, 1775, Peter Force (ed.), *American Archives*, Washington, 1837–1853, III, 1387–1388.

53 For example, Mullin, *Flight and Rebellion*, 124, observes candidly, "The royal governor's 'Black Regiment,' little more than a group of fugitives temporarily welded together to perform a desperate holding action, was largely a creation of the planters' imagination and their newspaper press."

54 *Pennsylvania Evening Post*, December 14, 1775. (I am grateful to Steven Rosswurm for this reference.) In Hillsborough, North Carolina, Richard Bennehan, founder of one of the South's largest slaveholding dynasties, left these instructions before setting out to join patriot forces for the Battle of Cross Creek: "It is said the negroes have some thoughts of freedom. Pray make Scrub sleep in the house every night and [see] that the overseer keep in Tom." Letter of February 15, 1776, to James Martin at Snow Hill Plantation, Little River, in the Cameron Papers, Southern Historical Collection, University of North Carolina, Chapel Hill.

55 John C. Fitzpatrick (ed.), *Writings of George Washington from the Original Manuscript Sources, 1745–1799*, Washington, 1931, IV, 161, 172, 186, quoted in Noël Hume, *1775*, 417. For additional reactions, see Frey, "British and the Black," 227; and Hoffman, *Spirit of Dissension*, 148.

56 See Leon F. Litwack, *Been in the Storm So Long: The Aftermath of Slavery*, New York, 1979; and Vincent Harding, *There Is a River: The Black Struggle for Freedom in America*, New York, 1981. Charles Joyner, *Down by the Riverside: A South Carolina Slave Community*, Urbana, 1984, chapter 8, cites the recollection of Scipio that before the Civil War slaves near Georgetown had stayed up nights discussing secession and the prospect "dat if dey gwo to war de black man will be FREE," and he notes that blacks in the same area were thrown in jail at the start of the war for singing "We'll Soon Be Free" and "We'll Fight for Liberty."

57 *Virginia Gazette* (Pickney), November 30, 1775.

58 *Maryland Gazette*, December 14, 1775. This issue carried a report from Williamsburg, dated December 2, which read:

> Since Lord Dunmore's proclamation made its appearance here, it is said he has recruited his army, in the counties of Princess Anne and Norfolk, to the amount of about 2000 men, including his black regiment, which is thought to be a considerable part, with this inscription on their breasts:—"Liberty to slaves."—However, as the rivers will henceforth be strictly watched, and every possible precaution taken, it is hoped others will be effectually prevented from joining those his lordship has already collected.

59 *Virginia Gazette* (Purdie), March 29, 1776, quoted in Mullin, *Flight and Rebellion*, 133.

60 Dunmore to the Secretary of State, June 26, 1776, quoted in Mullin, *Flight and Rebellion*, 132.

61 "Journal of the Council of Safety," South Carolina Historical Society, *Collections*, III (December 6, 1775), 62–63. Milligan was preceded by Michael Bates, overseer for John Ash near

Haddrell's Point, who told the council "of a robbery which had last night been committed on the plantation of which he had the charge, by a man-of-war's boat, with a number of armed men, blacks as well as whites—among the former, Robinson who has the care of the pesthouse on Sullivan's Island, and among the Latter, one Swan, a mulatto; both [of] whom he declared he perfectly knew."

62 "Journal of the Council of Safety," South Carolina Historical Society, *Collections*, III (December 7, 1775), 64–65. Across the harbor at Fort Johnson a smaller but undoubtedly related drama was being played out. On the afternoon of December 6, Major Barnard Elliott of the Regiment of Artillery assumed command of the large-scale effort to build a redoubt on James Island west of the fort (using thick palmetto logs that could absorb cannonballs without splintering). From this battery he hoped soon to be able to bombard Governor Campbell and his British ships with red-hot cannonballs. Elliott arrived,

> expecting to see the work far advanc'd, but was much disappointed. I saw a number of Negroes perhaps 40: some tying the Palmetto Logs to a stake drove in the sand, others doing nothing. . . . I asked . . . that the Overseer . . . see the Palmetto's got out of the River before he went away he told me the Negroes w^d not do it, I desired he would insist upon their geting them up immediately, for a Western gale might break the rope & the Palmettos be drifted away before morning, as had to my certain knowledge happend before at Johnsons Battery, he refus'd obeying, words arose, I drew my hanger & slap'd him on the cheek . . . he cry'd out murth^r . . . he hasted away, during this the Negroes all went off, leaving the Palmettos to the surge.

With British ships in the harbor facing danger and fellow slaves across the way at Sullivan's Island hoping for evacuation to freedom, these blacks were apparently engaged in a calculated work slowdown. Elliott to the Council of Safety, December 7, 1775, *South Carolina Historical and Genealogical Magazine*, 3 (October 1902), 194–197.

63 Josiah Smith, Jr., to James Poyas, January 19, 1776, in Josiah Smith, Jr., Letter Book, Southern Historical Collection, University of North Carolina, Chapel Hill. (I am indebted to Jeffrey J. Crow for this reference.) Cf. "Journal of the Council of Safety," South Carolina Historical Society, *Collections*, III (December 14, 1775), 84:

> Capt. Alex. Wylly, master of a coasting scooner which had been seized about five weeks ago . . . declared that he saw a number of slaves belonging to the inhabitants of this town on board some of the ships of war, and on shore upon Sullivan's Island, several of which he knew; and that a few days ago, when a report prevailed, that they were to be attacked upon Sullivan's Island, they were taken off the shore in boats sent from the ships, and that he saw about twenty of them carried on board the scooner seized from him, which scooner, as well as two negroes he left behind, was his sole property.
>
> Capt. Wylly then signed the Association, declaring his frequent absence had prevented his doing so before.

64 Testimony of Mr. Fenwick Bull, "Journal of the Council of Safety," South Carolina Historical Society, *Collections*, III (December 10, 1775), 75.

65 Robert Wilson Gibbes (ed.), *Documentary History of the American Revolution . . . Chiefly in South Carolina*, New York, 1853, I, 266–267.

66 Ibid., 268–269. This remarkable document of March 14, 1776, which constitutes the missing half of the correspondence cited by Aptheker in *Negro Slave Revolts*, 204, goes on.

> Some of the Council of Safety are timid, particularly one Mr. Andrews, from St. John's Parish, Sunbury, who has influence, and through whose means Gov. Wright has been enable to carry on his plans of late. There are a few others in the same way, but, notwith-

standing that, you may depend the business shall be done agreeable to the orders of Congress; but it will be best the Council of Safety here should give the orders, at least, if they have not men of their own to do the business. I am told my coming here, with my command and orders from our Congress, had great good effect.

I have just this moment had proper and certain assurance, that a good leader and party of the Creek Indians are willing and desirous of going to take the runaway negroes upon Tybee Island, if I choose it; but as I have no authority from you to send the Indians on such an errand, I must decline it, but still think the Council of Safety will do it. The two of that board, who I a few minutes ago had a private interview with, seem to doubt whether they will have a majority from it. But it must be kept a profound secret, lest the negroes should move off, or they should ask for arms, and so lay an ambuscade for the Indians. I have something farther to say on this subject, but defer it until I come to Charles Town.

I have the honor to be, sir,

Your most obedient servant,

STEPH'N. BULL.

67 Quoted in Aptheker, *Negro Slave Revolts*, 204.
68 Letter from Shelden, March 26, 1776, Gibbes (ed.), *Documentary*, I, 273.
69 Kaplan, "'Domestic Insurrections,'" 244.
70 Ibid., 253.

12

Black Women in Resistance: A Cross-Cultural Perspective

ROSALYN TERBORG-PENN

People of African descent have resisted oppression throughout history, whether resistance originated within or outside the African continent.* From the fifteenth through much of the nineteenth centuries, Africans were enslaved by people both indigenous and foreign to Africa. Men and women resisted internal African slavery and enslavement in the institutions developed by Europeans in the Western Hemisphere, or New World societies. Despite resistance, the centuries-long African slave trade resulted in the enslavement and dispersal of millions of Africans, especially throughout the Western Hemisphere. Their descendants have been called Africans abroad, or people of the African diaspora. The resistance activities found among African women on the continent, in the New World, and among their descendants reveal common patterns. These patterns reflect the heritage and world view of traditional African women, especially those from the western and central regions, and the adaptive behavior of African women transplanted to New World communities. For those who study the diaspora, certain unifying conceptual issues can be applied to the study of African and African diaspora women's resistance. One concept is that the study of African descendants abroad is an extension of African history. Another uni-

* Several individuals read and made suggestions about this essay. I thank them all, but express special appreciation to Linda Heywood, Lucille Mathurin Mair, Debra L. Newman, Rayna Rapp, and Andrea Benton Rushing.

fying concept is that there exists a tradition of identity with Africa among people of the diaspora. Both conceptual issues negate the conventional Eurocentric interpretation of Africa as a recipient and not a donor of cultural heritage. In the context of this discussion, studying black women's resistance includes a review of the ways in which African heritage is viewed or reflected in the lives of those of African descent.

The field of African diaspora studies as a viable scholarly endeavor has been developing since the late 1960s. Since then, scholars of African-American history have addressed these issues—African diaspora history as an extension of African history, and identity with Africa among people of the diaspora.[1] The focus upon women of the diaspora as a distinct area of inquiry developed about a decade later, for the most part among anthropologists. Among them, Filomina Chioma Steady pioneered in this cross-cultural approach to the study of black women's lives by viewing the experiences and the responses of women of the African diaspora as part of a continuum, wherein common themes are significant in the experiences of black women, past and present, in various parts of the world. Steady emphasizes how women's position was important in maintaining the biological, physical, and cultural survival of the people.[2] Hence, within traditional societies throughout the regions of Africa, common values in women's experiences provided a synthesis, which can be used by scholars of New World experiences for establishing a model to study women of the diaspora. Among the common values Steady identifies are an ideology of self-reliance among women who rely upon one another for various forms of support, and the creation of survival imperatives designed by women to oppose social, economic, and political threats to their communities. Both of these values represent strategies needed to fight oppression on the African continent. Self-reliance encouraged the development of networking or bonding among women, whether for economic or political survival. African and later African-Brazilian, African-Caribbean, and African-American women relied upon their own strengths, wits, organizational abilities, and spiritual powers to resist the forces that endangered their physical and cultural existence. Unlike women of Western societies, who by the nineteenth century had been socialized to depend upon their men for survival, traditional African women and New World women of African descent were encouraged by members of their respective societies to depend upon themselves to a great extent. In addition, African women were traditionally the key to cultural survival, because they were the bearers of tradition. They were the primary agents in maintaining conventional behavior among their families and the community at large. In addition, African women were important to the economic life of their communities, for it was the women who produced the food their families consumed. Not surprisingly, Steady finds that several of these functions survived enslavement and, where possible, gained new meaning among Africans in the New World.[3]

Within this conceptual framework, Africa becomes the donor of a cultural heritage that spreads into the diaspora subcultures, changing or adapting with time and circumstance. In addition, women in the African diaspora, whether consciously or unconsciously, identify with African traditions. This theoretical construct can be used to study resistance among women in the diaspora. Resistance, in the context of this essay, includes women's involvement in the organized struggle against slavery, peonage, and imperialism. Strategies included open and guerrilla warfare, marronage, slave revolts, and peasant revolts. The societies discussed in this study include representatives from Africa, the United States, South America, and the Caribbean. The period varies from the seventeenth century through the nineteenth century. The common characteristics shared by many of the resistance movements include women as warriors, the leadership of older women, and women of rank emerging as political leaders as well as warriors. Furthermore, several of the women, or symbols representing female resistance, have been revered in stories or celebrated in ritual by later generations of African or African diaspora people. Variations on these themes can be traced through time and from African to New World societies. In tracing these themes, several questions emerge about the women under study. First, what combination of circumstances caused these women to resist? Were they individuals who were working for their own survival, or were they chosen by others to resist on their behalf? How and why did the leaders achieve their positions? Finally, what caused some of these women to be revered by future generations?

Women as Spiritual Leaders and Warriors

Rebelling against foreign invasion, colonization, and slavery may be among the oldest causes of resistance among African women and their descendants. Resistance took covert and overt forms among women on the continent of Africa, as well as in New World societies. In cases of women leading community resistance, respected older women often assumed leadership or were chosen as leaders. These women were revered generally because of supernatural or spiritual powers, which their followers believed were strong enough to combat the oppressive forces against which their society was struggling. The roles of women in traditional African religious organizations are important to the understanding of these cases, because they differ significantly from the Western religious traditions into which African women were placed throughout the diaspora. Female deities are powerful and highly respected in traditional West African societies, as is the belief that women enable the spiritual forces that communicate with the people. Among the Yoruba, for example, Gelede dances are performed to pay homage to all women, who are believed to have innate power to benefit the community.[4] The belief that African women have spiritual power and strength is not limited to the Yoruba, but found among the various ethnic groups in Africa, many of whose people were captured and subsequently enslaved in the New World. Among African and African diaspora people, effective resistance often was strengthened by the spiritual "power" of religious women.

Perhaps the most celebrated African woman to resist European colonization was Nzinga Mbunde, the leader of four decades of warfare against the Portuguese in Angola. She is popularly known as Queen Ann Nzinga. A controversial figure, whose leadership and warfare lasted from the 1620s to the 1660s, Nzinga has been portrayed paradoxically as a protonationalist resistance leader, a devout Christian and Portuguese ally, a superb but ruthless Mbunde politician, and a vicious slave trader. Despite the contradictory interpretations, scholars have not failed to praise her skill as a negotiator and military strategist who was directly responsible for limiting the Portuguese colony at Luanda to a few square miles.[5] The scholarly debate about Nzinga does not deny that she has been revered as a heroine by nationalistic African-Americans for several generations. Historian Chancellor Williams gives the popularly accepted view of Nzinga, portraying her as a woman who fought the slave trade as well as the Portuguese. She assumed leadership when she was in her forties, and held varying degrees of influence and power until she was in her eighties.[6]

Why has Nzinga remained a heroine among African-Americans? Several of her characteristics may explain why. First, she was a leader who could inspire her people to resist the Europeans. Second, she had unusual strength, which appeared to increase with time, almost supernaturally. Third, Nzinga's role as a warrior and an anticolonialist is an excellent example of the commitment of African women to certain values: self-reliance and survival strategies. Both of these values are revered by African-Americans. As to her role as a slave trader, many African-Americans just do not want to believe that allegation. In the end, Nzinga recanted her pledge to fight the Portuguese to the end, eventually signing a treaty with them, believing that peace would foster the survival of her people. Seemingly this compromise has become acceptable to those who revere her, African-Americans and black Caribbeans, past and present.[7]

Taradoba (also called Sandemande) was another African woman with military and political skill. She lived in the late nineteenth and early twentieth centuries and was revered as a warrior by her people, the Vai of Liberia. Taradoba was said to have been the favorite wife of a ruler of a Vai region. When Taradoba's husband died in the late 1870s, she chose to continue his rule. Her brother-in-law was the ruler of another section of Vai country, northwest of Bendoo, Taradoba's capital, and attempted to claim her throne. His plan did not succeed because Taradoba led five hundred to six hundred warriors against him, successfully capturing a southern province of the kingdom. Her brother-in-law attempted to subdue Taradoba three times, but she repelled his forces in each case. It is said that she commanded her troops in person, "distinguishing herself with valor and success." Taradoba ruled the province for many years thereafter.[8]

Although the two women—Nzinga and Taradoba—differ in period, ethnic group, and region in Africa, they are similar in that both assumed positions as military leaders and became political leaders as a result. Unlike Nzinga, there appears to be no scholarly debate about the motives and ambitions of Taradoba.

African women warriors were not limited to Angola and Liberia. European travelers in Dahomey reported the existence of groups of female soldiers as early as the 1730s, during wars among the ethnic groups in present-day Nigeria and Benin. After conquering the coastal regions, Agadja, who had ascended the Dahomey throne in 1708, and his forces were attacked and nearly devastated by the Oyo (of Nigeria). By 1734, the conquered coastal monarchs decided to launch a campaign to retake the towns from which they had been driven by Agadja. In response to the threatened attack, Agadja was reported to have ordered a large number of women to be dressed as soldiers and armed. Then ordering the army to march, he sent the women to the rear. When the opposition army beheld the Dahomey force, they were surprised at the large numbers and many retreated. Anthropologist Melville Herskovits quoted several other European observers who, throughout the eighteenth and nineteenth centuries, noted units of Dahomey women soldiers, whom Europeans called Amazons.[9] Although Agadja was an expanionist rather than a liberator, those Dahomians enslaved and taken to the New World during the period from the mid-1700s until the end of the European slave trade accepted women as warriors and knew of women's role in the Dahomey army.

In New World societies, where adaptations of traditional African rituals were practiced and where descendants of the Dahomian people were enslaved, evidence of women as warriors is symbolized in the traditional dances and religious ritual. In Brazil, African-Brazilian religious rituals were practiced by African captives in various regions as early as the late sixteenth century. Although some changes occurred, the African-Brazilians attempted to conserve the essence of their traditional beliefs. Changes in various rituals occurred by the nineteenth century, because the different religious groups contained members of several African ethnic groups. Exclusiveness gave way as members sought less to preserve their respective ethnic characteristics and more to enhance African cultural attributes, which differed from those of whites. Africans who were brought to Bahia, for example, came largely from Nigeria, Dahomey, Angola, and Guinea. The Dahomey people began the custom of worshiping their deities separately from the white religious forms, although Europeans encouraged conversion to Catholicism. Among the Dahomey, mothers of the saints were quite common and Candombles is the cult most commonly practiced. Iansa is one of the female deities worshiped; she is the wife of Xango, a powerful male deity, and is portrayed in dance "aggressively brandishing a cooper scimitar." During a Candombles celebration in Bahia in 1974, anthropologist Seldon Rodman witnessed the women dressed for their roles as saints. All but one represented a female. For the most part, the dancers brandished "battle-axes, poniards, power horns, mirrors, and bundles of sticks." Rodman interpreted the Candombles goal as an effort to keep "Africa pure," resisting cultural change.[10]

Conserving cultural continuity or resisting cultural change, the Candombles cult, whose officials are usually women, reflect several important aspects of women's roles in traditional African culture that were transformed in New World societies. First, the religious power of African women is immediately apparent. The warrior nature of the deities portrayed in the celebration connects African women soldiers to enslaved Africans in Brazil. Once enslaved, women's roles as warriors could be permitted only through rituals and ceremonies, which were passed down through generations thereafter by women. Women's resistance to white cultural imperatives is covertly shown through the aggressive dances that honor the warlike nature of African women. Further, the symbolically powerful African women warriors represent female deities. Europeans revered female saints, not female deities. Among the African-Brazilian women of Bahia, ritual maintains belief in female deities in defiance of Euro-American religious traditions.

Women in Slave Revolts and Maroon Societies

Values that encouraged African women to develop leadership abilities to aid in the survival of their people were carried to New World societies by African women. From the late seventeenth century until the abolition of slavery, women of the African diaspora demonstrated their abilities as leaders and as supporters of slave resistance and revolts in the Western Hemisphere.

The women involved in slave plots and revolts in Jamaica were sometimes called queens. As early as 1680 a slave conspiracy in the Jamaica parish of Vere was uncovered. The leaders were said to be a king, a queen, and a chief, all of whom were revered by the slaves involved in the plot. Although women appeared to be less prominent in the execution of slave insurrections, at least one woman participated in most reported conspiracies. This was true for the thwarted 1745 Jamaica slave plot; one of the eleven slaves found guilty and transported from the island was a woman. Another Jamaica uprising involving six parishes was planned in 1760 and led by a slave woman, Queen Cubah. She was reported to have presided over the slaves while seated under a canopy, dressed in a robe and a crown. The plot was uncovered and Cubah was captured. After a trial, she was exiled from the island for life. Determined, Queen Cubah furtively returned to Jamaica, where she was recaptured and hanged.[11]

How Cubah became the leader of this insurrection, why she returned to Jamaica after banishment, and what became of her memory remain unanswered questions. It appears that Cubah's "power," whether religious or political, was greater than her ability to plan a slave insurrection, and that her realm was broad enough to attract a following from her own community and five others. Perhaps the commitment she made to those who selected her to lead compelled Cubah to return to Jamaica to complete her task, despite the threat of death. It would not be surprising to learn that the descendants of people living in the Jamaica parishes involved in the 1760 conspiracy remember and revere her name today.

Similar cases of militant slave women involved in insurrection plots were reported in the United States over a hundred-year period beginning in 1712. In the infamous New York City slave conspiracy of 1712, it was said that the conspirators bound themselves to secrecy by sucking the blood from one another's hands and using a charm for reassurance, both rites of African derivation. The slaves then set fire to a building and succeeded in attacking nearly twenty white men, nine of whom they killed. Seventy slaves were arrested, most of whom were alleged to know of the conspiracy. Twenty-seven slaves were condemned to death; six were eventually pardoned, including a pregnant woman.[12] As in the Jamaica revolts of the period, at least one woman was identified as a conspirator, although quite possibly more were involved. Subsequent revolts also included slave women. In two of the most famous nineteenth-century revolts, Gabriel Prosser's conspiracy of 1800 and Nat Turner's insurrection of 1831, women were among the conspirators. Prosser's wife, Nancy, was actively involved in that Henrico County, Virginia, plot. Nat Turner's wife, Cherry, is said by her descendants to have been a strong force in planning this revolt in South Hampton, Virginia.[13] Neither Nancy Prosser nor Cherry Turner was brought to trial. Perhaps the male conspirators refused to implicate the women who were part of the insurrection plan. In addition, there was an insurrection of ninety slaves who were being transported for sale in Kentucky during the summer of 1829. One of the six leaders was a pregnant woman who was sentenced to hang, but not until after her child was born. The militancy of this woman was not unusual.[14]

Public outcries against slavery were forms of resistance used by women in the United States as well as in Africa. In an essay on slave resistance, historian Herbert Aptheker noted the militancy of African-American slave women during the early nineteenth century, when reports appeared about several women who publicly called for rebellion. Slaveholders' periodicals reported these outcries with alarm. For example, in 1812, reports from Virginia noted a slave woman's saying that slaves "could not rise too soon for her, as she had rather be in hell than where she was." In 1835, reports from Mississippi noted the sentiments of a slave woman calling for revolt: "She wished to God it was all over and done with; that she was tired of waiting on white folks." Aptheker attributes rebellious statements made by women to the harsh oppression they suffered under slavery.[15] Still, the form of their protest goes deeper than the slave experience in America. For African women, traditionally, "the role of ridicule" has been institutionalized in most societies, where, unlike the United States, women are not looked upon negatively for it. Among Africans, ridicule allows a mechanism for releasing tensions between the sexes; in the case of Asante queen mothers, it is a tool for criticizing questionable male decisions. In Sierra Leone and Liberia, the secret societies among the men and women of the Mende and Temne provide a means for diffusing tensions. According to Steady, ridicule can take the form of direct taunts, group pressure, or ritual satire.[16] The women cited by Aptheker ridiculed slavery, and perhaps also their men who did not rebel against enslavement. Ridicule may not have remained institutionalized in slave communities in the United States, but black women continued in the militant traditions of their foremothers in various regions of the diaspora.

Evidence of African women's use of ridicule to resist slavery was noted by Benjamin Anderson, a black American explorer who settled in Liberia. During the 1860s he noted that the Mandingoes in Boporu, Liberia, had many slaves who were used primarily as carriers in the trade of salt and cloth. In 1866, at the death of one of the Mandingo king's relatives, several of his slaves were to be sold in order to settle the relative's debts. The slaves resisted sale and a revolt took place involving all the slaves in the town. The enslaved, who outnumbered their captors, took over the town, seized arms, and barricaded their fortress. It was apparent that the rebellion had been well planned and that the slaves waited for the right opportunity to stage the revolt. The Mandingo king sent word informing the slaves that if they surrendered and returned to their masters, all offenses would be pardoned. While the rebelling men deliberated on what to do, one of their women publicly harangued them against listening to any proposals for reconciliation. She warned that the king only wished them to submit so that he might more easily punish them. She concluded "that if their hearts began to quail, they had better give their spears into the hands of the women."

Her speech settled the debate and the slaves held fast, continuing to resist. Unfortunately they lost their battle to the king's forces. Afterward the king ordered all the male slaves and the woman who had publicly called for continued revolt to be executed. In the words of Anderson: "The woman was executed with circumstances shocking to humanity and decency. All the women in Boporu were compelled to go out and witness her fate" so that they would be discouraged from rebelling against male authority.[17]

In this case, the public taunts of a slave woman urging enslaved men to rebel were not recognized as a legitimate form of ridicule by the king. Implicit in his insistence that all women of the community witness her execution is the king's fear that other women may attempt a similar form of protest. Nonetheless, it is not surprising that the enslavers did not recognize the traditional roles of African women when they conflicted with roles as slaves. Similarly, white enslavers in the United States were upset by the public outcries against slavery by enslaved women of African descent.

In Grenada, the African-Caribbean women involved in the most infamous slave rebellion were both enslaved and free. Historian Edward L. Cox called the rebellion the Revolution on Grenada, because the aim was to overthrow the political system as well as slavery. It was led by a "free colored," Julien Fedon, and involved members of his class, free blacks, and slaves, and lasted from March 1795 to June 1796. Cox discloses several reasons why free coloreds, or mulattoes, free blacks, and slaves joined to take over the island to drive the whites away. The French and Haitian revolutions had significant impact upon the entire Caribbean, especially in areas, like Grenada, with a sizable French-speaking population. In addition, the free mulattoes of Grenada had been rebuffed when they attempted to gain full citizenship and civil rights equal to the other landowning and educated persons in Grenada, who were white. The goal of the revolutionaries was to turn the government over to the French, to extend civil and political rights to all free people, and to emancipate the slaves. The Grenada rebellion failed, mainly because the revolutionaries were unable to realize outside support for their cause. Before the end of the fighting, seven thousand slaves had lost their lives. Fedon made good his escape to either Trinidad or Cuba. Of his captured supporters, those who were not executed were banished to Honduras, several of them leaving property later confiscated by the government.[18]

Women were suspected of supporting and participating in the rebellion. Shortly after the government regained control of the island, the governor appointed a committee to investigate the free mulatto women who were "under strong suspicion of having taken an active part with the insurgents and rebels during the insurrection." Some women had fled to Trinidad as the revolutionary forces collapsed. For the most part, these were free mulatto women, whose families had owned land in Grenada. In 1797, when these women attempted to return to Grenada from Trinidad, the Grenada council advised the governor to refuse the women permission to enter. The governor complied with the council's request. The same year the legislature passed an act empowering the governor to question all inhabitants of the island, in an effort to single out illegal immigrants and *personae non gratae*. Any resident who had left the island during the rebellion was deemed a vagabond unless he or she obtained permission to remain thereafter, or to reenter. The act was probably aimed at the women suspected of having condoned or aided the revolutionaries. Aid could very well have been supplied by free or enslaved women of color who spied on the whites or by women planning strategy.[19]

Unlike the Grenada rebellion, in Haiti the slaves fought successfully against the whites and the mulattoes, driving many of both groups to surrounding Caribbean islands and to the United States. As a result, in 1791 a black republic emerged in Haiti. Here we can speculate about the involvement of African women in the Haitian Revolution. Religious practices among women in Haiti remain similar to the Yoruba cults in West Africa and to the Candombles in Brazil, in all of which women take leadership roles. An examination of the Haitian voodoo celebrations of the revolution practiced today gives clues about women's involvement in the revolutionary movement. The iconography used in contemporary voodoo ceremonies reflects symbols of the revolution. In a 1978 ceremony witnessed by this writer in Port-au-Prince, women celebrants brandished swords, daggers, pennants, and pictures of Toussaint-Louverture, the primary leader of the slave revolution. For now we can say that it is not likely that free mulatto women identified with slave women in Grenada after the revolution failed, just as the division among free mulattoes and slaves in Haiti caused the free population to flee the island in the wake of slave victory. Questioning the religious roles of women in both countries would help in future analysis. Was African religious survival in Grenada as significant as it was in Haiti on the eve of the revolutions and thereafter? Probably not. In Haiti today, black women and mulatto women participate in voodoo celebrations. In Grenada, however, for the most part the mulattoes are affiliated with British religious institutions. This process began shortly after the failure of the revolution, and represents a strategy initiated by the British. Furthermore, looking for African religious survivals in Grenada during the generation after the revolution would be difficult. The British divested the Catholic church of its property from 1763 to 1795. After the revolution, the government tightly controlled the activities of priests, fearful of their influence with individuals sympathetic to pro-French and pro-Catholic revolutionaries.[20] Probably any African religious practices were equally feared on the island and were forbidden or forced underground. The reverse occurred in Haiti, where African religions were celebrated along with the revolutionary victory. In Haiti, voodoo is similar to Candombles in Brazil, where women officiate in the ceremony.

Revolutionary activities against slavery rarely succeeded in the New World, as is well known. An alternative to destroying slavery as a system was flight from it. Directly confronting the slave system by waging war against it was found to be less successful than establishing maroon societies on the fringe of slave communities. Women were usually involved in the leadership and in the support of this type of resistance. Examples of such maroon societies, or *quilombos* as they were called in Brazil, can be cited for Jamaica, Surinam, Brazil, and the United States from the 1770s through the early 1800s. Hence, marronage was an alternative to enslavement, chosen by many Africans early in the history of New World slavery. Large-scale and long-lasting maroon communities were common among Africans throughout the Caribbean and the tropical areas of South America, but less common among Africans in the temperate climate of North America, where guerrilla warfare prevailed on the outskirts of slave communities.

One of the most successful series of maroon societies among Caribbean countries emerged in Surinam in the early eighteenth century, resulting in the largest maroon population, with several societies still in existence today.[21] Isolated maroon communities began to develop in Surinam shortly after the British first brought slaves to this mountainous rain forest area. The Dutch assumed control of the colony in the late seventeenth century; within less than fifty years, slave uprisings became numerous as Africans took to the rain forest. The Dutch were unable to crush these communities with military force and in 1730 decided to try terrifying the Africans into submission. Eleven slaves, captured in warfare between the Dutch and the Saramaka maroons, were barbarously executed. Eight of those executed were female. The six adult women were broken alive upon the rack, and the two girls were decapitated. Observers claimed that "such was their resolution under these tortures, that they endured them without even uttering a sigh." Instead of terrifying the maroons, the executions increased their determination to struggle for freedom. Finally, in 1749, the Dutch government negotiated a peace treaty with the Saramakas.[22]

No known records document how these women were captured. One may surmise that they were stolen from the maroon camp by Dutch soldiers. But this possibility seems remote, because the Dutch experienced no success in penetrating the forest to confront the permanent maroon settlements. Were the women captured as they waged battle to protect their community? This is a possibility, because women of Africa have participated in armed struggles from time to time. Regardless of how they came to be captured, the bravery of these Saramaka women has been passed down through time and is part of the folk tradition.

Day-to-day survival was imperative to these communities, and women provided the stability for the community. As in the African societies they came from, women cultivated and produced the food consumed by the community. Based upon a matrifocal social structure, a Saramaka proverb expressed the descent ideology as well as the cosmology of this African-derived society.

> Women are like hearthstones, men like axe handles. Once placed in a house, a set of clay hearthstones may never be moved; they endure. But an axe handle is made to travel, and once worn out from use, it is discarded on the spot; it leaves no traces.[23]

Thus, the Saramakan women descendants reflect traditional African values that encouraged women to be self-reliant and to develop survival strategies.

Maroon societies, or *quilombos*, appeared in Brazil with the beginning of the slave trade. The center of slave resistance was the state of Minas Gerais, where slaves were forced into hard labor in the gold and precious metals mines. Uprisings occurred frequently, and by the 1700s authorities blamed runaways in *quilombos* for inciting the uprisings, for the runaways often used guerrilla warfare against the white settlements. Some *quilombos* included fugitive African and Indian peoples, and among these, African women could be found as leaders during the 1700s. Sociologist Roger Bastide attributes African female leadership to the African belief that women have spiritual powers or magical qualities, resulting in a religious syncretism or mixture emerging among the African-Indian groups. The dominant cultural element in these African-Indian mixtures came from African beliefs. Groups of African and Indian fugitives have been found as far west of Minas Gerais as the state of Amazonas, near the Trombetas River. Here there was a *quilombo* led by an African woman, Filippa Paria Aranha, who was so powerful that the Portuguese had to make a treaty with her because they could not defeat her forces in battle. Her descendants survive in the area today and consider her the founder and spiritual and political leader of their community. Similarly, the inhabitants of a *quilombo* formed by the Malali Indians and fugitive Africans at Paranaiba in Minas selected an African woman as their leader. The descendants of these African-Indian people acknowledge African women as their ancestors. Bastide ties the leadership selection process in these *quilombos* to the African religious belief that women have powers that can be used to keep away evil or to protect the community. The success of Aranha, if no other, surely reinforced the *quilombo* belief in powerful African women.[24]

Other maroon societies thrived among Caribbean islands such as Cuba and Jamaica. One Jamaica community still in existence is Moore Town, originally called Nanny Town for the woman responsible for the survival of these Portland maroons. Nanny was an older woman and was said to have been an *obeah* woman, or leader of great spiritual and supernatural powers. Historian Lucille Mathurin Mair calls her "the first national heroine of the Jamaica people."[25] Much of what is known about "Grandy" Nanny, as she was called, comes through oral traditions of the Asante descendants of this windward maroon society. According to the traditions, Nanny was a free woman who had never experienced slavery. Said to be the sister of the renowned leeward maroon leader Cudgoe, Nanny, like Nzinga, became a military leader of great strategic abilities. When in 1730 her community was threatened by British attack, Nanny directed the successful campaign, communicating through a horn called the *abeng*. Nanny resolved never to come to terms with the Europeans, and in 1737 she was said to have taken a solemn pledge that she would fight to the death before making peace with the British. In the meantime, Cudgoe, who led the revolt of the maroon community on the leeward side of the island, made peace with the Europeans in 1739. Oral tradition says that while men negotiated the truce, the women stood by wearing the teeth of white soldiers killed in battle around their ankles—a sign of defiance. After the truce the windward maroons continued fighting, eventually splitting into two groups, one of which followed Nanny to a new settlement now called Moore Town, where they continued to fight a losing battle against the British. Finally in 1740, Nanny decided to come to terms with the British and applied for a land patent, which granted her followers five hundred acres in the parish of Portland. Once again, the desire for community survival overruled a pledge to fight the Europeans to the death. It is said that Nanny's body died in the 1750s, but not her spirit. Legend relates that this "queen mother" still keeps watch over her people.[26]

Writers today debate whether women like Nzinga or Nanny should be called heroines because of their compromises on the subject of slavery. Some claim that Nanny made an agreement with the British to return fugitive slaves to authorities. Others, like Mathurin, have searched the documents thoroughly and found no evidence of such an agreement. As far as the descendants of the Moore Town maroons are concerned, Nanny is their heroine, despite the attacks upon her credibility by outsiders.[27] Even if Nanny were not a positive legendary figure among the maroons, her abilities as a military leader and as a strategist make her significant to the history of Jamaica slave resistance against the British.

Survival, once again, was primary in the culture of this maroon society. Unlike the Saramaka maroons in Surinam's rain forest, the maroons in the Blue Mountains of Jamaica were more accessible to the European colonists. As a result, Jamaican maroons were constantly under the threat of attack. The women of this Jamaican society were of Akan-speaking people, particularly the Asante and the Fanti, where matrilineage determines the descent structure. It is not surprising that Nanny emerges not only as the symbol of survival but also as the original queen mother of the society. The queen mother is an institution in Asante culture. Historian Agnes Ahosua Aidoo described the queen mother as the co-ruler, jointly responsible with the male chief for affairs of state. Hence, the queen mother held a vital political office. She was obligated to advise the chief, to criticize and to rebuke him in public, if necessary. In the event that there was no male ruler or heir, the queen mother ruled alone as chief. These Akan values were transferred to the New World, where maroon women shared in the day-to-day struggle for survival, especially in food production, and provided the basic stability needed for community survival. Nanny represented the standard for physical survival not only through her power as a religious leader but also through her ability as a warrior. To the maroons and their descendants, Nanny became the mythical ancestress from whom all descended. According to the myth, Nanny rebelled, fleeing to the mountains, where she began a guerrilla war against the Europeans. Her sister, Sekesu, remained a slave on a plantation and from her descended the plantation slaves. In another legend, Nanny's mystical and supernatural powers are extolled and the great maroon military victories are attributed to Nanny's supernatural powers or her survival strategies. Here the powers of Nanny can be compared to the powers of Aranha of Brazil.[28]

The establishment and survival of large maroon societies in North America was more difficult. Small groups of fugitive slaves attempted to subsist on the fringes of plantations located near swamps throughout the colonial and the antebellum periods of United States history. In the Dismal Swamp between Virginia and North Carolina about two hundred fugitive slaves and their offspring lived for several generations. Survival was said to be based upon an illegal trade they maintained with whites living on the borders of the swamp. The women who were a part of these communities helped to plan insurrections. One of these plans was uncovered in 1811 among the maroons of Cabarrus County, North Carolina. The maroons were attacked and the community wiped out. Two of the four fugitives captured during the ensuing battle were women.[29]

Female leadership, though difficult to establish from the accounts that have survived, should not be surprising among maroons in the United States, for similar survival mechanisms worked for women of African descent throughout North America. Even if women were not leaders, they were almost always participants in resistance movements. In 1818, for example, one member of a group of over thirty guerrillas captured in Princess Anne County, Virginia, was an old woman. Although she was not acknowledged by authorities to be a leader, her presence at least raises questions about the possibility of this role, especially when we consider the leadership roles older women of African descent have assumed. Whether in leadership positions or not, female resistance among maroons attacked by slaveholders was common. A group of men, women, and children near Mobile, Alabama, for example, resisted valiantly in 1827, but the lack of sufficient weapons resulted in the defeat of the maroons and the demise of their settlement.[30]

From the little that is known about African-American women in maroon societies, it appears that both older and younger women played a role in defending these communities. Maroon survival was imperative to these women, just as it was for their sisters elsewhere in the diaspora. Several questions remain about the spiritual role of maroon women in the United States, the numbers involved in maroon societies, and the names, if any, of women leaders.

Women Leaders in Postemancipation Resistance

Resisting oppression continued in similar ways after emancipation. Examples of female leadership in warfare can be found in the United States and the Caribbean, for in both areas peonage was later substituted for the slave labor system. The patterns were similar. Peonage followed slavery in less than a generation after emancipation in the United States and in the Danish Virgin Islands. Resistance in both societies was initiated by older women, the acknowledged leaders in their communities.

During the Civil War in the United States, slaves used the opportunity of war to free themselves, escaping to Union army lines even before 1863, when President Lincoln emancipated the slaves in rebelling states. Harriet Tubman, the foremost conductor of the Underground Railroad before the war, stepped out of this role shortly after the war began to assist in the Union effort. Tubman was known as Moses in the biblical sense, rather than as queen or queen mother. She, like Moses, was believed to be the deliverer of her people. She, like Moses, was believed to have mysterious powers. She was plagued by the disease somnolence, which was said to strike her at any time, leaving her asleep for hours. Despite this affliction, Tubman was never caught transporting slaves illegally through the Underground Railroad.[31]

Although a fugitive slave herself, Tubman went South in 1862 and attached herself to Major General David Hunter's forces in Beaufort, South Carolina. The perfect intermediary, Tubman bridged the gap between the two worlds of the Northern white and the Southern black soldiers. Quickly she won the respect of the South Carolina freedmen, by bringing their problems to the attention of military authorities and by nursing the sick. Using survival techniques learned from other slaves, Tubman acquired a special reputation for curing dysentery with roots, a practice inherited from African ancestors.

As if nursing were not enough, Union officers relied upon her knowledge of guerrilla warfare and espionage. Her most notable accomplishment in this area was her victory against the Confederate army in the Combahee River campaign. In July 1863, a news dispatch from the *Boston Commonwealth* noted that Colonel James Montgomery and his band of three hundred black soldiers surprised the Confederate army troops camped on the river and destroyed millions of dollars worth of supplies while liberating nearly eight hundred blacks, who had been illegally detained after the Emancipation Proclamation of January 1863. This news dispatch noted that the Union forces were "under the guidance of a black woman," who, not surprisingly, remained nameless to readers. She was Harriet Tubman, who at the time was forty years of age. She had formulated the Combahee campaign strategy herself, requested Colonel Montgomery as commander, and instructed the forces to place torpedoes in key places in the Confederate lines. The success of the battle resulted from not only her skill in planning the attack but also her espionage ability. Tubman's preliminary survey of the river enabled her to know where to attack as well as the capacity of the enemy.[32]

Once the news of the Union success began to spread, droves of blacks left the nearby plantations for the gunboats. Despite the attempts by plantation overseers to whip them into submission, hundreds of former slaves headed for the river. In later years, Tubman reminisced about the women she saw there.

> I never saw such a sight. . . . Here you'd see a woman with a pail on her head, rice a-smoking in it from the fire; young ones hanging on behind, one hand around her forehead to hold on, the other hand digging into the rice pot, eating with all its might; a hold of her dress two or three more; down her back a bag with a pig in it. . . . I never saw so many twins in my life; bags on their shoulders, baskets on their heads and young ones tagging behind, all loaded, pigs squealing, chickens screaming, young ones squealing.[33]

Harriet Tubman painted a picture of self-reliant African-American women creating their own survival mechanisms. It stands to reason that for these women, escaping the plantation meant taking their children and the means to feed them. Tubman's oral account of these South Carolina women was one of the few about their activities during this crucial transition in their lives. War correspondents had not thought enough to record Tubman's name as a battle leader for posterity; they would not be likely to record the actions of these soon to be peasant women. Tubman's Civil War exploits faded quickly from the memories of the Union army officials. In 1869 Sarah Bradford, a white philanthropist, collected Tubman's oral account of her life on the Underground Railroad, and wrote *Scenes in the Life of Harriet Tubman*. This little book was designed to raise funds for the impoverished veteran forgotten by the government she had served.[34]

Aside from the Bradford book, which did not include the Civil War experiences, Tubman's memory was kept alive by a network of black women who continued to sing her praises into the late nineteenth century. Occasionally, these praises would find their way into print. For example, in an 1896 issue of *The Woman's Era*, a black women's periodical, the story of Tubman's Combahee River campaign was related. This issue recorded the proceedings of the National Federation of Afro-American Women's convention, which met in the District of Columbia that year. Tubman, by then in her late seventies, was honored at this convention, where she spoke about the need for adequate care and housing for the elderly. Thus, as the nineteenth century drew to a close, African-American women revered one of their legendary, older women leaders. Reverence for Harriet Tubman continues into the present. She is one of the few African-American women of the nineteenth century who is universally known and respected in black communities across the nation.[35]

Slavery ended in the United States as a result of a civil war between slaveholding and nonslaveholding states. In the Danish Virgin Islands, slavery ended in 1848 as a result of a massive slave revolt on the island of St. Croix. The insurrection was precipitated by a gradual emancipation decree announced by the Danish king the year before. The slaves did not want to wait; they wanted their freedom immediately, not gradually, and took action to achieve it. Freedom, in reality, meant a quasi-free peonage system imposed shortly after emancipation by the sugar planters, who dominated the island's economy. By 1878, thirty years later, a generation of peons realized that they were still enslaved by the new labor regulations, which required laborers to sign yearly contracts that were forced on black workers. As a result, on October 1, 1878, the day the new yearly contracts were to be signed, a "labor riot" broke out in Frederiksted as laborers burned and looted the town. By the dawn of the next day, half of Frederiksted was gone. From the town the rebels headed for the countryside, where they burned nearly all the sugar plantations between Frederiksted and Christiansted.[36]

Men, women, and children took part in this rebellion, with several women taking leadership roles. Mary Thomas, known as Queen Mary, led the band of women and children, aided by her lieutenants, Queen Agnes and Queen Matilda. Together they were responsible for the rum and kerosene fires that demolished Frederiksted factories, including the rum factory that exploded, killing fourteen women. They also set fire to the sugar estate houses where the plantation owners lived. Some accounts say that this was a riot that erupted spontaneously with no particular leadership. Others speak of a well-organized rebellion of masses of discontented peasants. Let us consider a few other facts. None of the livestock was killed; all were removed from the estates. One estate was not burned because its architecture resembled a chapel (and the slaves thought it was a church). The range of evidence indicates that a plan must have been put into effect. Despite the controversy over whether it was a planned or spontaneous rebellion, oral traditions of the labor rebellion today sing the praises of one leader, Queen Mary.

> Queen Mary away ya go burn.
> Don't ask me nothin' 't all.
> Just give me match and oil.
> Bassin jailhouse ata we go burn.[37]

Queen Mary was among the four women imprisoned in the Bassin Jail for her role in the rebellion. She, Queen Agnes, and Queen Matilda were sent to Denmark for trial, but later returned to St. Croix. Over four hundred laborers were arrested and tried over a one-and-a-half-year period. (The number of women in this group remains to be determined.) Eventually, three hundred and thirty-six of them were freed. Interestingly, of the leaders imprisoned, only the four women were native born. Their exploits are still celebrated by common folk and in schoolbooks in St. Croix.[38]

Virgin Islands black female leadership represents a continuing stream of protest among women, whose African roots were still apparent a generation after slavery had been abolished and perhaps two generations after the arrival of their last African foremothers. The three women were older women who probably had been slaves as children. But age was not the reason they were called queens. According to folklore, they earned their positions as leaders among the women laborers in their communities.

During the same period, Asante queen mothers were exerting political and military resistance against British colonialism in West Africa. One such woman, Afua Kobi, attempted to avert war through negotiations with the British in 1873. She realized that a full-scale war with the British would be disastrous for her people at the time. Her counsel was overruled, however, and the Asante went to war with the British and were defeated at Kumasi.[39] The tradition of political and military astuteness among women had continued through diaspora history, despite the horror of the slave trade and slavery itself. In both the St. Croix and the Kumasi cases, women joined men in the discussion and execution of war strategies. In resisting common forms of oppression, such as slavery, women initiated survival strategies and utilized self-reliance mechanisms—both values rooted in African cosmology. Hence their activities not only reflected a tradition of identity with Africa but also provided an extension of African history— diaspora history. In essence, Africa becomes the donor of cultural heritage.

IN THE CASES CITED, four themes recur through a period of over two hundred years. One theme is the identification of women leaders with titles given by their own people or by later groups that revere them. The terms used for spiritually or politically militant women in the United States changed over time from the terms found in the Caribbean, such as *queen* and *queen mother*, to include terms such as *Moses*, or *Mother*, as in Mother Bethel Church, the name given the first African Methodist Episcopal church founded in 1794. In addition, twentieth-century African-Americans know the name Queen Mother Moore, founder of the Universal Association of Ethiopian Women and an American woman who was born in 1898. Her title is one of the few among African-American women that represents a conscious identification with Africa.[40]

Another theme found in Africa and throughout the diaspora is the emergence of militant women warriors willing to die for a cause. This seemingly universal resistance theme can be observed in the history of female participation in slave, maroon, and peasant rebellions, as well as their roles in fighting declared wars. The feats of warrior women are celebrated in the religious and cult rituals practiced by Africans and African diaspora peoples.

A third theme is the supernatural or spiritual power attributed to many of the women leaders of resistance movements. Reflecting the religious power attributed to traditional African women, strengths are extolled visually through religious ritual and verbally in oral traditions, which keep alive the legends of certain women among later generations in Africa, in the Caribbean, in South America, and in North America. The power attributed to women leaders was used to resist military attacks against their communities or to mount attacks against potential aggressors.

The final theme is the emergence of older women as strategists, advisers, and warriors in resistance movements in Africa and throughout the diaspora. Identifying a person's age is one of the most difficult tasks unless the person, like Nzinga, "Grandy" Nanny, or Tubman, remained in the struggle for so long that she clearly became middle-aged or older.

In every case of resistance cited, at least two of the four themes can be noted. In addition, the values of self-reliance and developing survival strategies can be measured in varying degrees throughout the period identified. For the most part, the accounts of these experiences are derived from the oral tradition and the religious rituals, maintained primarily by the women of these African diaspora societies. In this way, diaspora history brings the process of historical inquiry full circle, for a major source of traditional African history is oral history.

This survey of resistance activities among women in Africa and of the African diaspora is a preliminary exercise toward the work that needs to be done to answer the questions raised in the beginning of this essay. The reconstruction of the activities of women in the African diaspora is only beginning. Scholars have few models from the historical discipline to follow and must rely upon anthropological studies for the groundwork. Nonetheless, the available data provide insights into how women of African descent have resisted forces that threaten their survival or the survival of their people. In-depth studies of women's resistance throughout the countries of the diaspora and of African nations that donated the persons enslaved in the New World are essential to further the work now being done on women of African descent.

Notes

1 See the essays in Lorraine A. Williams (ed.), *Africa and the Afro-American Experience*, Washington, DC, 1977; and Joseph E. Harris (ed.), *Global Dimensions of the African Diaspora*, Washington, DC, 1982.
2 Filomina Chioma Steady (ed.), *The Black Woman Cross-Culturally*, Cambridge, 1981, 1–3.
3 Ibid., 15–23. On the ambiguities of African women's relation to production and place within the family, see Margaret Jean Hay and Marcia Wright (eds.), *African Women and the Law: Historical Perspectives*, Boston, 1982; and the special issue entitled "The History of the Family in Africa," *Journal of African History*, 24:2 (1983).
4 Henry John Drewal and Margaret Thompson Drewal, *Gelede: Art and Female Power among the Yoruba*, Bloomington, 1983, 7–9.
5 Joseph C. Miller, "Nzinga of Matamba in a New Perspective," *Journal of African History*, 16:2 (1975), 201–216.
6 Chancellor Williams, *The Destruction of Black Civilization: Great Issues of a Race from 4500 B.C. to A.D. 2000*, Chicago, 1976, 276–289. Although historian Joseph Miller found no oral traditions concerning Nzinga in Angola, Williams said they existed. In addition, Georgina Anne Gollock, in *Daughters of Africa*, London, 1932, 12, noted that Livingston saw a great rock at a Portuguese fort in "Congoland," where there was carved a woman's footprint. The African people there told him it was the footprint of the "great queen Nzinga."
7 See Walter Rodney, "European Activity and African Reaction in Angola," in Terence O. Ranger (ed.), *Aspects of Central African History*, London, 1968, 56–59; and Monroe Majors, *Noted Negro Women: Their Triumphs and Activities*, Chicago, 1893. This nineteenth-century collection of biographical sketches, primarily about African-American women of prominence, includes sketches of four African women, one of whom is "Queen Anna Zinga."
8 George W. Ellis, *Negro Culture in West Africa*, New York, 1914.

9 I. A. Akinjogbin, "The Expansion of Oyo and the Rise of Dahomey, 1600–1800," in J. F. Ade Ajayi and Michael Crowder (eds.), *History of West Africa*, New York, 1972, I, 323–333; and Melville J. Herskovits, *Dahomey: An Ancient West African Kingdom*, Evanston, 1967, II, 84–85.

10 Maria Isaua Pereira de Queiror, "Religious Evolution and Creation: The Afro-Brazilian Cults," *Diogenes*, 115 (Fall 1981), 2–3; Seldon Rodman, "African Brazil and Its Cults: Batugue, Candombles, and Umbanda," *Americas*, 27 (June 1975), 9–11; and Hector Bernabo, "Candombles of Bahia," *Americas*, 2 (January 1959), 16–19.

11 Lucille Mathurin, *The Rebel Woman in the British West Indies during Slavery*, Kingston, 1975, 21.

12 Herbert Aptheker, *American Negro Slave Revolts*, New York, 1970, 172–173.

13 Ibid., 220; and Evangeline Grant Redding, *Nothing: The Mentality of the Black Woman*, Tillery, NC, 1976, 7, 11.

14 Herbert Aptheker, "Slave Resistance in the United States," in Nathan I. Huggins et al. (eds.), *Key Issues in the Afro-American Experience*, New York, 1971, I, 171–172.

15 Aptheker, "Slave Resistance," 172.

16 Steady (ed.), *Black Woman*, 33. See also, Irene V. Jackson-Brown, "Black Women and Music: A Survey from Africa to the New World," in Steady (ed.), *Black Woman*, 396–397.

17 Benjamin Anderson, *Narrative of a Journey to Musardu, The Capital of the Western Mandingoes*, London, 1971, 41–43. For discussions about African women enslaved in Africa, see Claire C. Robertson and Martin A. Klein (eds.), *Women and Slavery in Africa*, Madison, 1983.

18 Edward L. Cox, *Free Coloreds in the Slave Societies of St. Kitts and Grenada, 1763–1833*, Knoxville, 1984, 76–77.

19 Cox, *Free Coloreds*, 89–90.

20 Ibid., 117.

21 Surinam maroon societies are Kwinti, Matawai, Saramaka, Djuka, Paramaka, and Aluku.

22 Graham W. Irwin (ed.), *Africans Abroad: A Documentary History of the Black Diaspora in Asia, Latin America, and the Caribbean during the Age of Slavery*, New York, 1977, 308–309.

23 Richard Price, *Saramaka Social Structure: Analysis of a "Bush Negro" Society*, Rio Piedras, Puerto Rico, 1973, 55.

24 Roger Bastide, *The African Religions of Brazil: Toward a Sociology of the Interpenetration of Civilizations*, Baltimore, 1978, 90–94.

25 Mathurin, *Rebel Woman*, 34.

26 Ibid., 36–37.

27 Interview with Lucille Mathurin Mair, New York, January 1985.

28 Kenneth Bilby and Filomina Chioma Steady, "Black Women and Survival: A Maroon Case," in Steady (ed.), *Black Woman*, 454–459; and Agnes Ahosua Aidoo, "Asante Queen Mothers in Government and Politics in the Nineteenth Century," in Steady (ed.), *Black Woman*, 65–66.

29 Herbert Aptheker, *To Be Free: Studies in American Negro History*, New York, 1948, 11–16.

30 Ibid., 18, 21.

31 See Sarah Bradford, *Harriet Tubman: The Moses of Her People*, Secaucus, NJ, 1980.

32 Earl Conrad, *Harriet Tubman*, New York, 1969, 69–72; and *Boston Commonwealth*, July 10 and 17, 1863.

33 Conrad, *Harriet Tubman*, 174–175.

34 Bradford, *Harriet Tubman*, introduction and preface.

35 *The Woman's Era*, 3 (July 1896), 3.

36 Florence Lewisohn, *Divers Information on the Romantic History of St. Croix: From the Time of Columbus until Today*, St. Croix, 1964, 51; and Isaac Dookhan, *A History of the Virgin Islands of the United States*, St. Thomas, 1974, 227–231.

37 Lewisohn, *Divers Information*, 55–57; and Dookhan, *History of the Virgin Islands*, 227–231.

38 Lewisohn, *Divers Information*, 54; and Dookhan, *History of the Virgin Islands*, 231. See Roger Hill, *Clear de Road: A Virgin Islands History Textbook*, St. Croix, 1983, 153. This text is used in the Virgin Islands public elementary schools. It depicts Mary Thomas as the leader of the "Fireburn," the popular name given by the Crucian peasants for the labor rebellion.

    The Danish court records from the labor rebellion are currently in the National Archives, Washington, DC, where they remain in old Danish, without an English translation.

39 Aidoo, "Asante Queen Mothers," in Steady (ed.), *Black Woman*, 72–73.

40 *Black Scholar*, 4 (March-April 1973), 47.

13

Bibliographical Comment

BETTINA APTHEKER

Herbert Aptheker's first published work appeared in his high school newspaper in 1932. He was seventeen years old and in his senior year at Erasmus Hall High School in Brooklyn, New York, when he wrote a series of articles entitled "The Dark Side of the South." The series contained impressions of his first trip to the Southern states. He had traveled by car, accompanying his father and brother-in-law; Herbert was appalled at the poverty and suffering he saw among black folk. During the same year the trial of the black Communist Angelo Herndon took place in Georgia. Herndon was charged with insurrection as a consequence of his activities in the movement of the unemployed. He was convicted and sentenced to death. A mobile exhibit in Herndon's defense toured the neighborhood in which Herbert lived. It made a strong impression on him. The exhibit displayed a cage with the figure of a black man chained inside, to dramatize the Herndon case. A defense committee, organized by the Communist party, ultimately won Herndon's release.

The next year, Herbert entered Columbia University. He majored in geology, and finished his B.S. degree in only three years. He was then invited by one of his professors to accompany him on an exploration for oil under the auspices of the Italian government; but it was 1936 and Herbert couldn't see looking for oil for Mussolini. His professor had no such reservations, and it occurred to Herbert that maybe he ought to give up a career in geology. He turned to American history, and reentered Columbia as a graduate student. Drawn into Afro-American history by the humanitarian and socialist impulses already evident in high school, he wrote his master's thesis on the Nat Turner revolt, and embarked upon the research for a dissertation on American Negro slave revolts.

By 1938, Aptheker was again in the South. He was now twenty-three years old, and engaged as an educational worker for the Food and Tobacco Workers Union. He worked with the black Communist and leader of the Southern Negro Youth Congress, Louis E. Burnham. Aptheker joined the Communist party in 1939. In the same year he served as secretary of the Abolish Peonage Committee, established to force an end to the widespread debtors' slavery in the South. While in the South he also pursued the research for his dissertation. Some of the white archivists and librarians, however, were not sympathetic to his subject matter, and they deliberately kept materials from him. As a consequence, he had great difficulty locating documents he requested, and only limited opportunities to find others through the more rewarding discoveries of chance. Support for the project existed in the black communities, and from these quarters help was often forthcoming. During one memorable search a janitor led Herbert into an archival collection in the dead of night, and found the materials he had otherwise been unable to obtain.

Two months after the United States entered the Second World War, Aptheker enlisted in the army. While in training as an officer, he continued his work on *American Negro Slave Revolts*. It was completed and published by Columbia University Press in 1943, and only a few months before he was shipped overseas. Aptheker asked to be assigned to black troops. He fought in the European theater. His outfit took Dusseldorf, and he was in Paris on V.E. Day. After he returned from the war, he plunged back into his research and was awarded a Guggenheim fellowship to work on a documentary history of the Negro people.

When Herbert Aptheker began his scholarly work in Afro-American history, there was no such discipline in the white universities. Pioneering studies by black historians led by Carter G. Woodson, Charles H. Wesley, and W. E. B. Du Bois had established the field, but it remained unrecognized within the historical profession. The predominant view of Afro-American people among the white intelligentsia in this period may be summarized by quoting from William E. Woodward's then best-selling biography, *Meet General Grant* (New York: H. Liveright, 1928; repr. 1946). "The Negro," Woodward explained, "is lovable as a good-natured child, with a child's craving for affection, but his easy temper is deceptive. It is merely the pliability of surrender, the purring of a wild creature that has been caught and tamed." Woodward continued, "Negroes are the only people in the history of the world, so far as I know, that ever became free without any effort of their own. . . . It [the Civil War] was not their business. They had not started the war nor ended it. They twanged banjos around the railroad stations, sang melodious spirituals and believed that some Yankee would soon come along and give each of them forty acres and a mule."

Herbert Aptheker's lifework has been a refutation of those assertions. He believed, as he wrote in the introduction to one of his earliest books, *To Be Free* (1948), that only "prolonged and rigorous research . . . into the still largely untapped source material" would provide for an "overall history worthy" of the Afro-American people. "Nothing can replace this basic procedure in scientific investigation," he continued, "and it is only on the strength of such digging and probing, such sifting and weighing, that the discipline of Negro historical writing will be lifted from the level of fantasy, wish-fulfillment and bigotry, into the realm of fact and reality."

Aptheker's work reflects this meticulous attention to detail. First in seventeenth-century archives in states along the Eastern seaboard, and the slave states in particular, Aptheker combed through newspapers, journals, diaries, military and naval records, police reports, court cases, and congressional and state legislative records and continued the painstaking reconstruction of black history begun by Du Bois, Woodson, and Wesley. He began assembling and publishing his findings in 1937. Between then and the end of the Second World War, Aptheker completed his master's thesis, his dissertation, and additional essays on slavery and the struggle against it:

Nat Turner's Revolt: The Environment, the Event, the Effects (New York: Humanities Press, 1966; Grove Press paperback, 1968). Originally submitted as a master's thesis, Columbia University, 1937.

"American Negro Slave Revolts," *Science and Society*, 1 (Summer 1937), 512–538, and 2 (Summer 1938), 386–392.

"Class Conflicts in the South: 1850–1860," *Communist*, 18 (February-March 1939), 170–181, 274–279. Written under Aptheker's pseudonym, H. Biel. Later published in *Toward Negro Freedom* (New York: New Century Publishers, 1956); and in *The Unfolding Drama*, ed. by Bettina Aptheker (New York: International Publishers, 1979).

The Labor Movement in the South during Slavery (New York: International Publishers, 1954); reprinted in *The Unfolding Drama* (1979); cited here because the work is related to the previous entry on class conflicts in the South.

"Maroons within the Present Limits of the United States," *Journal of Negro History*, 24 (April 1939), 167–184. In slightly revised form Aptheker published this under the title "Slave Guerrilla Warfare," in *To Be Free* (1948).

"Negroes Who Served in Our First Navy," *Opportunity*, 18 (April 1940), 117.

"The Quakers and Negro Slavery," *Journal of Negro History*, 25 (July 1940), 331–362. This essay, under the same title, appears in Aptheker's *Toward Negro Freedom* (1956).

"They Bought Their Way to Freedom," *Opportunity*, 18 (June 1940), 180–182. Revised and lengthened, this appears under the title "Buying Freedom" in *To Be Free* (1948).

"Negro History: A Cause for Optimism," *Opportunity*, 19 (August 1941), 228–231.

"Militant Abolitionism," *Journal of Negro History*, 26 (October 1941), 438–484.

"Negroes in the Abolitionist Movement," *Science and Society*, 5 (Winter 1941), 2–23. This was also published as a pamphlet, *The Negro in the Abolitionist Movement* (New York: International Publishers, 1940); and it appeared as one of the chapters in Aptheker's *Essays in the History of the American Negro* (1945; 1964).

Between 1938 and 1941 Aptheker published four pamphlets: *The Negro in the Civil War; Negro Slave Revolts in the United States, 1526–1860; The Negro in the Abolitionist Movement;* and *The Negro in the American Revolution.* All of these were based upon the journal essays cited above, and then combined into a book, *Essays in the History of the American Negro* (New York: International Publishers, 1945). The pamphleteering especially reflected Aptheker's desire to disseminate his findings in forms accessible to people in black and working-class communities.

American Negro Slave Revolts represented, as historian Herbert Shapiro has suggested, "a new point of departure, and whatever the responses to [Aptheker's] work, the discussion of slavery has never been quite the same." Shapiro goes on to note that "at the time of publication there was some variation in the critical response but the general drift [of reviews in the historical profession] was markedly favorable." By 1952, however, with the onset of the cold war, Columbia regretted its copyright, and happily allowed its transfer to International Publishers, which has since reissued the book on five occasions (1963, 1969, 1974, 1978, and a fortieth-anniversary edition in 1983).

Having tunneled so deeply into the archival sources, Aptheker mined a veritable mountain of priceless nuggets in the form of petitions, appeals, pamphlets, and letters attesting to the black quest for freedom. Without benefit of duplicating facilities as we know them today, he copied the documents he found—totaling some two million words—by hand. And in 1951 Aptheker published the first volume of *A Documentary History of the Negro People in the United States, from Colonial Times to the Founding of the NAACP in 1910*. Volumes II and III were completed in 1973 and 1974, respectively—Volume II covering the period between the founding of the NAACP and the New Deal, and Volume III spanning the FDR years through the end of World War II (New York: Citadel Press, 1951; Secaucus, NJ: Citadel Press, 1973 and 1974).

Also after the war, *To Be Free: Studies in American Negro History*, which Aptheker marks as his favorite book, was published (New York: International Publishers, 1948). It included the previously cited essays on guerrilla warfare, buying freedom, and abolitionism. Hitherto unpublished chapters on aspects of the Civil War and Reconstruction completed the work.

Additional works in Afro-American history by Herbert Aptheker include the following:

> *Toward Negro Freedom: Historic Highlights in the Life and Struggles of the American Negro People from Colonial Days to the Present* (New York: New Century Publishers, 1956). Especially consequential here is the essay "America's Racist Laws," originally published under that title in *Masses and Mainstream*, 4 (July 1951), 40–56.

> *Soul of the Republic: The Negro Today* (New York: Marzani and Munsell, 1964). The volume contains a particularly useful analysis of the status and conditions of black people nationally and in the various states, compared and contrasted to the report of the United States Civil Rights Commission of 1963.

> *And Why Not Every Man? Documentary Story of the Fight against Slavery in the U.S.* (Berlin: Seven Seas Publishers, 1961; New York: International Publishers, 1970). Often mistaken as being a selection from Aptheker's *Documentary History*, this is, in fact, a separate effort and there is little overlap between the two works.

> *Afro-American History: The Modern Era* (Secaucus, NJ: Citadel Press, 1971). Focusing on the freedom struggle in the twentieth century, this work contains several significant essays, including "Afro-American Superiority: A Neglected Theme in the Literature," originally published in *Phylon*, 31 (Winter 1970), 336–343; "American Imperialism and White Chauvinism," originally published in *Jewish Life*, 4 (July 1950), 21–24; and "The Black College Student in the 1920's: Years of Preparation and Protest."

Another volume of Aptheker's writings edited by the present writer is *The Unfolding Drama: Studies in U.S. History* (New York: International Publishers, 1979). In addition to works already cited, this volume reproduces three of his pamphlets long out of print: "On the Centenary of John Brown's Execution" (1959); "Class Consciousness in the United States" (1959); and "The Civil War" (1961). Also reprinted in this volume are "The History of Anti-Racism in the United States," which originally appeared in *Black Scholar*, 6 (January-February 1975), 15–22, and "The Emancipation Proclamation," *Political Affairs*, 42 (January 1963), 17–26. Two of Aptheker's more polemical pieces conclude this volume: "Falsification in History," originally published in *Political Affairs*, 59 (June 1970), 53–59; and "The American Historical Profession," presented to the opening of the Sixth Annual Northern Great Plains History Conference, Moorehead State College, Minnesota, November 1971, and published in *Political Affairs*, 51 (January 1972), 45–54.

Other essays by Aptheker in Afro-American history not otherwise reprinted include:

"The Negro Woman," *Masses and Mainstream*, 2 (February 1949), 10–17.

Negro History: Its Lessons for Our Time (New York: New Century Publishers, 1956), a pamphlet of 23 pages.

"Slavery, the Negro, and Militancy," *Political Affairs*, 46 (February 1967), 36–43.

"Historical Roots of Violence in the United States," *Labour Monthly* (London), 49 (March 1967), 124–128.

"A Fabulous Black Woman," *Political Affairs*, 49 (March 1971), 54–57, on Ida B. Wells-Barnett.

"The Challenge to Dominant Religion in the U.S. from the Black Experience," *Journal of Religious Thought*, 41 (Spring-Summer 1984), 83–90.

Aptheker contributed a chapter to the book edited by Nathan I. Huggins, Martin Kilson, and Daniel M. Fox, *Key Issues in the Afro-American Experience*, Vol. I, *To 1877* (New York: Harcourt Brace Jovanovich, 1971), titled "Slave Resistance in the United States," 161–173. He also wrote the introductions for the following three historical reprints:

Booker T. Washington and W. E. B. Du Bois, *The Negro in the South: His Economic Progress in Relation to His Moral and Religious Development*. William Levi Bull Lectures, 1907 (New York: Citadel Press, 1970).

G. Spiller (ed.), *Inter-Racial Problems: Papers from the First Universal Races Congress Held in London in 1911* (New York: Citadel Press, 1970).

"Frederick Douglass Calls for Black Suffrage in 1866," *Atlantic Monthly*, 19 (1866), 112–117, reprinted in *Black Scholar*, 5 (December 1973-January 1974), 10–16.

Aptheker's review essays or commentaries in the field of Afro-American history include the following:

A review of eleven current books on Afro-American protest in *American Quarterly*, 21 (Spring 1969), 133–137.

A review of a half-dozen books dealing with slavery and abolitionism in the *American Historical Review*, 78 (February 1973), 151–163.

"Slave Revolts, Resistance, Marronage, and Implications for Post-Emancipation Society," a commentary on eight essays in Vera Rubin and Arthur Tuden (eds.), *Comparative Perspectives on Slavery in New World Plantation Societies*, Annals of the New York Academy of Sciences, 292 (New York: New York Academy of Sciences, 1977), 491–495.

"New Historians and a New History," Parts 1 and 2, *New South Student*, 5 (November-December 1978), 15–23, 7–23.

Aptheker was first named as a Communist by an informer testifying before a New York State investigating committee in 1938, a year before he actually joined the Party. When he returned from Europe at the end of World War II, he sought employment, first at Columbia University, where he had been one of their most outstanding graduate students, and then elsewhere. He was bluntly told that his politics made his employment impossible. He was to be blacklisted for almost thirty years, indeed, until the 1960s, when black students threatened a sit-in at Bryn Mawr College to force his appointment in Afro-American Studies. By the mid-1950s, in response to his own ostracism from the profession and the intense persecution of the Left, Aptheker's writing assumed an explicitly polemical mode, in contrast to his earlier work. This is first evident in his *Laureates of Imperialism: Big Business Re-Writes American History* (New York: Masses and Mainstream, 1954), and in a similar though much briefer critique of historial writing introducing his essay "Was the American Revolution a Majority Movement?" *Political Affairs*, 35 (July 1956), 1–10. Additional writings of this genre relevant to Afro-American and U.S. history are cited below.

"Legacy of Slavery: Comments on Eugene D. Genovese," *Studies on the Left*, 6 (November-December 1966), 27–34. This essay with some additions appeared under the title "Slavery, the Negro, and Militancy," *Political Affairs*, 46 (February 1967), 36–43. At the Socialist Scholars Conference in New York City in the fall of 1966 Eugene Genovese presented a paper entitled "The Legacy of Slavery and the Roots of Black Nationalism." This paper together with comments by Aptheker and C. Vann Woodward appeared in the issue of *Studies on the Left* cited above. Genovese's paper represented the main ideas in his book *The Political Economy of Slavery: Studies in the Economy and Society of the Slave South* (New York: Pantheon Books, 1965).

"Styron Turner and Nat Turner: Myth and Truth," *Political Affairs*, 46 (October 1967), 40–50. This was Aptheker's criticism of Styron's novel *The Confessions of Nat Turner* (New York: Random House, 1967). Subsequently, Aptheker published an addendum to the first review, "Styron's Nat Turner—Again," *Political Affairs*, 47 (April 1968), 47–50. Another of Aptheker's reviews appeared in *New Student South*, 5 (May 1968), 3–7, and in *The Nation*, 206 (April 22, 1968), 543–547. The review that appeared in *Political Affairs* was subsequently published in his *Afro-American History: The Modern Era* (1971).

"Racism and Historiography," *Political Affairs*, 49 (May 1970), 54–57.

"Banfield: The Nixon Model Planner," *Political Affairs*, 49 (December 1970), 34–45. This is a review essay of the book by Edward Banfield, *The Unheavenly City: The Nature and Future of Our Urban Crisis* (Boston: Little, Brown, 1970).

"Black Studies and U.S. History," *Political Affairs*, 50 (December 1971), 50–57, reprinted in Aptheker's *Afro-American History: The Modern Era* (1971).

"Southerners on Southern History," *Political Affairs*, 49 (February 1971), 50–59.

"John Brown and the Writing of History," *Political Affairs*, 53 (September 1973), 48–54.

"Heavenly Days in Dixie; or, The Time of Their Lives," *Political Affairs*, 53 (June-July 1974), 40–54, 44–57. This is a review essay on the book by Robert W. Fogel and Stanley L. Engerman, *Time on the Cross: The Economics of American Negro Slavery*, 2 vols. (Boston: Little, Brown, 1974).

"Marxism and Scholarship in the U.S.," *Maxwell Review*, 11 (Winter 1974), 1–11.

"No Welcome Mat for Marxist Scholars," *New York Times*, August 27, 1976, op. ed. page.

"The Struggle against Racism: Myths and Realities," *Political Affairs*, 56 (April 1977), 28–34. A review essay of Nathan Glazer's attack on affirmative action in his book entitled *Affirmative Discrimination: Ethnic Inequality and Public Policy* (New York: Basic Books, 1975).

"Affirmative Action: A Response to Critics," *Political Affairs*, 60 (June 1981), 23–27.

"Marxism and Social Sciences in the U.S.: A Brief Appraisal," *Political Affairs*, 62 (June 1983), 14–17.

Utilizing his basic focus on Afro-American history as a special vantage point from which to view American life in general, Aptheker, in the midfifties, conceived of a twelve-volume Marxist history of the United States. The first three of these were completed and published by International Publishers. Volume I, *The Colonial Era*, appeared in 1959; volume II, *The American Revolution, 1763–1783*, was published in 1960; and volume III, *Early Years of the Republic: From the End of the Revolution to the First Administration of Washington (1783–1793)*, came out in 1976. This work, however, was interrupted.

For the last twenty years Herbert Aptheker has devoted the major portion of his time to editing the *Collected Works* and letters of W. E. B. Du Bois. Aptheker's first encounter with Du Bois was in 1940. He wrote a critical review of Du Bois's *Dusk of Dawn: An Essay toward An Autobiography of a Race Concept* (New York: Harcourt, Brace and World, 1940), in *Masses*. Du Bois sent him a brief, handwritten note acknowledging the review. After the war, when Aptheker resumed his work on *A Documentary History of the Negro People in the United States*, he spent some time at the New York offices of the NAACP, and occupied a temporarily vacant desk next to Du Bois. Recalling the experience, Aptheker said it was like sitting next to an encyclopedia on Afro-American history. If he had a question about a person or event, he simply turned to Du Bois. They lunched together every day—Herbert learning to enjoy an apple, the only midday refreshment Du Bois permitted himself at the time. As the years progressed, the two developed a warm and intimate friendship.

The first discussion about publishing the Du Bois correspondence occurred in 1946. Letters between them in 1947 confirm the desirability of the project, but the want of a publisher. The matter was pushed aside by the inexorable pressures of repression brought on by the fifties. When Du Bois left the United States in 1961 to live in Ghana, the letters were stored in the basement of Aptheker's home; and in his will Du Bois named Aptheker as literary executor. By the late sixties Aptheker's work on the Du Bois project was well under way; it is now nearing a conclusion. Aptheker edited and wrote the introductions for several of Du Bois's works published posthumously.

The Autobiography of W. E. B. Du Bois (New York: International Publishers, 1968).

The Education of Black People: Ten Critiques, 1906–1960 (Amherst: University of Massachusetts Press, 1973).

Prayers for Dark People (Amherst: University of Massachusetts Press, 1980).

Against Racism: Unpublished Papers, Essays, Speeches, 1887–1961 (Amherst: University of Massachusetts Press, 1985).

Aptheker also edited the *Selected Correspondence of W. E. B. Du Bois*, a three-volume series published under the auspices of the University of Massachusetts Press. Volume I of the *Correspondence*, with selections from 1877–1934, was published in 1973. Volume II (1934–1944) appeared in 1976, and volume III (1944–1963) in 1978. Eric Foner, who reviewed the third volume of the *Correspondence* in the *New York Times*, noted that Aptheker had no financial assistance for this project, and bore the full responsibility himself. "For Aptheker," Foner concludes, "the essentially unassisted task of editing was very much a labor of love."

In addition to the *Correspondence*, Aptheker has completed all of the editorial work for the forty-volume *Collected Published Works of W. E. B. Du Bois*, to be published under the auspices of the Kraus-Thomson Organization, in Millwood, New York. In connection with this project, Aptheker produced a six-hundred-page *Annotated Bibliography of the Published Writings of W. E. B. Du Bois* (1973). Because of the depth of the annotations, the book provides not only a guide to his work but also an extraordinarily useful survey of Afro-American history in the twentieth century.

Finally, Aptheker has written a number of essays on Du Bois.

"W. E. B. Du Bois: The First Eighty Years," *Phylon*, 9 (First Quarter 1948), 59–62.

"By Way of Dedication: On the Meaning of Dr. Du Bois," in Aptheker's *Soul of the Republic: The Negro Today* (1964).

"W. E. B. Du Bois," *Harvard Journal of Negro Affairs*, 1:1 (1965), 42–51. Premier issue.

"Du Bois on Florence Kelley," *Social Work*, 11 (October 1966), 198ff.

"Du Bois and James Weldon Johnson," *Journal of Negro History*, 52 (July 1967): 224–227.

"Du Bois as Historian," originally delivered, in abridged form, at the 1968 meeting of the American Historical Association, and published in Aptheker's *Afro-American History: The Modern Era* (1971), 47–67.

"Du Bois: A Zest for Life," *CAAS Newsletter*, Center for Afro-American Studies, University of California, Los Angeles, 3 (May 1979), 6–8.

"W. E. B. Du Bois," in A. Walton Litz (ed.), *American Writers: A Collection of Literary Biographies*, Supplement II, Part 1, *Auden to O'Henry* (New York: Charles Scribner's Sons, 1981), 147–189.

"W. E. B. Du Bois: Man for Peace," *Political Affairs*, 61 (August 1982), 31–35.

"W. E. B. Du Bois and Religion," *Journal of Religious Thought*, 39 (Spring-Summer 1982), 5–11.

Du Bois and the Struggle against Racism in the World (New York: United Nations Centre against Apartheid, July 1983), a pamphlet of 17 pages.

This bibliography has been prepared in the summer of my father's sixty-ninth birthday. His most recent work is an essay entitled *"We Will Be Free": Advertisements for Runaways and the Reality of American Slavery*. It is Occasional Paper No. 1, published by the Ethnic Studies Program, University of Santa Clara, 1984. A few months ago he told me about this particular project as we walked near my home. He explained that a black scholar had collected and published all of the advertisements for fugitive slaves in the United States, without comment. It is a devastating indictment, Herbert said, as one reads the signatures of these ads: George Washington, Thomas Jefferson, James Madison, James Monroe. His eyes blazed as if he were finding this out for the first time. Herbert is a fierce polemicist, a dramatic speaker, and driven to produce. This bibliography, for example, includes only his work in history; I have omitted his efforts in sociology, foreign affairs, Marxist theory, and the Marxist-Christian dialogue in which he has been active for twenty-five years. He was a formidable mentor and an impossibly prolific writer to emulate. Underneath these outer fibers there is also a very sweet human being. His most treasured birthday present is still to be taken to a major league baseball game. He also loves to collect stamps, although he no longer has an active collection. He still, however, carefully saves the stamps from the envelopes of his overseas letters, and gives them to one of his adopted grandchildren, to whom he also gave his boyhood album. "To pass it on," he said to her on the occasion. His lifework, too, will be passed on in meaningful ways.

NOTES ON CONTRIBUTORS

BETTINA APTHEKER is a visiting lecturer in Women's Studies at the University of California, Santa Cruz. She is the author of *Woman's Legacy: Essays on Race, Sex, and Class in American History* (1982); *The Morning Breaks: The Trial of Angela Davis* (1975); and *The Academic Rebellion in the United States: A Marxist Appraisal* (1972). She has edited several works and has published numerous essays and reviews. Her major scholarly interests are in women's history and culture, Afro-American women's history, and lesbian studies. She is currently working on a manuscript entitled "A Labor of Love: Women's Work, Women's Consciousness, and the Meaning of Daily Life."

HERBERT APTHEKER is the author of thirty volumes in history, philosophy, sociology, and contemporary events. He is best known for his work in Afro-American history, especially *American Negro Slave Revolts* (1943) and the three-volume *Documentary History of the Negro People in the United States* (1951–1975). He is editor of the three-volume *Correspondence of W. E. B. Du Bois* (1973–1978) and of the forty-volume *Collected Published Writings of Du Bois* (1973–1985). Aptheker has taught at Bryn Mawr College, City University of New York, Yale University, University of Santa Clara, Humboldt University (Berlin), and the University of California Law School, Berkeley. He has been director of the American Institute for Marxist Studies since its founding in 1964.

BARBARA BUSH teaches Third World Studies for the Open University and is completing a doctoral dissertation at the University of Sheffield, entitled "Britain and Black Africa in the Inter-War Years: Responses to the Growth of Race and Political Consciousness." She has lived and worked in both the Caribbean and Canada, where as a postgraduate student at the University of Waterloo she carried out research for her book on slavery, *'Lost Daughters of Afrik': Slave Women in British West Indian Slave Society* (1985). She has published other relevant articles in *Slavery and Abolition* and *Immigrants and Minorities*.

MICHAEL CRATON is professor of history at the University of Waterloo, Ontario, Canada, where he has taught since 1966. He is the author of *A Jamaican Plantation: The History of Worthy Park, 1670–1970* (with James Walvin, 1970); *Sinews of Empire: A Short History of British Slavery* (1974); *Searching for the Invisible Man: Slaves and Plantation Life in Jamaica* (1978); and *Testing the Chains: Resistance to Slavery in the British West Indies* (1982). Currently he is at work on a history of the people of the Bahamas.

ELIZABETH FOX-GENOVESE, professor of history at SUNY Binghamton, has written *The Origins of Physiocracy: Economic Revolution and Social Order in Eighteenth-Century France* (1976); *The Autobiography of DuPont de Nemours* (1984); articles in women's history and literature; and, with Eugene D. Genovese, *Fruits of Merchant Capital* (1983) and articles in the history of antebellum slave society and problems of the expansion of Europe.

EUGENE D. GENOVESE is professor of history at the University of Rochester, fellow of the American Academy of Arts and Sciences, and past president of the Organization of American Historians. His most recent books are *From Rebellion to Revolution: Afro-American Slave Revolts in the Making of the Modern World* (1979) and, with Elizabeth Fox-Genovese, *Fruits of Merchant Capital* (1983).

PAUL E. LOVEJOY, professor and chairman of the Department of History, York University, is the author of *Caravans of Kola: A History of the Hausa Kola Trade (1700–1900)* (1980); *Transformations in Slavery: A History of Slavery in Africa* (1983); and *Salt of the Desert Sun: A History of Salt Production and Trade in the Central Sudan* (1985). He has also edited *The Ideology of Slavery in Africa* (1981) and *The Labor of African Trade* (with Catherine Coquery Vidrovitch, 1985). He is also co-editor of *African Economic History* and series editor for African Modernization and Development, Sage Publications, Beverly Hills.

GARY Y. OKIHIRO is associate professor of history and director of the Ethnic Studies Program at the University of Santa Clara. He has published in African and Asian American history, including articles in the *International Journal of African Historical Studies, African Historical Demography, Phylon, Oral History Review, Journal of Ethnic Studies,* and *Amerasia Journal.* He is author of *Japanese Legacy: Farming and Community Life in California's Santa Clara Val-*

ley (1985), and is currently working on a manuscript on the Kwena (Botswana) precolonial social formation and on a comparative history of Japanese-Americans in Hawaii and on the West Coast during World War II.

CORA ANN PRESLEY is associate professor of Afro-American and African history at Loyola University (New Orleans). Her research interests include African nationalism, African women in rebellion and revolution, and black women in the United States. Her publications include "African Women, Culture, and Nationalism," *Chico State African Studies Journal* (1981); and "Labor Unrest among Kikuyu Women," in *Women, Race, and Class* edited by Iris Berger and Claire Robertson (1985). Her doctoral dissertation is entitled "The Transformation of Kikuyu Women and Their Nationalisms" (Stanford, 1985). She formerly taught at Humboldt State University.

TERENCE RANGER is professor of modern history at the University of Manchester and past president of the African Studies Association (United Kingdom). In 1983, he was Smuts Commonwealth Lecturer at Cambridge University. His most recent books are *The Invention of Tradition* (edited with Eric Hobsbawm, 1982), and *Past and Present in Zimbabwe* (edited with John Peel, 1982). His forthcoming books include *Sons of the Soil: The History of the African Peasantry of Makoni District, Zimbabwe, 1900 to 1940*, and *From Peasant Nationalism to Guerrilla War, Makoni District, Zimbabwe, 1940 to 1982*.

HERBERT SHAPIRO is associate professor of history at the University of Cincinnati. In the field of Afro-American history, his articles have appeared in the *Journal of Negro History, Phylon, Crisis, Science and Society, Journal of Ethnic Studies*, and the *Negro American Literature Forum*. His essay "The Populists and the Negro: A Reconsideration" is included in the Meier and Rudwick collection, *The Making of Black America*. He has recently completed work on the first volume of a study of racist violence and black resistance since the Civil War. He previously taught at Morehouse College.

ROSALYN TERBORG-PENN is associate professor of history and director of the African/Afro-American Studies Program at Morgan State University. She is a co-founder of the Association of Black Women Historians and an editor of *Feminist Studies*. In 1980 she received a Ford Foundation Post-Doctoral Fellowship for Minorities for the research she is conducting in African-American women's history and women in the African diaspora. Among her recent publications are "Discontented Black Feminists: Prelude and Postscript to the Passage of the Nineteenth Amendment," in *Decades of Discontent*, edited by Lois Scharf and Joan M. Jensen (1983), and "Survival Strategies among African-American Women Workers: A Continuing Process," in *A Century of Women's Labor History*, edited by Ruth Milkman (1985).

PETER H. WOOD teaches at Duke University and works with the Highlander Center in Tennessee. He wrote *Black Majority* (1974) concerning slavery in early South Carolina, and he is preparing a general history of the colonial South. In December 1984 he helped edit a special history issue of the progressive journal *Southern Exposure*, in which a shorter version of his essay published in this book appeared.

INDEX

abolitionism, 25, 28, 83, 85, 86, 87, 118, 119, 140, 141, 152, 161, 162, 172, 193, 214
Adams, John, 176, 180
African, 3–4, 7–9, 32–50, 53–69, 71–91, 188–207, passim
African National Congress, 46, 47
Afro-American, 2–3, 4, 5–9, 10–20, 133–142, 143–162, 166–181, 188–207, passim
Afro-Caribbean, 4, 5, 100, 102, 105, 106, 107, 110, 112–113, 117–129, 188–207, passim
agrarian protest, 35–50, 53–69
American Negro Slave Revolts, 1, 2, 7, 10, 11, 15, 21, 22, 24, 26, 32, 43, 139, 144, 166, 167, 211, 213
American Revolution, 6, 23, 151, 152, 168, 173, 181
Amerindian, 4, 5, 96–113
Angola, 7, 34, 191–192, 193
Antigua, 107, 110, 111, 112
antiracism, 2, 8–9, 16–20
Aptheker, Bettina, 7, 14
Aptheker, Herbert, 1, 2, 5, 6, 7, 8, 21–33 passim, 43, 44, 45, 50, 72, 96, 133, 134, 138, 139, 140, 144, 152, 153, 159, 166, 167, 170, 175, 195, 210–218
Arawaks, 98, 99, 100, 101, 105, 112
arson as resistance, 6, 16, 143–144, 150, 158
Asante, 75, 90, 117, 122, 195, 200, 201, 205

Barbados, 100, 103, 104, 109, 112
Bauchi, 77, 81, 82, 84
Beinart, William, 39, 43, 46, 47
Benue River, 77, 81, 83, 84, 87
Black Caribs, 4, 5, 97, 112, 113
Blassingame, John, 13, 14, 133

Boston, 169, 171, 174, 203
Bozzoli, Belinda, 41, 42
Brazil, 192, 193, 197, 198, 199, 201
Brenner, Robert, 40, 41, 42
Brown, John, 11, 19
Bull, Stephen, 179, 180
Bundy, Colin, 39, 43, 46
Bush, Barbara, 5, 8

caciques, 97, 99, 100
Candombles, 193, 197, 198
capitalism, 3, 5, 6, 34, 35, 38, 41, 42, 49, 50, 90, 113, 134, 137, 139, 140, 141
Caribs, 4, 96–113
Catholicism, 97–98, 100–101, 102, 193, 197
Charleston, 19, 136, 156, 157, 169, 171, 175, 176, 178, 179, 180
cimarrones, 100, 102
Clapperton, Hugh, 81, 87
class struggle, 4, 5, 29–30, 49; slave resistance as, 22–24, 133–141
colonialism (European): anticolonial struggle, 4, 8, 49, 53–69, 96–113, 191; rise of slave resistance, 74–77, 82–91
Columbus, Christopher, 5, 98, 99, 113
Committee of Safety: New Bern, N.C., 173; Orange County, Va., 171; Pitt County, N.C., 175; Williamsburg, Va., 177
Communist party, 10, 27, 211, 216
Communists, 2, 21, 22, 26, 27, 29, 210, 211, 216
concubinage: African, 78–79, 84–85, 87; Afro-Caribbean, 118, 124; Amerindian, 99
Connelly, John, 174, 177
Continental Congress, 176, 178, 180

continuities of resistance, 3, 4, 6, 8, 22–23,
  29, 33–34, 46, 49, 96–97, 113, 118, 127,
  128–129, 140–141, 147, 189–190, 193,
  206, 207
Cooper, Frederick, 36, 76
Council of Safety: Georgia, 180; South Carolina, 178, 180
Craton, Michael, 4, 5, 8
Crummey, Donald, 34, 40, 42, 45
Cuba, 100, 196, 200
cultural resistance, 5, 28, 55–56, 117–129,
  145–146, 148, 189–190, 193

Dahomey, 192, 193
dan Fodio, Usman, 79, 80, 82, 86, 88
Declaration of Independence, 168, 180, 181
deculturation, 3, 5, 55–56, 97–98
Diagourou, Seeku, 82, 84
diaspora, African, 7, 188, 189, 190, 191, 193,
  195, 202, 205, 206, 207
Dominica, 108, 109, 110, 111, 112
Du Bois, W. E. B., 14, 21, 24, 27, 28, 133,
  137, 138, 139, 211, 212, 218
Dunmore, Governor John, 170, 173, 174, 176,
  177, 178
Dunmore's proclamation, 168, 177, 178, 180

East African Association, 54, 55, 56
Elkins, Stanley, 10, 11, 22, 133, 136, 141
Española, 99, 100

female circumcision (Kikuyu), 55–56
flight, slave: geographical factors, 4, 74, 77,
  81, 91; political factors, 4, 74–77, 82–91;
  religious factors, 79–82; as resistance, 4, 8,
  12, 15, 44, 45, 71–91, 150–151, 198
Fox-Genovese, Elizabeth, 5, 6, 8, 137, 138
French Revolution, 6, 23, 74, 90, 152, 196

Gabriel conspiracy. *See* Prosser, Gabriel
Gage, Governor Thomas, 170, 174, 177
gender relations, 53–69, 117–129, 143–162,
  passim
Genovese, Eugene, 2, 7, 8, 13, 15, 79, 85, 86,
  90, 133, 134, 135, 137, 138, 153
Georgia, 19, 154, 157, 172, 173, 176, 179,
  180, 210
Gold Coast, 79, 90, 218

"Grandy" Nanny, 7, 151, 200, 201, 206
Grenada, 103, 108, 109, 196, 197
Guadeloupe, 12, 107, 108
Gutman, Herbert, 123, 133, 136, 137

Haiti, 12, 99, 197, 198
Haitian revolution. *See* St. Domingue
  revolution
Harding, Vincent, 14, 28, 133, 152, 159
Hobsbawm, Eric, 29, 30
Homeguard (Kenya), 58, 65

Isaacman, Allen, 35, 39, 43, 44
Islam, 77, 78, 79, 80, 81, 82, 84, 85, 86, 88, 90

Jamaica, 7, 12, 99, 100, 106, 107, 122, 123,
  124, 125, 126, 151, 193, 194, 198, 200, 201
James, C. L. R., 23, 137
Jefferson, Thomas, 180, 220
jihad, 77, 79, 80, 81, 82, 86, 88

Kamiti Prison, 54, 59, 61, 62
Kano, 77, 81, 82
Kenya, 53–69, 76
Kenya African Union, 58, 59, 60, 63
Kenyatta, Jomo, 58, 59
Kiambu District, 54, 55, 58, 59, 60, 62, 63, 68
Kikuyu Central Association, 56, 57, 58
Kikuyu women. *See* women's resistance
kinship, 5, 79, 90, 117, 120, 124, 128, 136,
  149; fictive, 5, 120, 158
Klein, Martin, 36, 39, 75, 79, 90

Labat, Père, 107, 112
Lesser Antilles, 101, 106
Liberia, 191–192, 195
Liptako, 80, 82, 86
Lovejoy, Paul, 4, 8, 15
Lugard, F. L. (Lord), 84, 88, 89

McSheffrey, G. M., 79, 90
Madison, James, 171, 220
Mahdism, 87, 88
marronage, 12, 15, 28, 75, 85, 86, 91, 100,
  102, 109, 112, 147, 151, 152, 190, 198, 199,
  200, 201, 202, 206
Martinique, 107, 108, 109
Marxism, 2, 7, 10, 26, 29, 30, 41, 134, 220

Marxist-Leninist, 2, 26, 29, 30
Marxists, 26, 27, 29, 30, 35, 36, 38, 218
Maryland, 17, 173, 174, 175, 178
matrifocality, 118, 119, 120, 121–122, 151, 199
"Mau Mau" rebellion, 3, 53–69
May, Robert E., 11–12, 14
mestizo class, 97, 100, 109
millennial movements, 81, 82, 86, 88, 89, 90
miscegenation, 4, 17, 97, 104, 106, 107, 118, 127
Miskito Indians, 105, 106, 112
Moultrie, Colonel William, 178–179
Mozambique, 34, 38, 43, 45, 48
Mullin, Gerald W., 12, 133, 150
Mumbi Central Association, 3, 57, 58, 60

nationalism (Kenya), 53–69
nationalist history, 3, 33
New Orleans, 17–18, 19, 159, 170
Niger River, 77, 81, 83, 84, 87
Ningi, 74, 81, 82, 86
nitaino aristocracy, 97, 99
North Carolina, 13, 45, 150, 161, 171, 173, 175, 201
Nupe, 80, 81, 83, 84
Nzinga, Ann (Queen), 7, 191, 192, 200, 206

Paine, Thomas, 172, 180
Patterson, Orlando, 4, 10, 71, 72
peasants: defined, 37–38; resistance of, 34–50 passim, 88
Philadelphia, 170, 171, 172, 176, 177, 180
Phillips, U. B., 11, 18, 21, 28, 139
Plessy vs. *Ferguson* (1896), 18, 20
poisoning as resistance, 6, 16, 150, 155–156, 158
polygyny, 79, 118, 121, 127
Ponce de León, Hernán, 99, 100
Presley, Cora, 3, 8
property, destruction of, as resistance, 72, 73, 74, 91
Prosser, Gabriel, 15, 145, 194
psychological resistance, 143–144, 156–157, 161, 195, 196
Puerto Rico, 99, 100, 101
Pym, John, 105, 106

queen mother, 193, 195, 200, 201, 204, 205, 206
quilombos, 198, 199

Ranger, Terence, 3, 8, 45
Roberts, Richard, 75, 79, 90
rural protest. *See* agrarian protest

St. Croix, 101, 107, 204, 205
St. Domingue revolution, 74, 85, 90, 152, 196, 197
St. Kitts, 12, 103, 104, 106, 107, 108, 109, 110
St. Lucia, 103, 107, 108, 109, 110, 112
St. Vincent, 108, 109, 110, 111, 112, 113
Saramaka, 198, 199, 200
Satiru, 88, 89, 90, 91
Shapiro, Herbert, 5, 8, 213
slave family: Afro-American, 28, 136–137, 145; Afro-Caribbean, 117, 118, 119–122, 124, 127, 128–129
slavery, African, nature of, 78, 79
slaves: as a class, 49, 78; as property, 8, 71, 72, 73
slave women, African: childbearing, 73; concubines, *see* concubinage, African
slave women, Afro-American: childbearing, 157–158; as leaders, 146, 159–160, 201; oppression of, 13
slave women, Afro-Caribbean: childbearing, 5, 119, 125, 126, 127, 128; as leaders, 193–194, 201; mothering, 119, 124, 125; "promiscuity" of, 118, 119, 120, 122–123, 126, 127, 128
Smith, Captain John, 103, 104, 106
Sokoto Caliphate, 4, 71–91
South Carolina, 12, 19, 24, 25, 123, 149, 150, 156, 157, 170, 171, 173, 175, 176, 178, 179–180, 202, 203
Stampp, Kenneth, 21, 133, 135
Steady, Filomina Chioma, 189, 195
Stono Rebellion, 12, 150, 151, 152
Styron, William, 11, 27, 136
Sudan: central, 81, 86; western, 75, 79, 83, 87, 90
Surinam, 198–199, 200

Taradoba (Sandemande), 191, 192
Tegreman, 103, 104

Terborg-Penn, Rosalyn, 7, 8
Thomas, Mary (Queen Mary), 204, 205
Thuku, Harry, 55, 56
Trinidad, 100, 101, 103, 196, 197
Tubman, Harriet, 7, 143, 202, 203, 204, 206
Turner, Nat, 15, 23, 25, 135, 137, 145, 194, 210
Tybee Island, 179, 180

underdevelopment theory, 3, 35, 36, 40, 42, 50

Velázquez, Diego, 99, 100
Vesey, Denmark, 19, 136, 145
Vidrovitch, Catherine Coquery, 37, 38, 42–43, 47, 48
Virginia, 15, 16, 17, 19, 24, 149, 150, 151, 169, 170, 171, 173, 174, 175, 176, 177, 178, 180, 194, 195, 201
voodoo, 159, 197, 198

Wagarama, Wambui, 58, 59
wa Kore, Nduta, 59, 60
Wanjiko, Mary, 59, 61, 65, 66
Warner, Colonel Philip, 111–112
Warner, Sir Thomas, 103, 104, 109, 111
Warner, Thomas "Indian," 109, 110, 111

Washington, George, 178, 220
Wesley, Charles H., 211, 212
women, African, as leaders, 190–192, 205–206
women's resistance: African, 3–4, 7, 8, 53–69, 73, 78–79, 87, 188–207, passim; Afro-American, 5, 14, 143–162, 188–207, passim; Afro-Caribbean, 5, 117–129, 188–207, passim; as armed fighters, 63, 67–68, 146, 192–193, 206; gender-specific, 6, 8, 53–69 passim, 144, 145, 152–162 passim; as individualistic, 6, 144–145, 148, 153, 159–161; Kikuyu, 3, 8, 53–69; as laborers, 154–155; as leaders, 144–145, 149–150, 202–206; religious, 7, 159–160, 190–193, 197, 198, 199, 206; self-reliance, 7, 189, 191, 199, 203, 206; as support network, 62–66, 68; white, 19, 160–162
Wood, Peter, 4, 6, 8, 12, 15, 133, 150
Woodson, Carter G., 11, 20, 21, 133, 138, 211, 212
work slowdowns as resistance, 16, 72, 85

Zaria, 81, 83, 84
Zimbabwe, 33, 43, 45, 48